Abuse of Law in the European Union

Luca Pantaleo

Abuse of Law in the European Union

The Rise of a Special General Principle

ASSER PRESS

Springer

Luca Pantaleo
Department of Political and Social Sciences
University of Cagliari
Cagliari, Italy

ISBN 978-94-6265-730-4 ISBN 978-94-6265-731-1 (eBook)
https://doi.org/10.1007/978-94-6265-731-1

Published by T.M.C. ASSER PRESS, The Hague, The Netherlands www.asserpress.nl
Produced and distributed for T.M.C. ASSER PRESS by Springer-Verlag Berlin Heidelberg

This T.M.C. ASSER PRESS imprint is published by the registered company Springer-Verlag GmbH, DE, part of Springer Nature.
The registered company address is: Heidelberger Platz 3, 14197 Berlin, Germany

Acknowledgements

In the acknowledgements to my first monograph, written more than six years ago, I noted how many people I was indebted to for its completion. The same holds true for this second monograph. Despite being more experienced (read: older) and, hopefully, a little wiser, writing a scholarly book remains a journey filled with its fair share of obstacles and challenges. My first thanks go, therefore, to all the friends and colleagues who, over these years, shared a smile, a kind word, or an encouraging message when I most needed it.

I began working on this book in the spring of 2021, that is, four years ago. It was a dark time, not just for me, but for much of the world. We were cautiously emerging from the Covid-19 pandemic and the unprecedented restrictions it brought, not long after we had all briefly feared that the extinction of the human race might not be such a far-fetched scenario after all. Curiously, this book owes its very inception to that moment in time. The idea was born in the midst of the first lockdown, in May 2020. I spent those days in my makeshift home office, alternating childcare shifts with my wife while trying to carry on with work. During one of the countless online meetings that defined that period, I was discussing possible monograph topics with my friend and colleague Amedeo Arena. Somewhere in that exchange, the idea for this book emerged—and stuck. I recently met Amedeo in Helsinki, where we served as judges at the Regional Final of the ELMC. He no longer remembers that conversation, but I remain sincerely grateful to him for sparking the inspiration, whether consciously or not.

I am also deeply indebted to Graham Butler. Graham co-authored an excellent book chapter on abuse of Union law, which is repeatedly cited throughout this book. It was published when I was about a year into this journey, at a time when I was far from convinced of my choice of topic and was even considering abandoning it altogether. Graham, who understood the potential of the topic far better than I did then, encouraged me to persevere and offered valuable guidance. Without his encouragement, this work might never have seen the light of day.

As always, my deepest thanks go to Paolo Palchetti. What I wrote in the first monograph still holds true, word for word. I am grateful to him for being both a lifelong academic mentor and a dear friend. Without his constant guidance, neither this book nor indeed my academic path would have taken shape. I first met Paolo as a young law student in 2006, and ever since, through all that life has brought, he has always been there. I am especially thankful to him this time for hosting me as a visiting professor at the *Institut de recherche en droit international et européen de la Sorbonne* (IREDIES), Université Paris 1 Panthéon-Sorbonne, in 2024. A considerable portion of this book was written in Paris, benefiting from the studious environment and the exceptional bibliographic resources of the city.

I also owe a special debt of gratitude to Enzo Cannizzaro, another guiding figure throughout my career. His thoughtful advice has always been available whenever I asked, and I am truly fortunate to have him as a mentor. If I were to offer one piece of advice to a young researcher embarking on an academic career, it would be this: seek out good mentors. I have been lucky enough to find two outstanding ones in Paolo and Enzo.

Many colleagues and friends have provided valuable input, whether by commenting on earlier drafts, discussing ideas during seminars, or simply over coffee or a beer. In alphabetical order, I thank: Adriana Brusca, Alina Carrozzini, Daniele Amoroso, Dilara Khamitova, Federica Velli, Felipe Tomazini, Francesca Ippolito, Francesco Seatzu, Giacomo Biagioni, James Harrison, Mads Andenas, Matthew Happold, Rachele Marconi and Tarjei Bekkedal. A heartfelt thanks also goes to the team at T.M.C. Asser Press, especially Frank Bakker and Kiki van Gurp, for their professionalism and support throughout this process.

Precious support was provided by Federico Casolari, who kindly agreed to review the manuscript and offered many valuable insights. One of these is expressly acknowledged in a footnote, though several others, no less important, remain unmentioned.

Last but never least, I am grateful to the members of my family, whose presence has sustained me throughout my life. To my grandfather, Antonio, whose memory and example continue to inspire me. To my parents, Fiore and Rosa, for always being there when I need them. To my brother, Maurizio, who brought joy into the final stages of writing this book by giving me a beautiful niece. And above all, to my wife Raquel, my partner in everything, and to my children, Eduardo and Giovanna, of whom I am proud every single day.

Cagliari, Italy
June 2025

Luca Pantaleo

Contents

Chapter 1
At the Edge of the Law: Mapping the Terrain of Abuse in the EU Legal Order

Contents

Abstract This chapter outlines the content and structure of the book, clarifying its scope and the aspects it deliberately leaves aside, while offering a rationale for these choices. It also introduces a preliminary definition of abuse of law and offers a brief overview of its main features and role as a general principle of EU law.

Keywords Abuse of law · Good faith · Legitimate expectations · Proportionality · Estoppel

1.1 The Aim of This Book and Delimitation

This book focuses on the principle of abuse of law as it has developed within the EU legal order, primarily through the case law of the Court of Justice of the European Union (ECJ). The aim is not to demonstrate the existence of a general principle prohibiting the abuse of law in the Union's legal system. That question was open to debate until 2017, when the ECJ delivered its landmark ruling in *Cussens*.[1] Since then, the existence of the principle has been firmly established. Rather, the objective of this study is threefold. First, it aims to clarify the constitutive elements of abuse of law—that is, what makes the exercise of a right granted by EU law abusive. Second, it aims to determine the scope and reach of the principle. Third, it is aimed at examining the systemic function of abuse of law within the EU legal order—namely, the underlying reasons for its existence and its role in the broader legal framework. This is, in a nutshell, what the book sets out to explore. However, in this introductory section, it is equally important to clarify what this book does not aim to address—and why.

[1] See Chap. 3.

L. Pantaleo, *Abuse of Law in the European Union*,
https://doi.org/10.1007/978-94-6265-731-1_1

As the following analysis will show, a number of important legal concepts intersect with the principle of abuse of law. Some share conceptual affinities with it but serve distinct purposes, while others may stand in potential tension with it. Among the latter is the principle of legal certainty, of which the protection of legitimate expectations is a specific expression.[2] As is well known, the general principle of legal certainty embodies "the fundamental premise that those subject to the law must know what the law is so as to be able to plan their actions accordingly".[3] It is a key ingredient of a system based on the rule of law. As this book will argue in detail, abuse of EU law refers to situations where individuals, while formally complying with the rules, exercise their rights in a way that defeats or distorts the purpose of those rules.[4] This gives rise to the concern that it may, at times, be difficult for a right-holder to clearly distinguish between the lawful invocation of a right and its abusive exercise. This issue has arisen most prominently in tax evasion cases, where the principle of legal certainty requires that individuals must "know precisely the extent of the obligations which [the rules] impose on them",[5] particularly given the significant financial consequences. Nevertheless, the Court of Justice has consistently denied that abuse of law and legal certainty are actually in conflict. As will be demonstrated in Chap. 3, the Court has achieved this by carefully construing the constitutive elements of abuse of law. Where those elements are met, individuals cannot legitimately invoke legal certainty as a shield against the finding of abuse. In any case, a detailed examination of the precise scope of legal certainty and legitimate expectations, as well as their potential interaction with the principle of abuse of Union law, lies beyond the scope of this study. These issues will be addressed only to the extent necessary to clarify the scope and contours of abuse of law as established in the case law.

Among the legal concepts that share clear connections with abuse of law, the most prominent is good faith. The connection between these two principles will emerge consistently and explicitly throughout this book. For a detailed discussion, the reader is referred in particular to Chap. 2. At this stage, it is sufficient to note that the link between abuse of law and good faith has surfaced across a range of legal systems, both domestic and international. Perhaps the field where this connection is most vividly illustrated is international investment law, as discussed in Chap. 2, Sect. 2.4.2, though it is also present in general international law.[6] In municipal legal systems, the relationship between the two principles is sometimes explicitly codified,

---

[2] See Tridimas 2006, p. 242.

[3] Ibid.

[4] In fact, beyond the individual dimension highlighted in this brief definition, abuse of law also has an institutional dimension. As Chaps. 3 and 4 will show, the principle of abuse of Union law is likely to extend to institutional actors, including both EU institutions and Member States. Thus far, however, this dimension has found only limited expression in the practice, and the case law of the ECJ offers little support for such an interpretation. This issue will be revisited in greater detail below.

[5] CJEU, *Halifax plc, Leeds Permanent Development Services Ltd and County Wide Property Investments Ltd*, Judgment of the Court, 21 February 2006, case C-255/02, ECLI:EU:C:2006:121, para 72.

[6] See, in particular, the theory of abuse of law as elaborated by Bin Cheng, in Chap. 2, Sect. 2.4.1.

as in the Swiss Civil Code;[7] in other cases, it is either implicitly recognised or inferred through case law, as in the Italian legal system.[8] The basic idea is that abuse of rights is a specific manifestation of bad faith, just as legitimate expectations are a specific expression of legal certainty. Put simply, the exercise of a right in good faith cannot constitute abuse—or, conversely, an abusive exercise of a right necessarily involves some degree of bad faith. This is not to suggest that the principle of abuse of law is redundant or entirely subsumed under good faith—though that has been one of the principal arguments advanced by those who question the existence of a standalone principle prohibiting abuse of rights.[9] As Michael Byers insightfully observed: "the principle of abuse of rights is not redundant. Instead it is, in one small but important respect, supplemental to the principle of good faith: it provides the threshold at which a lack of good faith gives rise to a violation of international law, with all the attendant consequences".[10] Although Byers was referring specifically to international law, this reasoning is equally applicable to abuse of law more broadly, as the analysis in this book will seek to demonstrate.

Another concept that has connections with abuse of law, particularly in the context of international law,[11] is estoppel. Estoppel refers to situations where a "State that has taken a particular position may be under an obligation to act consistently with it on another occasion [or where a State] has acted to its detriment in relying on a formal declaration by another State, the latter may be estopped from denying its responsibility for any adverse consequences".[12] This principle is often encapsulated in the Latin maxim *venire contra factum proprium*. At its core, estoppel is grounded in the idea that expectations created by a previously held position or formal statement—when relied upon in good faith—may give rise to legal consequences. For this reason, estoppel is frequently understood as one of the duties that flow from reasonableness and good faith.[13] The relationship between estoppel and abuse of law has been noted most clearly in procedural contexts. For instance, a scenario in which "a State commences proceedings against another State contrary to a prior undertaking not to do so" lies at the intersection of estoppel and abuse of process.[14] While in some instances, a clear overlap between the two concepts is evident, this book will demonstrate that abuse of law remains an autonomous legal notion, distinct but occasionally intersecting with estoppel.

---

[7] See Chap. 2, Sect. 2.3.1.

[8] Ibid.

[9] This is the case of Schwarzenberger 1956, p. 148, who claimed that "abuse of rights is [...] obviously a postulate of reasonableness and good faith"; but also Birnie and Boyle 1992, p. 126.

[10] See Byers 2002, p. 411.

[11] There are similar legal concepts in domestic systems as well. In the Italian one, for example, there exists *acquiescenza* (acquiescence) in administrative law and in civil procedure. See Astone 2017, pp. 62–63.

[12] See Aust 2010, p. 8.

[13] Schwarzenberger 1956, p. 179.

[14] Mitchell and Malone 2018, para 10.

The final principle that shares clear affinities with abuse of law is proportionality. As Enzo Cannizzaro masterfully defined it, at its core, "proportionality is a legal technique mostly employed to determine the legality of unilateral measures taken by a state to protect certain interests protected by international law on the basis of the detrimental effect produced on other interests that are entitled to legal protection".[15] When this is read alongside Hersch Lauterpacht's definition of abuse of rights, the conceptual parallels become evident. Lauterpacht famously asserted that "there is […] an abuse of rights each time the general interest of the community is injuriously affected as the result of the sacrifice of an important social or individual interest to a less important, though hitherto legally recognized, individual right".[16] In both cases, a similar balancing exercise lies at the heart of the legal analysis.[17] However, there is a fundamental distinction between the two concepts. A breach of the principle of proportionality may render a measure unlawful, but it does not question the underlying right itself. Proportionality assumes that the State is entitled to act, but that the measure adopted may be excessive and therefore in breach of the law. In contrast, as this book will argue, abuse of law is of a different nature: an abusive act is performed *non iure*, that is, without a valid legal right. Acting abusively nullifies the legitimacy of the underlying entitlement. Moreover, abuse of law and proportionality are not mutually exclusive, but complementary, at least in the EU legal order. As the following analysis will show, proportionality is used (particularly by the ECJ) as a legal technique to assess the legality of anti-abuse measures taken by the Member States or the EU, precisely in the sense identified by Cannizzaro.

Before turning to the substance of this book, the next section will address a few remaining preliminary issues.

1.2 A Few Preliminary Issues

There are three characteristics commonly found across all legal systems in which the doctrine of abuse of law exists. First, there is or has been persistent debate surrounding the very existence of abuse of law as an autonomous legal principle. Second, judicial practice tends to be limited and often inconsistent, with relatively few decisions offering clear guidance.[18] Third, abuse of law is rarely invoked as the primary legal argument in a dispute. More often, it serves as a secondary line of reasoning or even as a last resort—a kind of desperate argument within a strategy of throwing everything at the wall to see what sticks.

One illustrative example is the *Chen* case. As discussed more in-depth in Chap. 3, Sect. 3.3.3, this case involved a newborn child of third-country nationals who

[15] See Cannizzaro 2016, p. 1068.

[16] See Lauterpacht 2011, p. 294.

[17] In this sense also Cannizzaro 2000, p. 448.

[18] As we shall see, the EU legal order now stands as an exception, given the relatively high number of abuse findings by the ECJ and the establishment of a clearly structured abuse test.

acquired Irish nationality—and thereby EU citizenship—as a result of the purposeful planning of the child's birth in Ireland by her parents. In response, the United Kingdom argued that the invocation of EU citizenship rights amounted to an abuse of rights, given the circumstances under which Irish nationality had been obtained. However, this argument was only a secondary line of reasoning in the first part of the UK's pleading. Moreover, it relied on an inappropriate precedent and was ultimately so unconvincing that the Court chose to sidestep it entirely. Among the cases analysed in this volume, there appears to be only one notable exception to this pattern. As we will see in Chap. 2, Sect. 2.4.3, France invoked abuse of rights as its primary argument—albeit unsuccessfully—in the *Immunities and Criminal Proceedings* case brought against it by Equatorial Guinea before the International Court of Justice. But even this exception reinforces the broader point: in most disputes, parties tend to rely on primary arguments they believe to be more persuasive, relegating abuse of law to a subsidiary or fallback role. If, in the context of litigation, even the parties themselves are reluctant to invest heavily in an abuse of law claim, it is hardly surprising that courts have approached the doctrine with caution. The reasons for this reluctance may vary, but one overarching challenge stands out: proving the existence of abuse of law is often a difficult task,[19] which makes it hard to weaponise the concept effectively in a courtroom setting. This difficulty is confirmed, among others, by the Italian legal experience, where the limited practical impact of Article 833 of the Italian Civil Code—the provision prohibiting spiteful acts—is frequently attributed to the evidentiary challenges associated with proving abuse of rights and particularly the intention to cause harm (so-called *animus nocendi*).[20]

Moreover, as we will see in Chap. 2, both domestic legal systems and international law tend to use the term "abuse of rights" more frequently than "abuse of law". This preference also emerges in the extensive case law of the ECJ, which we will examine in Chaps. 3 and 4, where the Court predominantly employs the expression "abuse of rights". Nevertheless, for the purpose of this book, we will adopt the alternative terminology: "abuse of law", "abuse of Union law" or "abuse of EU law". While some scholars have sought to distinguish between these expressions, this distinction has not been endorsed by the ECJ, and will therefore not be followed here. For example, Takis Tridimas has argued that a "general distinction can be drawn between abuse which occurs where a person seeks to derive excessive advantages by relying on a right, thus causing disproportionate harm to others, and abuse which occurs in the improper use of a rule [...] The first is primarily a concept of private law and derives from French law. It seeks to limit the exercise of private rights in the light of social objectives and, ultimately, curb the excesses of individualism. The second meaning is a broader one. Abuse is here understood as a circumvention or evasion and seeks to prohibit a person from deriving a benefit which, although

---

[19] I am grateful to my friend Dilara Khamitova, a practising investment lawyer at a prominent international law firm, for bringing this question to my attention during a lunch in Paris. It is the kind of insight that might well have eluded an academic—especially one as prone to living in his own world as yours truly.

[20] See Astone 2017, p. 6. For an analysis of the Italian legal system, see Chap. 2, Sect. 2.3.1.

the benefit may result from formal compliance with a rule, in fact pursues ends which are beyond its objectives".[21] Similarly, Saydé has proposed a classification distinguishing between "private-private abuse", which he terms "abuse of rights", and "private–public abuse", which he labels "abuse of law".[22] In his words, "abuses of law are essentially undesirable choices of law, whereas abuses of rights are undesirable exercises of rights".[23] These conceptual distinctions undoubtedly have analytical value. However, because the Court of Justice does not draw this distinction, this book will use the terms "abuse of law" and "abuse of rights" interchangeably, with a general preference for the former.[24]

The final preliminary issue to be addressed is the distinction between abuse and fraud. As will become apparent throughout this book, the ECJ does not draw a clear line between these two concepts and often treats them together in its reasoning. Even when fraud is addressed separately, the Court has applied a variation of the abuse of law test developed in its case law. Yet, despite certain commonalities, the two concepts are fundamentally different. The key distinction lies in the fact that fraud invariably involves a misrepresentation of reality, which may take the form of forged documents, false statements, or other forms of deliberate deception.[25] This element of misrepresentation is absent in cases of abuse of law. This raises the question of why the Court of Justice has not (yet) drawn a clearer conceptual boundary between abuse and fraud. On the one hand, it may simply be a matter of time before such a distinction is more explicitly articulated. On the other hand, the Court's approach may be influenced by the French legal tradition, in which *fraude à la loi* does not necessarily require a misrepresentation of facts,[26] making the distinction between abuse and fraud less rigid. Given the supranational character of the ECJ and the influence of multiple legal traditions within the EU legal order, this blending of concepts is perhaps unsurprising. It offers a plausible explanation for the current lack of firm demarcation between abuse and fraud in the Court's reasoning.

---

[21] See Tridimas 2011, p. 169.

[22] See Saydé 2016, pp. 23–31.

[23] Ibid., p. 28.

[24] It is worth noting that part of the terminological confusion may stem from linguistic differences. In Latin and the modern Romance languages, such as French and Italian, there is only one term corresponding to both the English law and right: respectively, *droit* in French and *diritto* in Italian. Thus, the law is *le droit* or *il diritto*, while a right is *un droit* or *un diritto*. This dual meaning derives from Latin, where *ius* referred both to law as a system and to an individual legal entitlement or right. By contrast, the term *lex*, from which the French *loi* and the Italian *legge* are derived, designated a specific piece of legislation. Famous examples include the *Lex Aquilia* (the Roman law on damages and wrongful harm to property), *la loi Veil* (which legalised abortion in France), and *la legge Basaglia* (which abolished psychiatric hospitals and revolutionised mental health care in Italy).

[25] See Saydé 2016, p. 24.

[26] See the considerations made by Gaillard 2017, p. 36.

1.3 Plan of the Book

The structure of the book is as follows.

Chapter 2 offers a comparative analysis of various domestic legal systems and international law. It opens with a brief survey of the historical origins of the concept of abuse of law, tracing it back to Roman law and its development in the 19th century. The chapter then turns to contemporary domestic legal systems, grouping them into three categories. The first group consists of civil law jurisdictions, where the doctrine of abuse of law is well-established, though variations exist between legal orders. The second group includes common law jurisdictions, where the admissibility of a general theory of abuse of law is highly contested. The prevailing view is that no such doctrine exists. However, the analysis will demonstrate that legal concepts serving similar functions—albeit under different names—are present in systems rooted in the common law tradition. The third group comprises legal systems with distinctive approaches to abuse of law, including the Nordic countries, Japan and the Islamic legal tradition, which will be briefly examined together.

Chapter 3 provides a comprehensive examination of the extensive case law of the Court of Justice, presented in chronological order to trace the gradual and sometimes convoluted evolution of the concept of abuse of law within the EU legal order. This evolution is structured into three phases: (a) the foundational period, beginning with *Van Binsbergen*, (b) a more structured development, starting with *Emsland-Stärke*, where the Court formulated an abuse test, and (c) the consolidation phase, initiated by the *Cussens* ruling in 2017, in which the Luxembourg Court explicitly recognised the prohibition of abuse of EU law as a general principle of the Union's legal order.[27]

Chapter 4 provides a doctrinal reflection on abuse of law as a general principle within the EU legal order. It tackles a number of key issues. First, it examines the distinction between fraud and abuse, as well as partial analogies with the *Keck* line of case law. Second, it presents a systematisation of abuse into two main types, corresponding to the two most frequent scenarios in which the concept arises in EU law. Third, it explores the application of the principle across different fields of EU law, highlighting both common features and divergences, and considers the impact of secondary legislation and harmonisation. The chapter also addresses open questions and unresolved challenges surrounding the doctrine.

Chapter 5 adopts a more theoretical perspective. It examines the purpose and function of abuse of law within the EU legal system and its broader implications for the general concept of abuse of law. It addresses fundamental questions concerning the normative function of the principle, its contribution to the understanding of abuse beyond the EU, and its ultimate purpose as a general legal concept. The chapter concludes that, in the EU context, abuse of law primarily serves to preserve the coherence and systemic integrity of the legal order—aligning with the function of abuse of law in other legal traditions. It argues that the emergence and consolidation of this principle is a clear indicator of the maturation of the Union's legal system.

---

[27] References to these rulings are provided in Chap. 3.

Finally, Chap. 6 summarises the main conclusions reached in the preceding chapters and closes with a reflection on abuse of law as an inevitable by-product of the consolidation of the rule of law and democratic governance.

References

Astone A (2017) Il divieto di abuso del diritto. Giuffrè, Milan.
Aust A (2010) Handbook of International Law. Cambridge University Press, Cambridge.
Birnie P, Boyle AE (1992) International Law and the Environment. Clarendon Press, Oxford.
Byers M (2002) Abuse of Rights: An Old Principle, A New Age. McGill Law Journal 47:389–434.
Cannizzaro E (2000) Il principio della proporzionalità nell'ordinamento internazionale. Giuffrè, Milan.
Cannizzaro E (2016) Proportionality and Margin of Appreciation in the Whaling Case: Reconciling Antithetical Doctrines? European Journal of International Law 27:1061–1069.
Gaillard E (2017) Abuse of Process in International Arbitration. ICSID Review 32:17–37.
Lauterpacht H (2011) The Function of Law in the International Community. Oxford University Press, Oxford.
Mitchell A, Malone T (2018) Abuse of Process in Inter-State Dispute Resolution. Max Planck Encyclopedia of Public International Law, Oxford University Press, Oxford.
Saydé A (2016) Abuse of EU Law and Regulation of the Internal Market. Hart Publishing, Oxford/Portland.
Schwarzenberger G (1956) Uses and Abuses of the "Abuse of Rights" in International Law. Transactions of the Grotius Society 42:147–179.
Tridimas T (2006) The General Principles of EU Law. Oxford University Press, Oxford.
Tridimas T (2011) Abuse of Rights in EU Law: Some Reflections with Particular Reference to Financial Law. In: De la Feria R, Vogenauer S (eds) Prohibition of Abuse of Law. A New General Principle of EU Law? Hart Publishing, Oxford/Portland, pp. 169–191.

Chapter 2
Abuse of Law in Municipal Legal Orders and International Law: An Overview

Contents

Abstract This chapter broadens the perspective beyond the EU legal order by offering a comparative overview of how the concept of abuse of law is treated across various legal systems. It examines continental European and common law jurisdictions, as well as other municipal legal traditions. The analysis shows that the doctrine of abuse of rights is well established in continental Europe, Japan, Islamic legal systems, and the Nordic countries. While differences exist, these systems share a core understanding of the concept. Even in common law jurisdictions, where the doctrine is not formally recognised, analogous legal notions reflect the underlying idea that rights can be misused. The chapter also explores international law, where the notion of abuse of rights has gained traction in certain areas, such as international investment law, though it has yet to achieve general acceptance as a principle of public international law.

Keywords Civil law jurisdictions · Common law · Islamic legal tradition · International law · Human rights law · International investment law

L. Pantaleo, *Abuse of Law in the European Union*,
https://doi.org/10.1007/978-94-6265-731-1_2

2.1 Introduction

As the analysis of the Court of Justice's case law in Chap. 3 will demonstrate, the development of the concept of abuse of law within the EU legal order has been gradual and has not followed a strictly linear trajectory. Before engaging with that analysis—the central focus of this monograph—it is appropriate to first examine the notion of abuse of law in other legal contexts, both domestic and international.

With a certain degree of abstraction, municipal legal systems can be categorised into three main groups. At one end of the spectrum are civil law jurisdictions, where the existence of a doctrine of abuse of law is undisputed. While its scope and breadth may vary across countries, the core elements remain largely consistent. At the other end are common law jurisdictions, where the admissibility of an abuse of law theory is highly contested. The default position in common law is that no such doctrine exists. However, as the analysis will demonstrate, legal systems rooted in the common law tradition contain legal concepts that, although operating under different names, essentially serve the same function as abuse of law in civil law jurisdictions. Beyond these two broad categories lies a third group of legal systems that exhibit distinct characteristics regarding their approach to abuse of law. This group includes the Nordic countries, Japan and the Islamic legal system, which will be briefly examined together.

In the context of international law, the analysis will demonstrate that abuse of law has been explicitly recognised in certain fields, such as international investment law and WTO law. However, despite being invoked multiple times before the International Court of Justice (ICJ), the doctrine has yet to be explicitly endorsed by this court. Scholarly opinion on this issue remains divided, though the prevailing view today is that rights conferred by international law can indeed be exercised abusively.

This chapter aims to provide an overview of abuse of law in legal systems beyond the EU legal order. We begin with a brief survey of the concept's origins, tracing it back to Roman law and the 19th century (Sect. 2.2). The analysis then turns to domestic legal systems (Sect. 2.3), following the groupings outlined above, with each group examined in a separate subsection. Section 2.4 explores abuse of law in international law, structured into subsections. Section 2.5 presents interim conclusions.

2.2 The Origins of the Concept of Abuse of Law from Roman Law to Modern Times

As is well known, the origins of the notion of abuse of law can be traced back to Roman law. While it may not be accurate to claim that Roman law contained a fully developed doctrine of abuse of law, its foundational principles undeniably laid the groundwork for what would evolve into the concept as we understand it today.

The Romans initially conceived individual rights as absolute, as reflected in the maxim *neminem laedit qui iure suo utitur* ("he who exercises his legal rights harms no one"). However, the rigidity of this principle was gradually tempered. Over time, the Roman legal order developed the principle *summum ius summa iniuria* ("the highest law is the highest injustice"), as well as the principle *sic utere iure tuo ut alterum non laedas* ("use your own right in such a way that you do not injure other people").[1] According to Josserand, this gradual evolution was attributable to "*le génie de la race latine, si impressionable, si volontiers accessible aux pensées altruistes*".[2] It culminated in the application of these principles to the Roman notion of *exheredatio* (the act of excluding a legitimate heir from receiving an inheritance). Initially regarded as an unrestricted right, *exheredatio* gradually became subject to justification requirements.[3] Despite these developments, Roman law ultimately fell short of formulating a comprehensive theory of abuse of law. However, it became evident that acts were not strictly divided into lawful and unlawful; a third category emerged—acts that, while formally lawful, were not protected by the legal order.

If the Romans laid the foundation for the edifice of abuse of law, the French completed its construction and gave it a modern form, despite the absence of any provision on abuse of law in the French *Code civil*, promulgated in 1804.[4] Although some developments occurred even earlier,[5] a judgment of the Court of Appeal of Colmar in 1855 is widely regarded as a watershed moment in this evolution. In this well-known case, an Alsatian property owner built a tall chimney solely to cast a shadow over his neighbour's property. The court was confronted with Article 544 of the *Code civil*, which—then as now—defines property rights in strong absolute terms: "*[l]a propriété est le droit de jouir et disposer des choses de la manière la plus absolue, pourvu qu'on n'en fasse pas un usage prohibé par les lois ou par les règlements*". Since no law or regulation explicitly prohibited the construction of a tall chimney, the case presented a legal dilemma. Nonetheless, the Court of Appeal famously held that exercising property rights malevolently and with no other purpose than to harm another person was an abuse of rights.[6] This judgment is widely recognised as the cornerstone of the modern doctrine of abuse of rights. It was followed by a series of French court decisions that gradually extended its application to other areas of private law, such as labour law and contract law. While

---

[1] According to Kiss 2006, p. 2, this principle is "the very fundament of the concept of abuse of right" in international law.

[2] See Josserand 1905, p. 10.

[3] Ibid., pp. 11–12.

[4] According to Restivo 2007, pp. 67–68, this omission was a logical consequence of the strong rationalist approach that permeated the Code. At the time, abuse of law was seen as reflecting a connection between law and morality, making it incompatible with the prevailing intellectual climate.

[5] For an earlier application of the theory of abuse of law in French case law, see Perreau 1913, p. 488 ff., who refers to a 1577 case in Aix involving labourers who sang loudly solely to disturb a nearby resident.

[6] See Josserand 1905, pp. 19 ff.

today this case law is primarily of historical relevance, it is extensively analysed by Josserand and does not require further discussion here.[7]

This idea, inaugurated by the mentioned French case law, constitutes the very foundation of the modern understanding of abuse of law, shaping its development across various legal systems. In the next section, we provide a brief overview of several domestic legal systems. We begin (Sect. 2.3.1) with continental European legal systems that have either explicitly codified abuse of law, recognised it through the case law, or adopted a combination of both, as in the Italian system. We then examine common law jurisdictions (Sect. 2.3.2) before concluding with the third mixed group mentioned above (Sect. 2.3.3).

2.3 Abuse of Law in Domestic Legal Systems

2.3.1 Continental Europe

The first group includes civil law systems in continental Europe that feature either an explicit or an implicit theory of abuse of law.

Germany provides the first example of a legal system where abuse of law is explicitly codified. Notably, the German Civil Code (BGB) was promulgated nearly one century after the French Civil Code,[8] allowing it to incorporate a more structured approach to abuse of law. The BGB includes an explicit prohibition in Article 226, which states: "the exercise of a right is impermissible if its sole purpose is to cause harm to another". Additionally, two other provisions indirectly reinforce the theory of abuse of law: Article 242 establishes a general principle of good faith, and Article 826 prohibits intentional harm *contra bonos mores* ("contrary to good morals"). Through the combined application of these provisions, German courts have developed a comprehensive doctrine of abuse of law. This doctrine not only prohibits the malicious exercise of rights intended to cause harm, as mandated by Article 226, but also extends to cases where an exercise of rights reveals bad faith or results in grossly inequitable outcomes.[9] A textbook illustration is the classification as abusive of a husband's repudiation of paternity after having previously consented to his wife's heterologous insemination.[10]

[7] Ibid., pp. 30 ff. For an English-language analysis of this case law, which includes judgments issued after the publication of Josserand's work and therefore not commented on by him, see Di Robilant 2014, pp. 68 ff.

[8] According to Bolgár 1975, p. 1023, this was a decisive factor, given that "the progress of ideas within this span of time, from the strictly individualistic towards the social-functional aspects of law - which affected legal thought in Germany as well - had its definite impact on the principles that lay at the foundations of the German code".

[9] For an overview, see Bolgár 1975, pp. 1029 ff.

[10] This case is referred to by Rescigno 1998, p. 280.

While the German BGB was the first to explicitly codify abuse of law, the Swiss Civil Code, promulgated a few years later, went even further.[11] It enshrined the principle of abuse of law in Article 2, a general provision placed in the introductory part of the code, making it generally applicable by definition. Article 2(1) establishes that "*chacun est tenu d'exercer ses droits et d'exécuter ses obligations selon les règles de la bonne foi*". Article 2(2) stipulates that "*l'abus manifeste d'un droit n'est pas protégé par la loi*". Here, abuse of law is explicitly linked to good faith. However, unlike the French and German systems, the Swiss approach introduces a qualification: abuse must be *manifest*. Building on this provision, Swiss courts developed an extensive abuse of law doctrine as early as the mid-1940s, with judges openly asserting their active role in combating injustice through this doctrine.[12]

The law of the Soviet Union presents a unique case. The Soviet Civil Code included a general provision on abuse of rights in Article 1, which stated: "the civil rights of citizens are protected by law, except when they are exercised in contradiction to their socio-economic purpose".[13] In line with socialist legal theory, this provision framed the exercise of a right as abusive if it undermined its broader social function. This approach reflects the collectivist nature of Soviet law, where individual rights were subordinated to socio-economic objectives. What is particularly noteworthy about the Soviet experience is that Article 1 gradually became irrelevant. In a socialist system, laws enacted by the Soviets were presumed to be morally impeccable. If one acted within the boundaries of socialist law, malevolence was theoretically impossible. As a result, the concept of abuse of law lost significance. This suggests that, in a socialist society, the problem of abuse of law is inherently temporary—a challenge that ceases to exist once socialism is firmly established.[14]

Several other European legal systems explicitly recognise abuse of law, including Spain, Portugal and Greece,[15] whose Civil Code provisions played a central role in the so-called Greek challenge saga that ultimately reached the ECJ.[16] However, this analysis will not dwell on these jurisdictions but will instead focus on two additional domestic systems before examining legal traditions where the doctrine was developed in the absence of explicit codification. The first is that of the Netherlands, where the new Civil Code came into force in 1992.[17] Abuse of law is explicitly recognised by Article 13 of Book 3, which primarily concerns property law. However, Article 15

[11] This is also the opinion of Politis 1925, p. 82.

[12] In a 1946 judgment of the Swiss Federal Supreme Court referred to by Bolgár 1975, p. 1034, it is said that Article 2 is related to the fact that "there will always be special cases in which a rigid application of the statutory principles would lead to injustice, and this the judge is not permitted to tolerate".

[13] I have translated into English from the French version of Article 1 cited by Nolde 1923, p. 239, which is, in turn, a translation from the original language.

[14] See, in this sense, Rescigno 1998, pp. 44–45.

[15] For an overview of abuse of law in these systems, see Gestri 2003, p. 29 ff.

[16] These cases are extensively examined in Chap. 3, Sect. 3.2.8 of this book.

[17] The previous version of the Civil Code, promulgated in 1838, was heavily influenced by the Code Napoléon and, unsurprisingly, lacked a provision on abuse. This, however, did not prevent the case law from developing the doctrine autonomously. See Hartkamp 1992, p. 566.

extends its application beyond this field, broadening its scope. The definition of abuse provided in these provisions is arguably the most comprehensive codification of the principle. According to Article 13, the exercise of a right is considered abusive in three situations: (a) when it is exercised with no other purpose than to harm another person, (b) when it is exercised for a purpose other than that for which it is granted, and (c) when, in any case, it must be prevented due to a disproportionate imbalance between the interests served by its exercise and the harm it causes. However, this principle does not apply to the law of obligations and contract law, where "its function is completely covered by the provisions on good faith".[18]

The next legal system under consideration is Italy, which I am particularly familiar with for obvious reasons. In Italy, the development of a theory of abuse of law has been shaped both by explicit legal recognition and judicial interpretation. The Italian Civil Code, promulgated in 1942, contains a provision on abuse of rights in Article 833, specifically concerning property rights: "a property owner cannot carry out acts that have no other purpose than harming or harassing other persons".[19] The provision clearly resembles Article 226 of the BGB and is traditionally associated with *atti emulativi* (spiteful acts), a term also reflected in its title (*atti d'emulazione*). Article 833 applies exclusively to property rights, prohibiting actions that provide no economic benefit whatsoever to the owner. For this reason, it has been deemed insufficient to serve as the foundation for a general doctrine of abuse of rights.[20] Consistently with this narrow scope, Italian courts have interpreted Article 833 restrictively, requiring proof not only that the owner derives no economic advantage from the disputed actions but also that s/he acted with *animus nocendi* (intent to harm). Since proving such intent is notoriously tricky in litigation,[21] Italian case law had to look elsewhere to construct a broader theory of abuse of rights. This theory gradually emerged by extrapolation from the general principles of good faith and fairness. The evolution culminated in a landmark ruling by the *Corte di Cassazione* in 2009,[22] which inaugurated a new line of case law. In this decision, the Court affirmed in general terms that the exercise of a right for a purpose other than that for which it was granted constitutes an abuse of rights.[23]

Turning to legal systems where a general theory of abuse of law has been developed entirely through case law, in the absence of explicit statutory recognition, the prime example is France. Despite being credited as the jurisdiction where the modern concept of abuse of law first emerged, the French legal system lacks a general provision on abuse of law comparable to those in Switzerland, Germany or the Netherlands. Nevertheless, French courts have progressively extended the doctrine of abuse of law, originally developed in property law through the classic case law discussed

---

[18] Ibid.

[19] See Article 833 of the Civil Code (the translation is mine).

[20] See Rescigno 1998, pp. 51–52.

[21] See Astone 2017, p. 6.

[22] Commented on by Galgano 2011, p. 311 ff.

[23] See Astone 2017, pp. 62–63.

above, to virtually all areas of private law.[24] Additionally in public law, the notion of *détournement de pouvoir* is recognized as "*la variété de l'excès de poiuvoir qui [...] se rapproche le plus de l'idée représentée, dans le droit privé, par l'abus de droit*".[25] A similar evolution has taken place in Belgium, where courts have followed a comparable trajectory in the absence of a statutory provision explicitly addressing abuse of law.[26]

2.3.2 The Common Law Tradition

As previously noted, common law jurisdictions are generally perceived as rejecting the theory of abuse of law. It is often assumed, particularly by civil law scholars, that these systems adhere to a highly individualistic conception of rights.[27] However, the analysis in this section demonstrates that this assumption is not entirely accurate. First, abuse of law is recognised in common law systems, albeit sometimes under a different name. Second, and as a consequence, the dichotomy between individualistic and solidaristic conceptions of individual rights is largely misplaced.

Any analysis of abuse of law in common law jurisdictions must begin with the landmark judgment in *Bradford v. Pickles*.[28] The case concerned a landowner who carried out works on his property that disrupted the flow of underground water, fully aware that his actions would negatively impact the community's water supply. In a widely cited decision, the House of Lords held that a landowner's motives were immaterial—no matter how churlish or selfish, they could not transform a lawful act into an unlawful one. As a result, he was entitled to use his property as he saw fit. This case is often regarded as endorsing an absolute conception of individual rights in common law jurisdictions. It remains a leading authority to ground the absence of an abuse of rights doctrine.[29] However, as noted by Tridimas, "a more careful study [...] suggests a more nuanced approach".[30]

First, as aptly argued by Perillo, extensive US case law demonstrates that "the doctrine exists in American law and is employed under such labels as nuisance, duress, good faith, economic waste, public policy, misuse of copyright and patent

---

[24] See Ghestin and Goubeaux 1994, pp. 705 ff.

[25] See Politis 1925, p. 84.

[26] See Gestri 2003, p. 42 ff.

[27] See Politis 1925, p. 82, who wrote "[*là] où le droit reste, comme dans les pays anglo-saxons, très fortement individualiste, on est en principe hostile à l'idée de l'abus*". Along the same lines Ionescu 2012, p. 397.

[28] See *Bradford Corporation v. Pickles* [1895] AC 587.

[29] While writing this book, I have posed the question of whether abuse of rights exists in common law to numerous common law scholars and practising lawyers. With few exceptions, the response has been consistently that the common law has no need for such a doctrine. These answers frequently included a standard reference to *Bradford v. Pickles* as the leading authority on the matter.

[30] See Tridimas 2011, p. 170.

rights, lack of business purpose in tax law, extortion, and others".[31] However, Perillo also acknowledged that "the lack of an overt recognition of a doctrine of 'abuse of rights' creates injustices in cases not falling within one of these doctrines".[32] Di Robilant reached a similar conclusion two decades later.[33] Moreover, it is no coincidence that one of the earliest studies on abuse of law in the EU legal order was conducted by a common law scholar, Neville Brown. He recognised that, while a formal doctrine of abuse of law was absent in the British Isles—including Ireland—common law had developed specific torts, such as nuisance, to address cases where the exercise of rights leads to unreasonable outcomes.[34] Neville Brown also noted that the law of Scotland contains the concept of *aemulatio*—closely resembling Article 833 of the Italian Civil Code—and that abuse of process is widely acknowledged across common law jurisdictions.[35]

In conclusion, while common law scholars—particularly in earlier times—have been among the most vehement critics of the abuse of law doctrine,[36] it has been unequivocally established that common law jurisdictions contain legal concepts that share the same underlying rationale and serve an equivalent function.[37]

2.3.3 *Japan, the Islamic Legal System and the Nordic Countries*

The third and final group to be analysed here consists of a variegated group of legal traditions that are worth being analysed. We will begin with Japan, where the development of a doctrine of abuse of law has been particularly intriguing.[38]

Until the so-called Meiji Restoration of 1868, Japan lacked a formal legal system in the sense understood by civil law countries. A strong cultural emphasis on compromise and community harmony ensured that disputes were resolved internally within village communities.[39] The Meiji Restoration marked a watershed moment in Japanese legal history, ushering in a new era with the promulgation of the 1868 Constitution and the 1896 Civil Code. This period saw the westernisation of Japanese

---

[31] See Perillo 1995, p. 40.

[32] Ibid.

[33] See Di Robilant 2014, pp. 8–20.

[34] See Neville Brown 1994, pp. 514–515.

[35] See Neville Brown 1994, p. 515. See Mitchell and Malone 2018, para 13, who also point out that abuse of process has an established place in the common law.

[36] See Gutteridge 1933, pp. 43–44 and Schwarzenberger 1956, pp. 149–150.

[37] For an analysis of the purpose and function of abuse of law see Chap. 5.

[38] For this part, I am indebted to my colleague Felix Dröll, one of the few – perhaps the only Western expert on the topic, at least to my knowledge. Not only did he direct me to the predictably scarce sources available in a language I can read, but he also guided me through the evolution of the concept in Japan, from the early development to modern Japanese law. His assistance has been truly invaluable.

[39] See Dröll 2024, pp. 35.

law, with France and Germany serving as primary legal models.[40] The shift was nothing short of a cultural revolution, as it introduced a fundamentally new legal paradigm—the concept of individual rights, which had been foreign to Japanese tradition.[41] Despite this, it was not long before Japanese courts were confronted with cases involving the potentially abusive exercise of rights. The *Shinagawa v. Kurobe Railway Co.*, also known as the *Onsen* case, is widely regarded as a landmark ruling. Coincidentally, much like *Bradford v. Pickles*, it concerned the passage of water beneath private land. However, the outcome diverged significantly from its English counterpart. The case involved a plaintiff who purchased a vast tract of wasteland—previously unused—for a minimal sum. A small portion contained an underground pipeline supplying hot spring water to a spa resort operated by the defendant. The landowner demanded an exorbitant price for the fraction of land housing the pipeline, which the defendant refused to pay. In response, the plaintiff sued, seeking the removal of the pipeline. The court weighed the competing interests and concluded that the right to use property freely could not supersede the broader social benefit of maintaining the pipeline. The claim was therefore rejected as an abuse of property rights.[42]

The abuse of rights doctrine was later formally incorporated into the Japanese Civil Code with the 1947 reform, through the introduction of Article 1, which now states: "1. Private rights must conform to the public welfare. 2. The exercise of rights and performance of duties must be done in good faith. 3. *No abuse of rights is permitted*."[43] This reform established a general limitation on the abusive exercise of private rights, laying the foundation for a comprehensive theory of abuse in Japanese law. Among the various areas where the doctrine has been applied, its most significant influence is arguably in labour law, particularly in the protection of workers against dismissal. The leading case in this regard is the *Kôchi broadcasting* case,[44] widely regarded as a landmark ruling. The Japanese example is, therefore, particularly emblematic. It illustrates that abuse of rights is, in a sense, inherent to the very notion of subjective rights, even in a legal culture where such concepts remained foreign for a long time. It reinforces the idea, which will be closely examined in Chap. 5, that abuse of rights serves as a mechanism within legal systems to prevent the law from being exploited in the service of injustice.[45]

The concept of abuse of law is also well established in Islamic legal tradition and is now codified in the civil codes of most Arab countries. However, its origins lie in Shari'a principles and Islamic jurisprudence. A widely accepted general definition of abuse of law considers the exercise of a right abusive when it contradicts the purpose

---

[40] See Evans and Ramseyer 2021, p. 314.

[41] So much so that the Japanese language had to introduce a neologism—*kenri*—to articulate this concept. See Dröll 2024, p. 36.

[42] For a detailed account of this case, see Sono and Fujioka 1975, pp. 1041–1042.

[43] The English-language text is taken word for word from Hayashi 2008, p. 20 (emphasis added).

[44] From which English excerpts are available in Emerson 1987, p. 45.

[45] See Dröll 2024, p. 35.

for which it was granted.[46] This conceptualisation closely parallels the abuse of law doctrine in other legal traditions, particularly continental European systems. As we shall see in Chap. 3, where the ECJ's case law is examined in detail, this principle also represents the core essence of abuse of law in the EU legal order.

The connection between modern abuse of law and Shari'a principles is particularly evident in certain manifestations of abuse. One such example comes from traditional Islamic case law, which considers it abusive for merchants to purchase massive quantities of goods, particularly food, when there is no immediate shortage or price crisis, solely to resell them at significantly higher prices when supply diminishes or prices surge. While stockpiling goods is not inherently prohibited, it becomes abusive when the sole intent is to generate disproportionate and unjust profit. This notion is directly linked to the words of the Prophet Muhammad, who condemned hoarding and labelled those who engaged in it as "sinners".[47] In modern times, abuse of law in the Islamic legal tradition is typically identified in four specific situations: (a) when a right is exercised with the intent to harm others, (b) when the individual benefit of the right holder is grossly disproportionate to the harm caused to others, (c) when the individual benefit contradicts the public interest, and (d) when the harm caused by the exercise of a right is, in any case, severe and unjustifiable.[48] Hence, in conclusion, it can be said that abuse of law in the Islamic tradition ultimately serves the same fundamental ideal of justice observed in other legal traditions.

The final group under examination consists of the Nordic countries,[49] which, despite certain differences, seem to share a common core approach to the doctrine of abuse of law. Finland's legal system does not explicitly prohibit abuse of rights in a general manner. However, statutory manifestations of the prohibition can be found in tax law and bankruptcy law. Additionally, Finnish case law has developed a general doctrine through interpretation, establishing that formal rules cannot be exploited to achieve outcomes fundamentally at odds with the spirit of the law. This doctrine serves to protect both private rights and broader societal interests.[50] A similar situation can be found in Sweden, where no general codification of the prohibition of abuse of law exists, yet statutory provisions embodying the principle are present. Moreover, under the impulse of the *Högsta domstolen* (Swedish Supreme Court), case law has developed an overarching principle that prevents individuals from profiting from wrongful conduct they themselves orchestrated, even if the formal basis for their

[46] See Dawwas 1993, p. 1, citing, at footnote 1, another scholar who wrote in Arabic.

[47] Ibid., p. 10.

[48] Ibid., p. 14.

[49] For this part, I am deeply indebted to my colleague Pekka Pohjankoski, who generously shared his insights on the topic, and even more so to Katri Havu, whose guidance was invaluable in helping me understand the legal frameworks of the countries involved. Given the surprising scarcity of English-language sources on the subject, navigating the relevant literature and the case law would have been nearly impossible without Katri's assistance. AI should also be credited with helping me translate some texts into English. Unfortunately, I could not find any relevant material concerning Norway and Iceland.

[50] See Linna 2004, *passim*.

claim rests on an individual right.[51] The same reasoning largely applies to Denmark. While no single statutory clause systematically enshrines the doctrine of abuse of law, Danish courts refuse to uphold conduct that flagrantly contradicts the lawful purpose of a right or imposes disproportionate harm without legitimate justification. As a result, despite the absence of an explicit general clause, Danish case law and legal theory recognise an unwritten rule preventing the manipulative or malicious use of legally valid rights.[52]

In summary, the Nordic countries may appear to belong to the continental European legal tradition, where the doctrine of abuse of law has been developed through judicial interpretation despite the absence of an explicit statutory provision. However, what distinguishes them from countries such as France or Belgium is that, at least initially, they admittedly shared the same scepticism towards abuse of law that has traditionally characterised common law jurisdictions.[53] It is only in recent decades that they have shifted towards a more civil-law-oriented approach on this issue. It would be interesting to explore whether this shift is linked to the influence of EU law or, more broadly, to these countries' adherence to the European integration project. However, this question falls beyond the scope of this volume.

2.4 The Concept of Abuse of Law in the International Legal Order

As briefly noted above, the concept of abuse of law in the international legal order is not as firmly established as it is in domestic legal systems. While the possibility that rights granted by international law may be exercised abusively has been affirmed in some specific fields, such as investment law and WTO law, and is widely accepted by scholars, its recognition as a principle of general international law remains unresolved. In the following pages, we will trace the international development of this concept by beginning with its theoretical framing by scholars (Sect. 2.4.1), followed by an analysis of specific areas where it has been recognised (Sect. 2.4.2), including international human rights law (Sect. 2.4.3) where the concept of abuse of rights has an autonomous meaning only partly connected with the general one, and concluding with an examination of its status under general international law (Sect. 2.4.4).

[51] See Lennander 2019, *passim*.

[52] See Evald 2001, p. 335 ff., as well as the English summary provided at p. 369.

[53] See Neville Brown 1994, p. 515.

2.4.1 The Scholarly Dimension: A Theory of Abuse of Law in International Law

The first attempt to systematise abuse of law within a general legal theory of international law was arguably made by Nicolas Politis, whose work on the subject is widely considered foundational and has been referenced multiple times in this volume. Politis, a Corfiot Greek, completed his legal studies in France, where he held several academic positions before transitioning to a diplomatic career in the service of his native Greece.

Unsurprisingly, he was profoundly influenced by French legal thought, particularly the work of Louis Josserand, who shaped his understanding of abuse of law as a mechanism for *l'humanisation du droit* (the humanisation of law). According to Politis, the law in its early stages was simple and rigid. The Roman *maxim neminem laedit qui iure suo utitur* served as the fundamental rule governing social relations. However, as society and human interactions became more complex, law gradually lost its inflexibility, and what was once the exception became the rule: "*c'est la maxime 'summum ius summa iniuria' qui devient la règle*".[54] In Politis' view, this evolution of law ultimately provided the foundation for the theory of abuse of rights, a theory that, though modern in form, had very ancient origins: "*[t]héorie moderne en la forme, mais d'origine très ancienne, qui [...] constitue un merveilleux* ***instrument de légalité et de paix sociales***".[55] Thus, for Politis, abuse of law functioned as a general instrument for upholding the rule of law (*la légalité*) and ensuring social harmony.[56] When examining its application to international law, he argued that it was "*théoriquement concevable, [...] pratiquement possible et [...] déjà entrée dans le domaine de la réalité*".[57]

Regarding the theoretical foundations of abuse of law, Politis argued that the same rationale justifying the doctrine in municipal law also formed its basis in international law. He maintained that "*[l]'individualisme nationale est, comme l'individualisme privé, un véritable anachronisme dans la communauté internationale où la conception de l'indépendance a fait place à celle de l'interdépendance*".[58] Thus, an evolution in international law could be observed, paralleling developments in domestic legal systems. Sovereign rights could no longer be regarded as absolute prerogatives.[59] They had to be exercised in a manner that respected the general interest of the international community as a whole. This principle applied particularly when the general interest was infringed "*par le sacrifice d'un intérêt particulier très fort à un*

---

[54] Politis 1925, p. 78.

[55] Ibid.

[56] As we will see in Chap. 5, Marie Lemey also argued that abuse of law is connected with the protection of the international rule of law (see Chap. 5, Sect. 5.3).

[57] Politis 1925, p. 86.

[58] Ibid., p. 87.

[59] It should be recalled that Politis was writing about abuse of law in the context of a broader study devoted to the limitations on State sovereignty. See Chap. 5, Sect. 5.3.

autre intérêt particulier plus faible".[60] According to Politis, abuse of rights occurred whenever a right or liberty was exercised for "*des motifs blâmables, c'est-à-dire dans un but autre que celui dans lequel le droit international a conféré*"[61] the right or liberty in question. In his work, Politis examined State practice, which, in his view, demonstrated that abuse of law was already an integral part of general international law at the time. We will return to this analysis in Sect. 2.4.3.

Another early theorist of abuse of law in the international legal order was Hersch Lauterpacht. Born in East Galicia under Austro-Hungarian rule, in what is now Zhovkva, Ukraine, near Lviv, he later grew up and was educated in Britain, where he was influenced by British scholars. Having in mind the common law, he was particularly aware that abuse of law "plays a relatively small part in municipal law [where] it has crystallized its typical manifestations in concrete rules and prohibitions".[62] Lauterpacht, like Politis, began with the premise that law in its early stages was more individualistic in the sense that it refused to interfere with legally recognised individual rights and freedoms. This changed, he argued, with "the growth of civilization and of the social integration of the community".[63] At a certain point, he explained, the law—whether through legislative enactment or judicial pronouncement—declares that the exercise of a right has become abusive, not because of the malevolent intention of the doer, but because "the interests injuriously affected by the exercise of the hitherto perfectly legal right are socially and morally more important".[64] Central to this assessment was the existence of an *iniuria*. However, in Lauterpacht's view, the harm in question extended beyond the individual sphere. Unlike *aemulatio*, where the abuse concerns the damage suffered by another individual, he argued that harm could also be inflicted upon the collective interest of the community. Moreover, he contended that in some cases, the law itself determines when a more significant interest has been affected. In other cases, it is the courts, acting in their law-making capacity, that conduct this balancing exercise.[65] Like Politis, Lauterpacht also offered State practice in support of his arguments. We will get back to this analysis below.

The next author relevant to our study is Bin Cheng. He began with the premise that the doctrine of abuse of rights was merely an application of the principle of good faith to the exercise of sovereign rights.[66] Cheng built his theory of abuse of law on the Roman maxim *malitiis non est indulgendum* ("malicious acts should not be excused"). In particular, he argued that "[e]very right is the legal protection of a legitimate interest. An alleged exercise of a right not in the furtherance of such interest, but with the malicious purpose of injuring others can no longer claim the protection of the law".[67] As is evident, Cheng's conception of abuse of law is narrower

---

[60] Politis 1925, p. 89.

[61] Ibid., p. 87.

[62] See Lauterpacht 2011, p. 306.

[63] Ibid., p. 307.

[64] Ibid., pp. 303–304.

[65] Ibid., p. 304.

[66] See Cheng 1953, p. 121.

[67] Ibid., p. 122.

than that of his predecessors, as it appears to be limited to the notion of *aemulatio*, a concept also found in the Italian Civil Code and the Scottish legal system. Consistent with his view of abuse of rights as an offshoot of good faith, which is presumed in international law, he concluded that abuses of rights could not be presumed.[68]

A few years after Cheng, Georg Schwarzenberger published a passionate and meticulously argued critique of abuse of law in international law. A self-proclaimed European, born and raised in Germany, with British nationality and British loyalties,[69] he contested the existence of abuse of law in international law much like a common lawyer would reject its existence in common law jurisdictions. With subtle irony, he remarked that "what Politis had modestly termed a theory" would be "preferable to call a hypothesis".[70] His central argument was that any theory of abuse of law in international law is redundant, as customary international law already contains well-established, specific rules to address the very situations proponents of abuse of law characterise as abusive.[71] The application of these customary rules, he argued, does not render the exercise of rights abusive—instead, it marks the State's conduct as unlawful. Schwarzenberger provided several examples to substantiate his claim. For instance, he argued that while States have an unlimited right to expel foreigners, their ill-treatment is not allowed. If a State exercises its sovereign right to expulsion in contravention of the so-called international minimum standards, "it does not abuse its right of sovereignty. It simply breaks a prohibitory rule by which its right of exclusive jurisdiction is limited".[72] The same reasoning, he argued, applies to expropriation of foreign property, unilateral promises made by a State,[73] and other cases—including the naturalisation of foreigners without the required genuine link.[74] Notably, Politis cited this last example as a textbook illustration of abusive conduct by States.[75]

Over the years, abuse of law has been extensively examined by numerous international law scholars, who have expressed a wide range of opinions on the subject. Gradually, the concept has gained significant traction, to the point that Marie Lemey, author of the most recent comprehensive study on the topic, wrote in 2021: "*la doctrine semble admettre de façon quasi-unanime l'existence d'un 'principe d'interdiction de l'abus de droit' dans l'ordre juridique internationale*".[76] Among the prominent scholars who have advocated for this principle are Alexandre Kiss,[77] Vaughan

[68] Ibid., p. 136.

[69] See Steinle 2004, p. 663.

[70] See Schwarzenberger 1956, p. 147.

[71] Ibid., p. 149.

[72] Ibid., p. 154.

[73] If a State "acts contrary to its notified intent, it breaks the rule on the binding character of communicated unilateral acts". Ibid., p. 157.

[74] Ibid., p. 161.

[75] See Politis 1925, p. 91.

[76] See Lemey 2021, p. 69.

[77] See Kiss 2006, *passim*.

Lowe,[78] Michael Byers,[79] and the aforementioned Marie Lemey, whose exhaustive study on the matter stands as a remarkable example of erudite scholarship. Before turning to the analysis of international practice, it is worth recalling an interesting perspective expressed by Roberto Ago in his capacity as Special Rapporteur of the International Law Commission (ILC) working on State responsibility. In 1970, Ago observed that international scholars were somewhat polarised on the issue, noting the existence of both "firm supporters and determined opponents".[80] However, he concluded there was no compelling reason for the ILC to take a position on the theory of abuse of law. If abuse of law were to be recognised, it would imply that international law contains a primary rule limiting the exercise of State rights and that violating this rule would meet the objective criteria for an internationally wrongful act, thereby triggering the State responsibility legal framework, which was the ILC's primary focus under Ago's tenure.[81] The ILC ultimately agreed with Ago's proposal,[82] and the notion that abusive acts constitute neither lawful nor unlawful conduct but instead fall into a *tertium genus*[83] was not even considered by the Commission.

2.4.2 The Practice: Areas of International Law Where Abuse of Law Has Been Recognised

Regarding international practice supporting the existence of abuse of law, two key observations must be made. First, abuse of law has been expressly codified in several international treaties. Second, even in areas where no explicit codification exists, the doctrine of abuse of law has been invoked in international disputes and explicitly upheld by the dispute settlement body responsible for resolving such cases. This is particularly evident in international trade law and, even more emphatically, international investment law.

We begin with explicit codifications of the doctrine of abuse of law. Various sectoral international agreements contain provisions addressing this concept. Some treaties expressly recognise abuse in its procedural form, known as abuse of process. Notable examples include Article 22(2) of the United Nations Convention against Torture and Other Cruel, Inhuman or Degrading Treatment or Punishment, as well as Article 77(2) of the International Convention on the Protection of the Rights of All Migrant Workers and Members of Their Families, both of which are identically worded. Another example is Article 294(1) of the United Nations Convention on the Law of the Sea (UNCLOS). While this provision has been frequently invoked—or

[78] See Lowe 2000, *passim.*

[79] See Byers 2002, *passim.*

[80] See Ago 1970, p. 193.

[81] Ibid., pp. 193–194.

[82] See Ago 1976, p. 4.

[83] See *supra*, Sect. 2.2.

at least its invocation has been foreshadowed[84]—tribunals have "studiously avoided making any findings in relation to an allegation of abuse of process".[85] Other international treaties codify abuse of substantive rights. The most notable example is Article 300 UNCLOS, which states: "States Parties shall fulfil in good faith the obligations assumed under this Convention and shall exercise the rights, jurisdiction and freedoms recognized in this Convention in a manner which would not constitute an abuse of right". Although this provision has been repeatedly invoked, it has never served as the basis for a ruling that a right was exercised abusively.[86] Finally, provisions such as Article 18 of the Vienna Convention on the Law of Treaties, while not explicitly addressing abuse of law, are regarded by some scholars as closely linked to the prohibition of abuse of rights.[87]

In cases where the doctrine of abuse of law has been recognised despite the absence of an explicit provision, WTO law and international investment law stand out as notable examples. Starting with the WTO, the Appellate Body famously endorsed the doctrine in the *US-Shrimp* dispute, treating it as an offshoot of the principle of good faith. Specifically, the Appellate Body held that "[the] principle [of good faith], at once a general principle of law and a general principle of international law, controls the exercise of rights by States. One application of this general principle, the application widely known as the doctrine of *abus de droit*, prohibits the abusive exercise of a state's rights".[88] However, this ruling remains a relatively isolated exception within the extensive body of WTO case law,[89] which otherwise demonstrates a "reluctance on the part of the Appellate Body and WTO Tribunals generally to hold that Members have acted in bad faith".[90] As a result, while some scholars remain sceptical about the applicability of abuse of law in WTO law,[91] others have relied on the *US-Shrimp* decision to assert the existence of such a doctrine under WTO law.[92]

International investment law presents far less controversy, possibly making it the only area within the international legal order where abuse of law is both widely recognised by scholars and consistently upheld in practice. In this field, a distinction has emerged between abuse of process and abuse of substantive rights, with abuse of process regarded as the procedural manifestation of abuse of rights. Gaillard offered

---

84 For example, by India in the *'Enrica Lexie' Incident* case. See *The 'Enrica Lexie' Incident (The Italian Republic v. The Republic of India)*, India Written Observations of 30 March 2016, PCA Case No. 2015-28, para 3.6. For a comment on the award that settle the dispute, see Marotti 2020, *passim*.

85 See Mitchell and Malone 2018, para 48.

86 See, for example, *The 'Enrica Lexie' Incident (The Italian Republic v. The Republic of India)*, Award of 21 May 2020, PCA Case No. 2015-28, paras 719–730.

87 See Kiss 2006, para 16.

88 See Appellate Body Report, *United States—Import Prohibition of Certain Shrimp and Shrimp Products, Recourse to Article 21.5 of the DSU by Malaysia, WTO Doc* WT/DS58/AB/RW (22 October 2001), para 158 (emphasis in the original text).

89 See the considerations made by Nguyen 2016, especially pp. 125 ff.

90 See Mitchell and Heaton 2010, p. 619.

91 On the sceptical side of the debate are Nguyen 2016, pp. 124 ff., and Carmody 2021, pp. 26 ff.

92 On this other side of the debate are Kiss 2006, para 14, and Byers 2002, p. 401.

the following definition: "the doctrine of abuse of rights is founded upon the notion that a party may have a valid right, including a procedural right, and yet exercise it in an abnormal, excessive or abusive way, with the sole purpose of causing injury to another or for the purpose of evading a rule of law, so as to forfeit its entitlement to rely upon it".[93] In his seminal work on abuse of process, he developed a typology specifically applicable to international investment disputes. The first category of abuse of process arises when an investor seeks to establish the jurisdiction of an arbitral tribunal through artificial arrangements. A textbook example is the *Philip Morris* case, where the tribunal found that Philip Morris had committed an abuse of process by restructuring an investment to fall under the Hong Kong-Australia BIT at a time when a dispute with Australia was already reasonably foreseeable.[94] The second type of abuse occurs when an investor seeks to bring its claim before the tribunal where it believes it has the greatest chance of success. While this practice is not inherently objectionable, it becomes abusive when the investor initiates multiple claims simultaneously.[95] The third and final type of abuse of process in international investment law occurs when a claim is brought for a purpose other than resolving a dispute. Investment arbitration exists to adjudicate disputes, yet an abuse arises when an investor does not genuinely seek resolution but instead uses arbitration as a tool to exert pressure on the other party.[96]

The prevailing view in investment law, as confirmed by case law, is that "the theory of abuse of rights is an expression of the more general principle of good faith".[97] As is well-known, good faith is binding upon States as parties to international agreements, whereas investors themselves are not bound by it. Consequently, a breach of good faith through the abusive behaviour of an investor is indirectly connected with the conduct of the investor's State of nationality, effectively amounting to a restriction of State sovereign prerogatives. Linderfalk provides a compelling explanation of this mechanism using the *Philip Morris v. Australia* case as an illustration. In this case, the issue arose from the criterion set out in Hong Kong legislation for determining the nationality of companies incorporated in its jurisdiction. Under international law, Hong Kong is free to define the criteria by which a company acquires its nationality and, consequently, the ability to exercise rights under a BIT as a Hong Kong investor. However, under the principle of good faith, international law may decline to recognise that criterion for the purpose of applying an investment agreement. Accordingly, if Philip Morris acquired Hong Kong nationality solely to benefit from the BIT, that

---

[93] See Gaillard 2017, pp. 32.

[94] *Philip Morris Asia Limited (Hong Kong) v The Commonwealth of Australia*, PCA Case No 2012-12, Award on Jurisdiction and Admissibility (17 December 2015) para 554.

[95] See Gaillard 2017, p. 22.

[96] Ibid., pp. 26–27.

[97] See *Abaclat and Others (formerly known as Giovanna a Beccara and Others) v Argentine Republic*, ICSID Case No ARB/07/5, Decision on Jurisdiction And Admissibility, 4 August 2011, para 646. See the thoughtful study of De Brabandere 2012, *passim*.

acquisition may not be recognised as valid under the investment agreement, and the claim brought on that basis would be deemed abusive.[98]

Having concluded our analysis of the areas of international law where abuse of law has been recognised—whether explicitly codified or interpreted through case law—we now turn to general international law, where, perhaps surprisingly, the concept has encountered the greatest difficulty in gaining full acceptance.

2.4.3 Abuse of Rights in the Field of Human Rights Law

Human rights law is the one area of international law in which the concept of abuse of law has developed along a markedly different trajectory compared to other fields—arguably to the extent it constitutes a distinct concept sharing only the same name. This section offers an overview of this notion, highlighting both its points of convergence with, and divergence from, other understandings of abuse of law.

Most international human rights treaties include a provision designed to prevent the misuse of the rights and freedoms they recognise for purposes that would undermine those very rights. The most notable examples are Article 5 of the International Covenant on Civil and Political Rights (ICCPR) and Article 17 of the European Convention on Human Rights (ECHR) . The EU Charter of Fundamental Rights (EUCFR) follows this approach with Article 54, meaningfully titled "Prohibition of abuse of rights". According to the explanatory note, this provision mirrors Article 17 ECHR. As Article 54 has been cited in only one AG Opinion but not yet in any judgment of the ECJ, the analysis that follows will focus primarily on the ECHR, unless otherwise indicated.

Article 17 ECHR was admittedly inspired by Article 18 of the 1949 German Basic Law.[99] Like similar provisions adopted in the aftermath of World War II, its original purpose was to give "democracies the weapons to defend themselves against the rise of dictatorships".[100] It reflects the broader concept of militant democracy.[101] Although the ECHR has consistently maintained that Article 17 is applicable only on "an exceptional basis and in extreme cases",[102] its scope has gradually expanded over time. It now encompasses not only the threats to democratic freedoms but also the abusive exercise of rights that endangers the so-called *noyaux dur* of the Convention. For instance, invoking the right to freedom of expression or freedom of religion has been deemed abusive when aimed at promoting totalitarian ideologies, terrorism, Holocaust denial, antisemitism, or homophobia.[103] A similarly broad

---

[98] See Linderfalk 2017, pp. 419–420.

[99] See Bifulco and Celotto 2010, p. 344.

[100] See Woods 2021, pp. 1696–1697.

[101] See Harvey 2004, p. 407 ff.

[102] See *Paksas v Lithuania* App no 34932/04 (ECHR Grand Chamber, Judgment 6 January 2011), par. 87.

[103] See Woods 2021, p. 1698 ff.

reading of Article 54 EUCFR, in line with the evolving case law of the ECtHR, was endorsed in the only relevant EU case to date. In *Mesopotamia Broadcasting*, AG Bot argued that "the freedom of expression guaranteed in Article 11 of the Charter ceases to operate when the message infringes other principles and fundamental rights recognised by the Charter, such as the protection of human dignity and the principle of non-discrimination".[104] The ECJ, however, did not address this specific issue in its ruling.

In essence, within human rights law, including the EUCFR, the concept of abuse of rights refers to the prohibition on invoking fundamental rights and freedoms with the intention of undermining, threatening or otherwise jeopardising the very system of rights and freedoms they are meant to protect. In this sense, the abuse of a fundamental right appears to share a core element with the concept of abuse of Union law as it will be developed in this book: in both cases, the concern lies in the use of a legal entitlement for a purpose that defeats or distorts its original objective. However, as Lorna Woods aptly observed, "the similarity ends there".[105] Abuse of a fundamental right presupposes an intent to subvert or endanger the human rights framework by exploiting it from within.[106] By contrast, as this book will demonstrate, abuse of Union law serves a more systemic function, primarily concerned with preserving the internal coherence and the overall fairness of the EU legal order.

2.4.4 An Appraisal of Abuse of Law in General International Law

In Sect. 2.4.1, we have already examined scholarly efforts to formulate a general theory of abuse of law within international law. Over time, this idea has gained significant traction, to the extent that a vast majority of scholars now acknowledge that sovereign rights conferred by international law can be exercised abusively by States. Despite this broad scholarly consensus, the doctrine of abuse of law has yet to be formally upheld outside the specific areas discussed in the previous subsection.

As previously mentioned, Politis conducted a survey of State practice as it stood in 1925 to demonstrate the existence of an abuse of law doctrine in international law. While this discussion is now mainly of historical interest, it remains valuable in understanding how interpretations of the doctrine have diverged over time. Politis focused primarily on two case studies: the closure of ports and the expulsion of foreigners. The first example he presented in support of the doctrine of abuse of law was the

[104] CJEU, *Mesopotamia Broadcasting*, Opinion of Advocate General Bot, 5 May 2011, Joined cases C-244/10 and C-245/10, ECLI:EU:C:2011:284, para 68.

[105] See Woods 2021, p. 1708.

[106] The same view was expressed, with a more articulated reasoning, by Vitale 2017, p. 1113 ff., who argued that "la figura dell'abuso del diritto di cui all'art. 54, aldilà del *nomen iuris* utilizzato e di una logica di base che condivide con la più generale figura di abuso enucleata dalla giurisprudenza della Corte, se ne differenzi in modo sensibile, atteggiandosi a criterio giuridico autonomo e in parte diverso da essa".

Portendick Claims Award.[107] This case concerned the closure of the port granting access to Portendick Bay, Senegal, implemented as a wartime measure by France to counter rebels occupying the area. The blockade disrupted British commercial shipments, which had already departed before the measure was enacted—without prior notification, as required under international law. As a result, the British government filed a claim for compensation, which was ultimately granted by a sole arbitrator. For Politis, this case demonstrated the limits of sovereign prerogatives: "*la fermeture exceptionnelle d'un port au commerce international est licite, mais qu'elle engage en principe la responsabilité de son auteur si elle n'a été entourée de la publicité necessaire pour épargner aux tiers des prejudices inutiles, parce qu'alors la faculté de fermeture dépasse la mesur promise; elle dégénère en abus*".[108] A similar dispute arose a few years later in the *Closure of the Port of Buenos Aires* Award.[109] While the factual circumstances were comparable, the sole arbitrator—this time adjudicating a dispute between Argentina and Britain—reached the opposite conclusion. The claim was rejected on the basis of the principle that "*celui qui fait usage de son droit ne lèse personne*",[110] that is, the maxim *neminem laedit qui iure suo utitur*. According to Politis, this reasoning was plainly illogical, and the decision was patently incorrect.[111]

Interestingly, Schwarzenberger used the very same cases to argue the opposite position—namely, that abuse of law was not a standalone principle of international law. For Schwarzenberger, the *Portendick Claims* Award was not an application of the doctrine of abuse of law but rather a case of legal consequences arising from a unilateral declaration of intent, given that the French Minister of Marine had assured that no blockade was planned.[112] In his view, the *Closure of the Port of Buenos Aires* Award only further confirmed the irrelevance of abuse of law in international law.

The same polarisation was evident in disputes concerning the expulsion of foreigners. Politis saw these cases as a confirmation that State sovereignty could not be exercised abusively.[113] Conversely, Schwarzenberger interpreted them as evidence that a State's territorial jurisdiction was governed solely by the rule on the minimum standard of international law,[114] without any need for an abuse of law doctrine. This debate exemplifies the scholarly divide that Roberto Ago later referenced, reflecting deep-seated disagreements over the role of abuse of law in international legal theory. In reality, Politis and Schwarzenberger may have been closer in their views than they themselves acknowledged. Both agreed that international law imposed limits on the arbitrary exercise of otherwise perfectly lawful rights. Where they diverged was in their conceptualisation of the legal framework addressing this issue. Politis viewed abuse of law as a general principle underpinning the legal order's response to

[107] See de Lapradelle and Politis 1905, p. 512.

[108] See Politis 1925, p. 97.

[109] See de Lapradelle and Politis 1905, p. 637 ff.

[110] See Politis 1925, p. 100, citing the Award.

[111] Ibid.

[112] See Schwarzenberger 1956, p. 171.

[113] See Politis 1925, p. 101 ff.

[114] See Schwarzenberger 1956, p. 172.

such situations, whereas Schwarzenberger maintained that international law already contained specific rules tailored to address particular instances of abuse. This fundamental distinction mirrors the traditional divide between civil law and common law jurisdictions, as discussed earlier.

Turning to more recent practice, abuse of law, or abuse of process, has been repeatedly invoked before the International Court of Justice (ICJ),[115] to the point that such arguments have become almost commonplace.[116] However, despite being routinely dismissed,[117] the ICJ has implicitly acknowledged the possibility of invoking abuse of law, albeit only under "exceptional circumstances".[118] In contrast, several dissenting opinions have endorsed this concept.[119] We will focus on the most notable one.

Recently, Judge Donoghue's dissenting opinion in the *Immunities and Criminal Proceedings* case provides a remarkable example. This case involved a dispute between Equatorial Guinea and France concerning the immunity from criminal jurisdiction of Equatorial Guinea's Second Vice-President, who was charged in France for misappropriating public funds, as well as the immunity of the building admittedly housing Equatorial Guinea's diplomatic mission, which had been searched and seized by French authorities. France contended that the case before the ICJ constituted an abuse of process, alleging that Equatorial Guinea had initiated proceedings to obstruct the criminal case against its Vice-President in French courts.[120] In addressing this argument, the ICJ distinguished between abuse of (substantive) rights and abuse of process. Regarding the latter, the Court held that "only in exceptional circumstances that the Court should reject a claim based on a valid title of jurisdiction on the ground of abuse of process".[121] Since no such exceptional circumstances were found in this case, the ICJ declined to dismiss the claim on this basis. The issue of abuse of substantive rights was reserved for the merits stage. France argued that Equatorial Guinea had deliberately altered the status of the building to shield it from criminal investigation.[122] The ICJ sidestepped the issue of abuse of law. Instead, it held that international law does not permit a sending State to unilaterally designate its mission premises if the receiving State objects. In her dissenting opinion, Judge

---

[115] For a comprehensive overview of the relevant ICJ's rulings, see Lemey 2021, p. 199 ff.

[116] See Kolb 2019, para 50.

[117] See Ascensio 2014, pp. 765–766.

[118] See International Court of Justice, *Jadhav (India v. Pakistan)*, Judgment of 17 July 2019, ICJ Reports 2019, p. 418, para 49.

[119] A notable early example is Judge Chagla's dissent in the *Right of Passage over Indian Territory* case, where he argued that Portugal's conduct constituted an abuse of process. See International Court of Justice, *Right of Passage over Indian Territory (Portugal v. India)*, Preliminary Objections, Judgment of 26 November 1957, ICJ Reports 1957, p. 125, pp. 171–172.

[120] See International Court of Justice, *Immunities and Criminal Proceedings (Equatorial Guinea v. France)*, Preliminary Objections of the French Republic, paras 74 ff.

[121] See International Court of Justice, *Immunities and Criminal Proceedings (Equatorial Guinea v. France)*, Preliminary Objections, Judgment of 26 November 1957, ICJ Reports 1957, p. 125, para 150.

[122] See International Court of Justice, *Immunities and Criminal Proceedings (Equatorial Guinea v. France)*, Preliminary Objections of the French Republic, paras 80 ff.

Donoghue took a different view, arguing that the sequence of actions undertaken by Equatorial Guinea did, in fact, constitute exceptional circumstances warranting a finding of abuse of rights. She further maintained that the ICJ should not allow itself to be used as a shield for abusive practices like those performed by Equatorial Guinea.[123] Despite its arguably disappointing outcome, the *Immunities and Criminal Proceedings* case remains a notable precedent. It is perhaps the only instance in which abuse of rights was not merely a secondary, subordinate argument, but rather one of the primary claims categorically asserted by one of the Parties.[124]

To date, the ICJ has yet to explicitly rule that a State has exercised a right abusively. However, given established case law in other areas of international law and the prevailing view in scholarship, it seems reasonable to assert that such a finding is a question of when, not if.

2.5 Concluding Remarks

At the conclusion of this survey of legal systems beyond the EU, several interim conclusions can be drawn.

Number one, the concept of abuse of law originated in Roman law as a response to the rigid, absolute conception of individual rights. Over time, Roman law gradually recognised that acts were not necessarily either lawful or unlawful but that a third category—a *tertium genus*—exists: acts that, while formally legal, do not enjoy legal protection under certain circumstances. However, Roman law did not develop a fully-fledged doctrine of abuse of law.

Number two, this further evolution was accomplished by French case law and legal scholarship in the 19th and early 20th centuries. The first major step occurred in the 1855 judgment of the Court of Appeal of Colmar, which we have described as a watershed moment—and rightly so. Under the influence of Louis Josserand, the doctrine was later expanded beyond property law, acquiring the general nature it holds today.

Number three, nearly all continental European jurisdictions in the civil law tradition recognise a principle of abuse of law, either codified in a formal rule (e.g., the Netherlands), developed through the case law and scholarship (e.g., France), or a combination of both (e.g., Italy).

Number four, although common law jurisdictions are traditionally perceived as resistant to the concept of abuse of law, they nonetheless feature legal doctrines—albeit under different names—that align with the underlying rationale of abuse of law. This is more apparent in the United States than in the United Kingdom, but even the latter is not entirely foreign to the idea.

---

[123] See International Court of Justice, *Immunities and Criminal Proceedings (Equatorial Guinea v. France)*, Dissenting Opinion of Judge Donoghue, paras 18–19.

[124] See, in this sense, Lemey 2021, p. 210.

Number five, in Japan, the doctrine of abuse of law was initially developed through case law and later codified in the Civil Code. In Islamic legal systems, the doctrine traces its roots to Shari'a law—and ultimately to the teachings of the Prophet Muhammad—but is now codified in many national codes. In the Nordic countries, the absence of explicit statutory provisions has been overcome through case law and legal scholarship, gradually shaping a functional doctrine of abuse of law.

Number six, international law remains the field where the doctrine of abuse of law has faced the most significant difficulties in gaining explicit recognition. While international investment law—and, to a lesser extent, international trade law—have fully embraced the concept, general international law has seen only sporadic and indirect acknowledgements of abuse of law. Moreover, the ILC's work on State responsibility has cast doubt on whether a third category of acts—neither lawful nor unlawful—can exist within the current framework of internationally wrongful acts.

This analysis confirms that the idea that legal entitlements cannot be exercised abusively is as old as the very concept of legal systems. The remainder of this book will focus on examining the existence, scope and application of this doctrine in EU law, as well as identifying the circumstances under which the exercise of a right is considered abusive within the EU legal order.

References

Ago R (1970) Second Report on State Responsibility. Yearbook of the International Law Commission 2:177–197.

Ago R (1976) Firth Report on State Responsibility. Yearbook of the International Law Commission 2: 3–54.

Ascensio H (2014) Abuse of Process in International Investment Arbitration. Chinese Journal of International Law 13:763–785.

Astone A (2017) Il divieto di abuso del diritto. Giuffrè, Milan.

Bifulco R, Celotto A (2010) Article 54 – Prohibition of Abuse of Rights. In: Mock W, Demuro G (eds) Human Rights in Europe. Commentary on the Charter of Fundamental Rights of the European Union. Carolina Academic Press, Durham, pp. 343346.

Bolgár V (1975) Abuse of Rights in France, Germany, and Switzerland: A Survey of a Recent Chapter in Legal Doctrine. Louisiana Law Review 35:1015–1036.

Byers M (2002) Abuse of Rights: An Old Principle, A New Age. McGill Law Journal 47:389–434.

Carmody C (2021) The New Normal: Abuse of Rights under WTO Law. International Trade Law and Regulation 27:7–27.

Cheng B (1953) General Principles of Law as Applied by International Courts and Tribunals. Steven & Sons, London.

Dawwas A (1993) Abuse of Rights in the Shari'a and Under Modern Arab Civil Codes: a Study in Comparative Jurisprudence. Islamic and Comparative Law Review 13:1–18.

De Brabandere E (2012) 'Good Faith', 'Abuse of Process' and the Initiation of Investment Treaty Claims. Journal of International Dispute Settlement 3:609–636.

De Lapradelle AG, Politis N (1905) Recueil des Arbitrages Internationaux Vol. I. Pedone, Paris.

Di Robilant A (2014) Abuse of Rights: The Continental Drug and the Common Law. Boston University School of Law Working Paper No. 14–28.

Dröll F (2024) The Abuse of Right Principle in Japan and Germany. Teisė 130:33–43.

Emerson M (1987) Regulation or Deregulation of the Labour Market: Policy Regimes for the Recruitment and Dismissal of Employees ln the Industrialised Countries. Commission of the European Communities – Directorate-General for Economic and Financial Affairs (https://aei.pitt.edu/36951/1/A2998.pdf).
Evald J (2001) Retsmisbrug i formueretten. Jurist- og Økonomforbundets Forlag, Randers.
Evans CDA, Ramseyer JM (2021) Negligence and Abuse of Rights in Early 20th Century Japan. Zeitschrift für Japanisches Recht 26:313–328.
Gaillard E (2017) Abuse of Process in International Arbitration. ICSID Review 32:17–37.
Galgano F (2011) Qui suo iure abutitur neminem laedit? Contratto e impresa 27:311–319.
Gestri M (2003) Abuso del diritto e frode alla legge nell'ordinamento comunitario. Giuffrè, Milan.
Ghestin J, Goubeaux G (1994) Traite De Droit Civil: Introduction Générale. LGDJ, Paris.
Gutteridge HC (1933) Abuse of Rights. Cambridge Law Journal 5:22–45.
Hartkamp AS (1992) Judicial Discretion under the New Civil Code of the Netherlands. The American Journal of Comparative Law 40:551–571.
Harvey P (2004), Militant Democracy and the European Convention on Human Rights. European Law Review 29:407–420.
Hayashi T (2008) Roman Law Studies and the Civil Code in Modern Japan: System, Ownership, and Co-ownership. Osaka University Law Review 55:15–26.
Ionescu RN (2012) L'abus de droit en droit de l'Unione européenne. Bruylant, Brussels.
Josserand L (1905) L'abus des droits. Rousseau, Paris.
Kiss A (2006) Abuse of Rights. Max Planck Encyclopedia of Public International Law, Oxford University Press, Oxford.
Kolb R (2019) General Principles of Procedural Law. In: Zimmermann A, Tams C, Oellers-Frahm K, Tomuschat C (eds) The Statute of the International Court of Justice: A Commentary. Oxford University Press, Oxford, pp. 963–1006.
Lauterpacht H (2011) The Function of Law in the International Community. Oxford University Press, Oxford.
Lemey M (2021) L'abus de droit en droit international public. LGDJ, Paris.
Lennander (2019) Rättsmissbruk genom att dra fördel av eget illojalt agerande. Insolvensrättslig Tidskrift 17:11–37.
Linderfalk U (2017) Philip Morris Asia Ltd. v. Australia. Abuse of Rights in Investor-State Arbitration. Nordic Journal of International Law 86:403–420.
Linna T (2004) Oikeuden väärinkäytön kielto ja sen sovelluksia. Lakimies 1:622–638.
Lowe V (2000) The Politics of Law-Making: Are the Method and Character of Norm Creation Changing? In: Byers M (ed) The Role of Law in International Politics: Essays in International Relations and International Law. Oxford University Press, Oxford, pp. 207–226.
Marotti L (2020) A Satisfactory Answer? The Enrica Lexie Award and the Jurisdiction over Incidental Questions. Italian Yearbook of International Law 30: 191–208.
Mitchell A, Heaton D (2010) The Inherent Jurisdiction of WTO Tribunals: Selected Application of Public International Law Required by Judicial Function. Michigan Journal of International Law 31:559–619.
Mitchell A, Malone T (2018) Abuse of Process in Inter-State Dispute Resolution. Max Planck Encyclopedia of Public International Law, Oxford University Press, Oxford.
Neville Brown L (1994) Is There a General Principle of Abuse of Rights in European Community Law? In: Curtin D, Heukels T (eds) Institutional Dynamics of European Integration. Essays in Honour of Henry G. Schermers, Martinus Nijhoff, Dordrecht/Boston/London, pp. 511–525.
Nguyen ST (2016) The Applicability of Comity and Abuse of Rights in World Trade Organisation Dispute Settlement. University of Tasmania Law Review 35:95–130.
Nolde B (1923) Le Code civil de la République des Soviets. Bulletin de la Société de législation comparée 51:232–257.
Perillo JM (1995) Abuse of Rights: A Pervasive Legal Concept. Pacific Law Journal 27:38–97.
Perreau EH (1913) Origine et développement de la théorie de l'abus de droit. Revue Générale du droit, de la législation et de la jurisprudence 37:481–507.

Politis N (1925) Le problème des limitations de la souveraineté et la théorie de l'abus des droits dans les rapports internationaux. Recueil des Cours de l'Académie de droit international de La Haye 6:1–122.

Rescigno P (1998) L'abuso del diritto. Il Mulino, Bologna.

Restivo C (2007) Contributo ad una teoria dell'abuso del diritto. Giuffrè, Milan.

Schwarzenberger G (1956) Uses and Abuses of the "Abuse of Rights" in International Law. Transactions of the Grotius Society 42:147–179.

Sono K, Fujioka Y (1975) The Role of the Abuse of Right Doctrine in Japan. Louisiana Law Review 35:1037–1057.

Steinle S (2004) Georg Schwarzenberger (1908–1991). In: Beatson J, Zimmermann R (eds) Jurists Uprooted: German-Speaking Emigré Lawyers in Twentieth Century Britain. Oxford University Press, Oxford, pp. 663–680.

Tridimas T (2011) Abuse of Rights in EU Law. Some Reflections with Particular Reference to Financial Law. In: De la Feria R, Vogenauer S (eds) Prohibition of Abuse of Law. A New General Principle of EU Law? Hart Publishing, Oxford/Portland, pp. 169–191.

Vitale G (2017) Divieto dell'abuso di diritto. In: Mastroianni R, Pollicino O, Allegrezza S, Pappalardo F, Razzolini O (eds) Carta dei diritti fondamentali dell'Unione europea, Giuffè, Milan, pp. 1098–1121.

Woods L (2021) Article 54. In: Peers S, Hervey T, Kenner J, Ward A (eds) The EU Charter of Fundamental Rights. A Commentary. Hart Publishing, Oxford/Portland, pp. 1692–1708.

Chapter 3
Analysis of the Court of Justice's Case Law

Contents

L. Pantaleo, *Abuse of Law in the European Union*,
https://doi.org/10.1007/978-94-6265-731-1_3

Abstract This chapter offers a comprehensive analysis of the case law of the Court of Justice concerning the principle of abuse of Union law. By examining the most significant judgments in chronological order, it demonstrates that while the development of the principle has been gradual, and at times uneven, it has ultimately led to a coherent and logically structured doctrine. The case law is divided into three phases: (a) the foundational period beginning with the *Van Binsbergen* ruling, (b) a phase of more structured development, initiated by the *Emsland-Stärke* ruling, and (c) the consolidation stage, marked by the *Cussens* ruling in 2017. The analysis culminates in a clear picture of the principle as it has progressively taken shape within the Union legal order.

Keywords Court of Justice · *Van Binsbergen* · *Emsland-Stärke* · *Cussens* · Abuse test · Abuse of EU law · Fraud

3.1 Introduction

The concept of abuse of law within the EU legal order has evolved significantly throughout the years. Since there is no mention of it in the Treaties,[1] its creation and development have been entirely in the hands of the Court of Justice, whose relevant

[1] Over the years, several anti-abuse clauses have been explicitly included in the EU secondary legislation. It can now be considered a widespread practice. To mention some of the most well-known examples, see Article 4 of Directive 2014/67/EU of the European Parliament and of the Council of 15 May 2014 on the enforcement of Directive 96/71/EC concerning the posting of workers in the framework of the provision of services and amending Regulation (EU) No 1024/2012 on administrative cooperation through the Internal Market Information System, OJ L 159, 28 May 2014, pp. 11–31; as well as Article 35 of Directive 2004/38/EC of the European Parliament

case law is relatively abundant nowadays. With some degree of approximation, this evolution can roughly be mapped through three distinct phases: (a) the foundational period beginning with the *Van Binsbergen* ruling,[2] in which the Court dealt with situations belonging conceptually to abuse of law, without necessarily qualifying them as such in explicit terms;[3] (b) a more structured development starting with the *Emsland-Stärke* ruling,[4] in which the Court started addressing abusive situations straightforwardly by equipping itself with a veritable abuse test designed to help the Court itself (as well as national courts) assessing whether a situation falls within the definition of abuse of EU law; and (c) the consolidation phase commencing in 2017 with the *Cussens* ruling,[5] where the Luxembourg Court explicitly and unequivocally recognised the prohibition of abuse of EU law as a general principle of the legal order.

However, one should not think the evolutionary trajectory outlined above was inherently coherent and linear, as is perhaps inherent in the development of legal discourse by means of the ECJ's case law. The case law on abuse of law remained ambivalent for quite some time and oscillated both conceptually and linguistically. Conceptually, the Court seemed to categorise abuse in different ways. In some cases, it has characterised it, directly or indirectly, as a motive justifying the imposition of a restriction to a fundamental freedom on the part of the Member State involved, employing a reasoning that is typical of internal market law.[6] In other cases, the Court seemed to employ a *Keck*-style reasoning by suggesting that abusive situations did not fall within the scope of EU law in much the same way selling arrangements do not.[7] Linguistically, the Court has resorted over the years to a variety of expressions. Sometimes, it would refer simply to abuse,[8] often in the plural, and other times to abusive practices.[9] Also, confusion was sometimes generated by the different

and of the Council of 29 April 2004 on the right of citizens of the Union and their family members to move and reside freely within the territory of the Member States amending Regulation (EEC) No 1612/68 and repealing Directives 64/221/EEC, 68/360/EEC, 72/194/EEC, 73/148/EEC, 75/34/EEC, 75/35/EEC, 90/364/EEC, 90/365/EEC and 93/96/EEC, OJ L 158, 30 April 2004, pp. 77–123.

[2] See CJEU, *Van Binsbergen*, Judgment of the Court, 3 December 1974, case 33/74, ECLI:EU:C:1974:131.

[3] For example, as we shall see in *Van Binsbergen*, the Court did not refer explicitly to abuse, even though the situation was clearly that of a legal person abusively invoking EU law in order to circumvent national law.

[4] See CJEU, *Emsland-Stärke*, Judgment of the Court, 14 December 2000, case C-110/99, ECLI:EU:C:2000:695.

[5] See CJEU, *Cussens*, Judgment of the Court, 22 November 2017, case C-251/16, ECLI:EU:C:2017:881.

[6] This is the case of the foundational *Van Binsbergen* ruling.

[7] This is the case, for example, of CJEU, *Sylvie Lair*, Judgment of the Court, 21 June 1988, case 39/86, ECLI:EU:C:1988:322. It should be noted that the analogy with *Keck* is no accident. As we shall see in this book, although not expressly treated as abuses by the Court, *Keck*-like situations have many things in common with abuse of EU law. See Chap. 4, Sect. 4.3.

[8] This is the case of *Lair*, para 43.

[9] This is the case, for example, of CJEU, *Cremer*, Judgment of the Court, 11 October 1977, case 125/76, ECLI:EU:C:1977:148, para 12 and para 21.

linguistic versions of the Court's judgments.[10] Not to mention that the Court often referred to abuse and fraud jointly, despite the fact that these two concepts are not precisely one and the same thing.[11]

This lack of clarity has significantly influenced the scholarship on abuse of EU law. For a long time, much of the discussion was centred on the legal nature of abuse in the EU legal order. Scholars have advanced the whole range of possible views, starting with those who maintained that "the prohibition of abuse in Union law does not possess 'the general, comprehensive character which is otherwise naturally inherent in general principles of [Community] law'".[12] Others admitted that a provision of EU law could be used inappropriately but that "a general principle of EU law prohibiting abuse in the technical sense of the term is not to be recognised".[13] Other scholars submitted that the prohibition of abuse of EU law was a general principle "capable of being used as an instrument of judicial review where national legislation falls within the scope of Community law".[14] From this perspective, I agree with Butler and Sørensen that the final, unequivocal and unquestionable recognition of (the prohibition of) abuse of law as a general principle is to be found in the most recent case law of the Court of Justice, that is, the third consolidation phase as described above.[15] Hence, the debate on the legal nature of (the prohibition of) abuse of Union law is to be considered closed. The aim of this chapter is to show how we got to this point.

To entirely grasp the evolution of this principle, a comprehensive analysis of the Court's case law is needed. As a consequence, the chapter will develop as follows. Section 3.2 will focus on the early cases that belong to the foundational period. Section 3.3 will deal with the more structured development phase that led to the establishment of an abuse test. Section 3.4 will examine the most recent consolidation period that clarified the legal nature of the principle. Section 3.5 will provide interim conclusions and prepare the floor for the discussion in Chap. 4, where the case law

---

[10] This is the case, for example, of CJEU, *Kofoed*, Judgment of the Court, 5 July 2007, case C-321/05, ECLI:EU:C:2007:408, para 38, where the English version says "[i]ndividuals must not improperly or fraudulently take advantage of provisions of Community law", while in other linguistic versions, for example the Italian one, "improperly" is translated as "abusively" *(abusivamente*, in Italian).

[11] This is the case, for example, of CJEU, *Paletta II*, Judgment of the Court, 2 May 1996, case C-206/94, ECLI:EU:C:1996:182, para 23. For a discussion of the conceptual differences between abuse and fraud, see *infra* Sect. 4.2.1.

[12] See Arnull 2011, p. 22.

[13] Kamanabrou 2018, p. 548.

[14] See De la Feria 2008, p. 438. It should be emphasised that two pioneering studies devoted to abuse of EU law already suggested that it should be recognized as a general principle of the legal order. See Neville Brown 1994a, p. 511, who affirmed that a "general principle, that of abuse of rights (*abus de droit*), while at present only latent or inchoate in Community law, deserves proper recognition by the Court of Justice" (emphasis in the original); as well as Gestri 2003, p. 199, who submitted that "it is reasonable to affirm that the control on the exercise of individual prerogatives based on the notion of abuse of law constitutes a principle inherent to the judicial function, which, as such, is an integral part of the Community legal order, as well as of the national legal orders" (original text in Italian, translation of the present author).

[15] See Butler and Sørensen 2022, pp. 406-407.

will be systematised in a coherent conceptual framework with a view to shedding light on the scope of the principle in question.

Before getting underway, one methodological clarification is necessary. As is perhaps natural in these cases, I read the relevant judgments multiple times. The more I went through them, the more I became convinced that the most effective way of examining the case law was to follow the chronological order. Since the case law lacks an entirely logical order, time is the only objectively verifiable factor that can help the writer and, hopefully, the reader navigate the routes followed by the Court. This differs from what other authors who have dealt with abuse of EU law in a comprehensive study have done so far. Previous authors have all grouped cases around the subject matter, such as internal market cases, common agricultural policy cases, and so forth.[16] However, I think that categorisation made sense when these authors were writing. Back then, one should not forget that it was still unclear whether abuse of EU law applied horizontally to all areas of the Union's legal order. Now that that has been clarified unequivocally by the Court, a case law analysis based on different EU law fields would not help in understanding how the core content of the principle in question came about. This is clearly not to say that the general principle of abuse of EU law applies in precisely the same way in all areas of the Union's legal order. There are indeed differences. However, these differences will be discussed in Chap. 4, which is devoted to examining the scope of the principle.

Needless to say, not all cases directly or indirectly related to abuse of EU law will be analysed. The examination will focus on a selection of the most relevant, meaningful judgments. All decisions containing a breakthrough or a (non-minor) development with respect to the previous state of the art will be taken into consideration.

3.2 The First Phase

3.2.1 The Foundational Stone: Van Binsbergen

When it comes to abuse of EU law, *Van Binsbergen* can be considered the foundational stone.[17] This is slightly ironic if one thinks that the Court of Justice did not refer explicitly to abuse in the ruling, nor did it use one of the alternative expressions mentioned above. Express reference to abuse is simply absent. However, this is the case in which the Court of Justice recognised for the first time that EU law can be used improperly and that such improper use must not be permitted.[18]

The case involved a so-called triangular situation, or U-turn situation, where individuals allegedly rely on the possibilities offered by Union law to circumvent national

[16] This was the criterion employed by Gestri 2003, Ionescu 2012, as well as Saydé 2016, although in a different manner.

[17] In this sense, see Carbone 2011, p. 69.

[18] For a comment, see Kjellgren 2002.

rules to which they would be subject had they not created the conditions to trigger the application of EU law. Mr. Kortmann, the lawyer of Mr. Van Binsbergen, moved his residence from the Netherlands to Belgium during the legal action he had brought on behalf of his client before a Dutch court. This ran counter to Dutch law, which mandated that all those wanting to practice legal professions in the Netherlands had to reside there legally. This raised the question of whether the Dutch rule was a restriction on the freedom to provide services across the border granted by EU law to Mr. Kortmann. If yes, the clear risk was that individuals could evade national legislation by creating the conditions to take advantage of the possibilities offered by Union law. For example, Dutch lawyers could circumvent the residence rule by moving to Belgium and claiming they provided legal services across the Belgian border.

In brief, the Court dealt with the relevant issue in a few paragraphs. In a typical internal market law reasoning, it stated that the Dutch rule constituted a restriction of the freedom to provide services. However, it was objectively justified. More specifically, it reasoned that the requirement imposed by Dutch law undermined the very essence of the freedom to provide services, thus constituting a restriction.[19] However, such a requirement, if binding for professionals established in the Member State in which the service was provided, was justified objectively by general interests, such as the need to ensure the observance of professional rules of conduct.[20] The Court also stated that a Member State could not be denied the right to take such measures, considering that the activity of the service provider was "entirely or principally directed towards its territory".[21] This last element, we must assume, was the criterion that allowed the Court to distinguish the situation of Mr. Kortmann from a genuine cross-border supply of services. The Court even said explicitly that "such a situation may be subject to judicial control under the provisions of the chapter relating to the right of establishment and not of that on the provision of services".[22] Thus, in the very first ruling on the matter, it already emerged the idea that abuse of EU law entails some degree of artificiality in the conduct of the alleged abuser. The Court would go back to this aspect multiple times in the future.

With this ruling, the idea that EU law can be misused by means, for example, of careful legal planning of a given economic activity, clearly started to emerge. The Court did not say that Mr. Kortmann's situation did not fall under the scope of the freedom to provide services.[23] It said that a Member State could not be prevented from taking measures that would allow an established national to become a service provider relying on the possibilities offered by EU law, thus escaping the national rules that would apply to him as an established professional. The Court did not explicitly talk about abuse, abusive practices or the like. However, it clearly demonstrated the awareness that EU law could be abused or improperly used to circumvent national

[19] See *Van Binsbergen*, para 11.

[20] Ibid., paras 12 and 14.

[21] Ibid., para 13.

[22] Ibid.

[23] Although this seems to be the view of Vanistendael 2020, p. 5.

law. For these reasons, *Van Binsbergen* is rightly considered the foundational stone of the doctrine of abuse in the EU legal order.

In addition, *Van Binsbergen* laid down two ideas that would later become standard features of the established case law on the matter. Firstly, the circumstance that the economic activity is entirely or principally directed towards the territory of a Member State different from the one in which the service provider is established was an indicator that the freedom to provide services was potentially being used improperly. Secondly, measures taken by the Member States to deal with such situations constitute restrictions to this freedom, but they are justified by the need to prevent similar practices. Put differently, the need to fight against abuse is a lawful justification for a restriction on free movement. Successive case law will develop and refine these concepts.

3.2.2 The **Knoors** *Ruling, aka* **Van Binsbergen,** *the Sequel*

The next episode took place again between Belgium and the Netherlands. Mr. Knoors was a Dutch national residing in Belgium, where he ran a business as a central heater, plumber and water fitter for several years. At some point, he asked for authorisation to conduct the same business in the Netherlands based on Council Directive No 64/427.[24] His request was denied on twofold grounds: on the one hand, he did not possess the qualifications required by Dutch law for that trade; on the other hand, as a Dutch national, he could not take advantage of the directive.[25] In short, the crux of the matter was whether a national of an EU Member State could invoke the fundamental freedoms and the legislation implementing them against their own Member State of nationality. The Dutch authorities denied it, based on a wholly internal situation reasoning. The Court disagreed and answered this question positively, affirming that individuals (more specifically, so-called free movers) could indeed invoke the fundamental freedoms against their own Member States of nationality under specific circumstances.[26] In those days, the Court of Justice was breaking new ground, but now we know this is an established principle of internal market law.[27]

---

[24] See Council Directive 64/427/EEC of 7 July 1964 laying down detailed provisions concerning transitional measures in respect of activities of self-employed persons in manufacturing and processing industries falling within ISIC Major Groups 23–40 (Industry and small craft industries), OJ 117, 23 July 1964, pp. 1863–1870 (no longer in force).

[25] CJEU, *Knoors*, Judgment of the Court, 7 February 1979, case 115/78, ECLI:EU:C:1979:31, paras 3–5.

[26] Ibid., para 24.

[27] The principle, in essence, is that an individual who has exercised free movement remains a free mover *vis-à-vis* her own Member State of nationality when she returns to the home State after such exercise. On this matter, see Nic Shuibhne 2002.

For the purpose of this book, the Court's answer to the wholly internal situation argument opened up the risk that individuals attempted "wrongly to evade the application of their national legislation as regards training for a trade".[28] In much the same way as in *Van Binsbergen*, the Court recognised that it was not "possible to disregard the legitimate interest which a Member State may have in preventing" these situations.[29] Unlike in *Van Binsbergen*, however, there was no such risk in the case at hand thanks to the precise conditions set out in the directive, which had "the effect of excluding, in the fields in question, the risk of abuse referred to by the Netherlands Government".[30]

In conclusion, *Knoors* is an important step forward from *Van Binsbergen*. First of all, this is so because the Court, for the first time, explicitly talked about abuse. Second, while recognising, in principle, that EU law may be improperly used (*rectius*: abused) to circumvent national law, the Court of Justice emphasised the role of secondary legislation, which, if detailed enough, can eliminate all risks. In this respect, the Court seemed to sort of reprimand the Member States when it stated that "it is always possible for the Council [...] to remove the causes of any abuses of the law by arranging for the harmonization of the conditions of training for a trade in the various Member States".[31] In other words, the Court seemed to say, more integration means less abuse. Less integration, more abuse.[32] The Court reminded everybody that this was ultimately a political choice of the Member States.

3.2.3 The Emergence of a Different Form of Abuse in the EU Legal Order: Abuse of Process

As we shall see in this book, abuse of process is in relation of species to genus with abuse of law. It is a specific (procedural) instance or category within the broader concept of abuse of law. Generally, the law regarding the process can be abused in much the same way as the law regarding the substance. We have seen in Chap. 2 that in recent times, abuse of process has sparked considerable controversy in the field of international investment law. In the EU legal order, abuse of process has emerged only in two cases, both of which date back to the early days. Perhaps surprisingly, the Court has recognised abuse of process quite straightforwardly from the very outset. Put differently, the emergence of the species (that is, abuse of process) in the Union's legal order has been much less contentious than the genus (that is, abuse of substantive law). This section will address these two cases relating to abuse of process conjunctively.

---

[28] *Knoors*, para 25.

[29] Ibid.

[30] Ibid., para 26.

[31] Ibid., para 27.

[32] But see the considerations made by Sørensen 2006, p. 459 when it comes to resorting to harmonisation as a means to prevent abuse.

The first relevant one is part of a long-lasting dispute between the Commission and Simmenthal, a well-known Italian canned meat producer, over the minimum price of imported frozen meat. The relevant ruling concerned the challenge brought by Simmenthal to a Commission's decision adopted on the basis of a prior ruling issued by the Court in the context of this long-term litigation. Without dwelling on the details of the dispute, suffice it to say that the Commission's decision at stake was a direct implementation of the Court's prior ruling. Based on that, the Court straightforwardly affirmed that "from the date of the judgment of 6 March 1979, and at the latest as from the date of the decision adopted by the Commission in implementation of that judgment [...] the applicant could foresee with certainty that its tender [...] would be rejected in view of the principles laid down by the above-mentioned judgment of the Court".[33] After calling the company's arguments "specious" in view of the predictability of the dispute as a result of its previous judgment, the Court declared the applicant's action "an abuse of process from the date when the judgment of 6 March 1979 was delivered and, at the latest, as from the date on which the decision adopted by the Commission in implementation of that judgment took effect".[34] In other words, in the EU legal order, bringing a dispute in a situation where the outcome is essentially predetermined is an abuse of process. This situation falls under the general legal category of frivolous litigation, which is common in many legal systems.[35] In the case at hand, the existence of a prior Court's ruling left no doubt about the outcome. However, the lesson to draw from the *Simmenthal* judgment is that, even in the absence of a prior ruling, a dispute whose outcome is easily predictable may constitute an abuse of process in the Union's legal system.

The other relevant case involved a different manifestation of frivolous claims, which usually fall under the category of vexatious litigation.[36] The case concerned two scientists who worked for an EU agency and were prevented by their Head of Division from presenting a scientific paper at an international conference.[37] Without dwelling on the merits of the dispute, the applicants' conduct throughout it was quite questionable. They filed a complaint "set out at great length" and involving "a number of allegations insulting to the head of division, some of which are capable of casting a slur on his personal, scientific and administrative reputation";[38] they requested multiple extensions of the normal procedural periods; and, more generally,

---

[33] CJEU, *SpA Simmenthal v Commission*, Judgment of the Court, 6 March 1979, case 92/78, ECLI:EU:C:1979:53, para 9.

[34] Ibid., para 11.

[35] In essence, claims whose probability of success is very small are usually considered frivolous. This is not to say that the definition of what constitutes frivolous litigation is obvious. For a discussion of its complexities see the seminal study of Bone 1997, pp. 529 ff.

[36] Vexatious claims are those brought primarily to harass, annoy, or subdue an adversary. See Lowe 1999, p. 203.

[37] CJEU, *Albertini and Montagnani v Commission*, Judgment of the Court, 17 May 1984, case 338/82, ECLI:EU:C:1984:181, paras 1–3.

[38] Ibid., para 6.

they conducted the proceedings in an "abnormal and abusive manner".[39] Although such conduct did not prevent the Court from addressing the merits of the case, it led it to order the applicants to pay the whole of the costs of the proceedings, in derogation from the general rule according to which "in staff cases institutions are to bear their own costs".[40] In short, the *Albertini and Montagnani* ruling confirmed the existence of abuse of process in the EU legal order. Unlike *Simmenthal*, which sanctioned as abusive the conduct of those who initiate proceedings where the outcome is predictable, *Albertini and Montagnani* added that even disputes that are not entirely devoid of legal merits could result in an abuse of process if the proceedings are not conducted fairly and correctly.[41] In such cases, abuse is not sanctioned by a declaration of inadmissibility, as in *Simmenthal*, but reverberates on the cost allocation decided by the Court.

As said above, the ECJ had little problem recognising abuse of process and even calling it by its name from the outset. It is fair to say that when it comes to abuse of process, the Court showed none of the conceptual or linguistic oscillation it experienced in the case law that eventually led to the establishment of a general principle of abuse of EU law. To be sure, the existence of an individual right to bring a case is not questionable. It is the way in which it is exercised that becomes problematic. In *Albertini and Montagnani*, there was no doubt that the claimants had the right to challenge the decision of their head of division before the Court of Justice. However, filing abnormally lengthy complaints filled with insulting allegations was an abusive manner of exercising an otherwise incontestable individual right. This is an abuse of rights *stricto sensu*, which is common to many legal systems[42] and easier for the Court to recognise for the reasons that will be discussed in depth in Chap. 5.

In conclusion, a first foundational distinction is starting to emerge. In the EU legal order, there are cases of abuse of rights *stricto sensu* consisting of a natural or legal person exercising in an abusive manner an otherwise indisputable individual right granted by EU law. This manifestation of abuse, which we have called abuse of rights *stricto sensu*, is relatively less problematic and reminiscent of abuse of rights as typically admitted in countries with a civil law tradition. In the EU legal order, this is exemplified by cases of abuse of process such as *Simmenthal* and *Albertini and Montagnani*. The EU legal order, however, experiences an additional type of abuse of law, which involves an element of circumvention. These are instances, such as *Van Binsbergen*, where EU law is (improperly) used to obtain an advantage that would be otherwise precluded under national law. This form of abuse is peculiar to the Union's legal order, being the consequence of what we could call its specific characteristics. It is in relation to this peculiar type of abuse that the Court has experienced the

---

[39] Ibid., para 52.

[40] Ibid., para 51.

[41] A similar line of case law has been developed by the ECtHR under Article 35(3)(a) ECHR. Applications are deemed abusive in cases of "vexatious or repeated applications, misleading or lying to the Court, use of offensive or provocative language, or deliberate breach of the Court's rulings". See Woods 2021, p. 1693.

[42] Although not all legal systems, as we have seen in the examination of common law jurisdictions carried out in Chap. 2.

conceptual and linguistic oscillation referred to above, as the next cases will further demonstrate.

Before turning to the next section, it is worth noting that the EU legal order features another distinctive manifestation of abuse of process, albeit one not explicitly labelled as such by the ECJ. As is well known, the Court of Justice has established that it may decline to give a preliminary ruling where the reference is tainted by serious defects, such as when it is artificial or hypothetical. This issue will be revisited in the following chapter, particularly in Chap. 4, Sect. 4.6.

3.2.4 *The Improper Invocation of Rights Granted by Secondary Legislation: A Matter of Abuse or of the Scope of Application of EU Law? The Court's Answer in* Cremer *and* Töpfer

The *Töpfer* ruling concerned the importation of wheat to the United Kingdom by a Danish trader, which received the so-called "accession" compensatory amounts upon completion in the UK of the customs import formalities.[43] The wheat was discharged and reloaded into the same vessel and shipped to its final destination, which had always been Germany, as clearly indicated in the instructions sent by the Danish trader to the British shipowner of the vessel in question.[44] The Danish authorities brought criminal charges against the trader and refused the payment of compensatory amounts for the wheat imported into the UK and immediately re-exported to Germany. The trader claimed to have formally completed the import formalities in the UK in accordance with the relevant EU secondary legislation and was, therefore, entitled to receive the amounts. The Danish referring court sought clarification from the Court of Justice on whether the compensatory amounts were due in the case at hand.[45] The Danish judge had doubts concerning the improper use of the rules on compensatory amounts. In the questions referred to the Court of Justice, however, there was no explicit mention of abuse or abusive practices.

It should be noted that a similar question had already emerged a few years earlier in the *Cremer* case.[46] In this case, a German trader claimed refunds for exporting to a third-country animal feeding stuff. The rules applicable at that time stipulated that

---

[43] When the first enlargement occurred in 1973, there were considerable price differences between the founding Member States and the (then) new Member States. Consequently, "accession" compensatory amounts applicable to trade between old and new Member States were introduced to avoid distortions in the internal market. For the cereals sector, see Regulation (EEC) No 229/73 of the Council of 31 January 1973 laying down general rules for the system of compensatory amounts for cereals and fixing these for certain products, OJ L 27, 1 February 1973, pp. 25–29 (no longer in force).

[44] CJEU, *Töpfer*, Judgment of the Court, 27 October 1981, case 250/80, ECLI:EU:C:1981:246, para 7.

[45] Ibid., paras 10–13.

[46] See CJEU, *Cremer*, Judgment of the Court, 11 October 1977, case 125/76, ECLI:EU:C:1977:148.

the refund was due where the feeding-stuff exported contained no less than 50% by weight of powdered milk or certain cereals or products expressly identified by the relevant rules, such as maize, barley, tapioca and sorghum. The problem in the case at hand was that the compound exported by the trader contained tapioca flour only in negligible amounts (less than 2%).[47] On that basis, the German authorities argued that the refund was not to be granted in full in order to prevent what they called "abusive practices" on the part of traders.[48] Cremer, supported (perhaps surprisingly) by the Commission, argued that "the full refund must be granted whenever a compound feeding-stuff contains an ingredient coming under the Community rules no matter what the amount is".[49]

It is interesting to note that the Court of Justice started off by saying that the rules in question were "difficult to understand from the point of view of their wording and context",[50] which is not exactly a panegyric to the EU lawmaker. Perhaps also to avoid the difficulties connected with the literal formulation of the rules, the Court resorted to their teleological interpretation. Since the main objective of the rules was to make up for the difference between the prices within the exporting Member State and those on the world market of the relevant cereals and products, the Court opted for a proportional calculation of the amount due. It concluded that the refund "can be granted only where [the relevant] cereals or products [...] are in fact contained in the mixture in significant proportions".[51] The underlying idea seemed to be that compounds not containing sufficient amounts of the relevant cereals or products were not included within the scope of the rules in question because, in such cases, there was no need to compensate for the price difference. In this way, the risk that traders purposefully added marginal amounts of covered cereals or products to their mixtures with the sole aim of getting a refund was eliminated altogether. In the Court's reasoning, abuse fell outside the scope of the relevant legislation. In fact, the Court pointed out that the rules in question "must in no case be extended to cover abusive practices of an exporter in taking advantage of the [system] in calculating the refunds".[52]

It is based on this precedent that the Court addressed the situation in *Töpfer*. The most significant difference between this case and *Cremer* was that the Commission, for the first time, explicitly argued that there was "an abuse or fraudulent exploitation of the Community system of 'accession' compensatory amounts",[53] offering the Court the perfect opportunity to tackle abuse expressly. The Court of Justice, however, did not pick up on the Commission's suggestion and, as in *Cremer*, focused on a teleological interpretation of the rules in order to exclude situations such as those at stake in *Töpfer* from their scope of application. More specifically, the Court started off

---

[47] Ibid., para 11.
[48] Ibid., para 12.
[49] Ibid.
[50] Ibid., para 13.
[51] Ibid., para 14.
[52] Ibid., para 21.
[53] Ibid.

by clarifying that the objective of the rules on "accession" compensatory amounts is to intervene where the "price-difference as may exist between [a new] Member State and the exporting Member State constitutes an economic factor which really affects trade between the two States".[54] Where the exported goods have been in the new Member State for the sole purpose of completing customs formalities without being effectively marketed in such State, "the objective of offsetting prices has not been attained" and "an essential condition for application of an 'accession' compensatory amount has not been fulfilled".[55] Therefore, the rules had to be interpreted as not including the mere transit of goods in a new Member State. The effective release of goods onto the market of that State was necessary to attain the objective of the system, which was, as clearly stated by the Court, to facilitate trade in agricultural products between new and old Member States where significant price differences existed between them. In the circumstances, the conditions to apply such rules did not exist.

The main takeaway of the case law analysed in this section is the following. The Court was confronted with traders invoking an individual right granted by EU secondary legislation, namely the right to receive a subsidy. In both cases, the conditions necessary to invoke such right were not unambiguously fulfilled but instead purposefully made up, more or less artificially, by the alleged beneficiaries. The German authorities in the first case suggested that the trader committed an abusive practice. The Commission, in the second case, argued that the trader's conduct amounted to an abuse or fraudulent exploitation of the rules. The Court had the option to state that the two situations came under the scope of the legislation in question, but that the traders' practice constituted an abuse of the rules. Instead, it decided to take a different turn. It held that practices like those at stake fell outside their scope by resorting to a teleological interpretation of the rules in question. The lesson we learn from these decisions is that abuse, or abusive practices, can be prevented by limiting the scope of EU law through its restrictive interpretation. As we shall see, the Court will often resort to this anti-abuse strategy in cases where an advantage granted by EU secondary law is invoked. Conversely, in so-called U-turn situations, the Court will often admit, at least in principle, that Member States can justify otherwise unlawful restrictions on free movement on the need to avoid circumvention of their national rules. These positions will come back and be further clarified in subsequent case law.

For the purpose of this book, it is also important to note that *Cremer* and *Töpfer* are the first two rulings concerning the secondary legislation on export subsidies that will eventually prove to be a field particularly prone to abusive exploitation on the part of traders. Over the years, the Court of Justice will gradually recalibrate its case law, culminating in the development of a veritable test for abuse in *Emsland-Stärke*,[56] which also concerned export subsidies.

---

[54] Ibid., para 15.

[55] Ibid., para 16.

[56] CJEU, *Emsland-Stärke*, Judgment of the Court, 14 December 2000, case C-110/99, ECLI:EU:C:2000:695. For a thorough analysis of this judgment, see infra, Sect. 3.3.1.

3.2.5 *The Emergence of* Fraus Legis *in the EU Legal Order:* Könecke *and the Use of Fraudulent Means to Exploit the Law*

The *Könecke* ruling concerned the case of a German undertaking that received a subsidy for the storage of fresh beef originating in the EU, for which it had to lodge a deposit in the form of a bank guarantee. Upon the expiry of the storage period, it obtained the release of such deposit in accordance with the relevant secondary legislation. However, German authorities later discovered that the undertaking had stored frozen meat originating in China rather than fresh European meat. Criminal proceedings were brought against the individuals involved, and the referring German court asked the Court of Justice whether the deposit could be recovered or a sanction equal to the amount of the deposit could be imposed in the alternative.[57]

After recalling that "a penalty, even of a non-criminal nature, cannot be imposed unless it rests on a clear and unambiguous legal basis",[58] the Court stated that in the relevant secondary legislation, no such clear and unambiguous legal basis was to be found. Therefore, the German authorities could not recover the wrongly released deposit nor impose alternative pecuniary penalties.[59] However, this finding did "not affect the right and the duty of the national authorities to take proceedings, in accordance with national law, against a trader who has obtained the release of the deposit by *fraudulent means*".[60] The fraudulent means in the case at hand consisted of the false statements issued by the trader to obtain the deposit release.

The importance of the *Könecke* ruling lies in the Court of Justice's finding that advantages deriving from EU law cannot be obtained in a fraudulent manner. Where fraud does occur, and the EU legal order does not offer the means to rectify the situation, the Member States have the right but also the duty to take action in accordance with national law. Although the Court did not say anything explicitly, it was clear that there was a significant difference between *Könecke* and the cases of abuse (or abusive practices) previously dealt with by the Court. In previous cases, formal compliance with the rules was not in question. In *Könecke*, there was instead a misrepresentation of reality. The facts presented by the trader to German authorities were not real. The trader declared that it stored fresh meat originating in the EU while storing frozen meat from China instead. In *Cremer* and in *Töpfer*, the facts corresponded with reality. Tapioca flour was indeed used, although in negligible amounts. The Danish wheat was effectively discharged and reloaded in the UK before eventually being shipped to Germany. Put differently, Konecke carried out an unlawful activity. Cremer and Töpfer did not. Their activity was in conflict with the objective of the rules invoked,

[57] CJEU, *Karl Könecke*, Judgment of the Court, 25 September 1984, case 117/83, ECLI:EU:C:1984:288, paras 1–6.

[58] Ibid., para 11.

[59] Ibid., para 17.

[60] Ibid., para 23 (emphasis added).

but it was lawful nonetheless. In this aspect lies the main difference between abuse and fraud, as we shall see below and in Chap. 4.[61]

However, none of these considerations were made by the Court of Justice. As we shall see, in the following case law, the Court will often address abuse and fraud conjunctively, as if they were the same concept, which is lamentable. As will be discussed below, fraud and abuse are closely related yet different legal concepts. Unfortunately, the Court of Justice has not been able to distinguish them clearly so far. The *Könecke* judgment is the first sign of the Court's direction in later cases.

3.2.6 *The Use and Abuse of the Free Movement of Goods to Circumvent National Legislation: The* Leclerc *Judgment*

Leclerc is the first case in which the issue of abuse emerged in connection with the Treaty rules on the free movement of goods.[62] In fairness, abuse of law was not directly addressed in the ruling. None of the parties involved brought it up. Neither did the Court. However, the possible existence of abusive practices resulting in an improper use of EU law on the part of the trader was clearly the elephant in the room.

The dispute revolved around the selling of books by the Leclerc Group at a price lower than the one fixed by the publisher or importer. According to French law, retailers had to abide by that price, selling books at a price between 95% and 100% of the fixed price. The rules also applied to imported books.[63] The Court distinguished two situations. For books published in other Member States, no doubt the rules in question amounted to a measure equivalent to a quantitative restriction (MEQR) contrary to (current) Article 34 TFEU.[64] No qualification was added to this finding. Hence, we must assume that there was no justification either. As regards books published in France and re-imported following exportation to another Member State, the relevant national provision also constituted a MEQR, for it "discourage[d] the marketing of re-imported books by preventing the importer from passing on in the retail price an advantage resulting from a lower price obtained in the exporting Member State".[65] In this case, however, the Court added a qualification. It stated that "the above finding is not applicable where it is established that the books in question were exported for the sole purpose of re-importation in order to circumvent legislation of the type at issue",[66] in which case the national rules could be justified

[61] Another case in which fraud is not unwarrantedly mixed up with abuse is *Kol*. See CJEU, *Suat Kol*, Judgment of the Court, 5 June 1997, case C-285/95, ECLI:EU:C:1997:280.

[62] CJEU, *Leclerc*, Judgment of the Court, 10 January 1985, case 229/83, ECLI:EU:C:1985:1.

[63] Ibid., paras 1–5.

[64] Ibid., para 25.

[65] Ibid., para 26.

[66] Ibid., para 27.

on the grounds set out in (current) Article 36 TFEU.[67] The Court stopped short of finding that no such ground could validly be invoked in the case at hand. However, a contextual interpretation of the Court's findings suggests that such was its view on the matter.[68]

For the purpose of this book, the following aspects must be pointed out. Although there was no explicit mention of abuse, it is clear that the relevant conduct of the trader, that is, exporting to another Member State for the sole purpose of re-importation in order to circumvent national legislation, was the kind of behaviour that the Court qualified as abusive practices (or improper use of the law) in previous cases. Just like in *Van Binsbergen*, which also concerned a (different) fundamental freedom, the Court affirmed that the Member States were, in principle, entitled to prevent such practices by imposing restrictions to free movement, provided such restrictions are justified on the grounds set out in the Treaty. The idea that anti-abuse measures were justified restrictions to the fundamental freedoms was thus becoming established case law.

However, so far, the Court of Justice has refrained from using expressions explicitly relating to abuse. In *Van Binsbergen*, it referred to the possibility of individuals "escaping" national law.[69] In *Leclerc*, the Court talked of "circumvention" of national legislation. The time to call things by their name was yet to come.

3.2.7 The Use of a Fundamental Freedom to Obtain a Benefit Granted by National Law: The Segers *and* Lair *Rulings*

So far, we have examined cases where the fundamental freedoms were invoked in order to circumvent, evade or escape national rules. In the two cases we will examine in this section, the fundamental freedoms are invoked to obtain an advantage deriving from national law. In *Segers*, the freedom of establishment was relied on in order to obtain a social benefit granted by national law. In *Lair*, the free movement of workers constituted the basis for claiming an unemployment allowance that the individual concerned would not be entitled to without being considered a free mover under EU law.

Let's start with the *Segers* judgment. Mr Segers was a Dutch national and director of a company incorporated under English law named Slenderose Limited. This company was formed by Segers and his wife in order to take over his one-man business named Free Promotion International, whose place of registration and operation was the Netherlands. Free Promotion International thus became the Dutch subsidiary (secondary establishment) of Slenderose Limited (primary establishment), whose

[67] Ibid., para 29.

[68] For a different reading of this ruling, see Weatherhill 2011, pp. 56 ff., who identified the situation in *Leclerc* as a purely internal one.

[69] See *Van Binsbergen*, para 12.

business was conducted solely and entirely by the subsidiary.[70] In other words, Slenderose was what many would call a letterbox company, the "real" company being Free Promotion International.[71] When Mr Segers fell ill, he applied for sickness insurance benefits in the Netherlands. Under Dutch law, the director of a company holding at least 50% of the shares was entitled to such benefits, provided that the company was registered in the Netherlands. Since its company (that is, Slenderose) was incorporated in the UK, Mr Segers was denied the requested insurance benefits. Therefore, the referring Dutch court sought clarification from the Court of Justice on whether the Dutch rules were compatible with the freedom of establishment.[72]

For the purpose of this book, it is interesting to emphasise that the Dutch authorities justified the refusal "by the need to combat abuse and to ensure that the Netherlands social security legislation is properly implemented".[73] To begin with, the Luxembourg Court clarified that the freedom of establishment means that "companies or firms formed in accordance with the law of a Member State and having their registered office, central administration or principal place of business within the Community [have the right] to pursue their activities in another Member State through an agency, branch or subsidiary".[74] As a consequence, "acceptance of the proposition that the Member State in which a company seeks to establish itself may freely apply to it a different treatment solely by reason of the fact that its registered office is situated in another Member State would deprive Article [54] of all meaning".[75] Although the Court did not say it explicitly, we can assume it meant to say that the Dutch rule in question constituted a restriction to the freedom of establishment. It remained to be seen, therefore, whether it could be justified by the need to combat possible abuses of the national social security legislation.

The Court of Justice recognised, in principle, that the "Treaty allows within certain limits special treatment for companies formed in accordance with the law of another Member State provided that that treatment is justified on grounds of public policy, public security or public health".[76] It also admitted that "the need to combat fraud may [...] justify a difference of treatment in certain circumstances" but found that "the refusal to accord a sickness benefit to a director of a company formed in accordance with the law of another Member State cannot constitute an appropriate measure".[77] Regrettably, the Court stopped short of clarifying what the "certain limits" it referred to were; what "special treatment" was admissible; why the refusal to grant sickness benefit was not "an appropriate measure".

The Court's terse statement on these points is regrettable. However, two main takeaways clearly emerged from the *Segers* judgment. On the one hand, it confirmed

---

[70] CJEU, *Segers*, Judgment of the Court, 10 July 1986, case 79/85, ECLI:EU:C:1986:308.

[71] See Cerioni 2010, pp. 789 ff.

[72] See *Segers*, paras 1–6.

[73] Ibid., para 10.

[74] Ibid., para 13.

[75] Ibid., para 14.

[76] Ibid., para 17.

[77] Ibid.

that the need to combat abuse, in principle, can constitute a valid justification for restrictions on free movement. So far, the Court only did so in relation to the freedom to provide services and the free movement of goods. *Segers* extended that case law to another fundamental freedom. On the other hand, the ruling is the first manifestation of what will become the Court's overall approach to this one particular fundamental freedom. More specifically, the Court opted for a formal interpretation of what is today Article 54 TFEU. It stated that the provision in question "requires only that the companies be formed in accordance with the law of a Member State and have their registered office, central administration or principal place of business within the Community".[78] If one of those conditions is satisfied, "the fact that the company conducts its business through an agency, branch or subsidiary solely in another Member State is immaterial".[79] Since Slenderose Limited was a validly existing company under British law, it had the right to exercise the freedom of establishment in the way most suitable to its business, including through a sole subsidiary in the Netherlands. This formalistic yet quite liberal and pro-integration stance will be repeated and strengthened in later cases, such as the well-known *Centros* ruling.[80]

One last aspect deserves to be pointed out. While the Dutch authorities argued that they needed to combat *abuse*, the Court recognised, although only in principle, that the need to combat *fraud* could, in principle, justify a restriction.[81] From a contextual interpretation of the ruling, we can assume that the Court, with this statement, did not intend to distinguish between fraud and abuse. Rather, it confirmed the Court's tendency to refer to abuse and fraud somewhat interchangeably despite the differences existing between these two concepts.

In *Lair*, the dispute revolved around the right of Ms Lair, a French national, to receive a maintenance and training grant for the pursuit of her university studies at the University of Hanover. Under German law, the grant could be awarded to German nationals but also to foreigners, provided they had resided and worked regularly in Germany for a total period of five years prior to the commencement of the studies for which assistance was sought. No such requirement was imposed on German nationals. Ms Lair had lived in Germany for over 5 years when she applied for the grant. During that time, she did not work regularly but rather went through alternate periods of employment, unemployment and retraining before eventually signing up to the University of Hanover. The referring court doubted whether the German rules in question were compatible with EU law.[82]

As far as the topic of this book is concerned, the *Lair* case's relevance lies in one of the arguments maintained by the three Member States that submitted observations

---

[78] Ibid., para 16.

[79] Ibid.

[80] The successive case law will be analysed below. See *infra*, Sect. 3.2.14.

[81] See *Segers*, para 17. The other linguistic versions of the judgment feature the same terminological choice. For example, the French version says "*lutte contre eventuels abus*" and "*lutte contre des opérations frauduleuses*"; the Italian version says "*prevenzione di eventuali abusi*" and "*lotta contro le pratiche fraudolente*".

[82] CJEU, *Sylvie Lair*, Judgment of the Court, 21 June 1988, case 39/86, ECLI:EU:C:1988:322.

in the proceedings, namely Germany, Denmark and the UK. According to them, the Member States were generally "entitled to require that a national of another Member State applying for a maintenance and training grant with a view to the pursuit of university studies must first have engaged in occupational activity for a minimum period [...] to prevent certain abuses, for example where it may be established on the basis of objective evidence that a worker has entered a Member State for the sole purpose of enjoying, after a very short period of occupational activity, the benefit of the student assistance system in that State".[83] The Court replied to this concern with (again) quite a terse statement. It merely observed that "such abuses are not covered by the Community provisions in question",[84] the provisions being the Treaty rules on free movement of workers and Regulation No 1612/68.[85] This statement was made right before finding that the Member States could not "make the right to the same social advantages provided for in Article 7(2) of Regulation No 1612/68 conditional upon a minimum period of prior occupational activity within the[ir] territory".[86]

In the *Lair* ruling, the Luxembourg Court used "abuse" as a noun for the first time rather than as an adjective to qualify something else (i.e. abusive practices, as in *Cremer*). In its abrupt statement, the Court seemed to suggest that abuses of the type feared by the Member States were outside the scope of the rules on free movement of workers. In terms of anti-abuse strategy, this position is the same as the one employed in cases of abuse of EU secondary law, such as *Cremer* and *Töpfer* (see above, Sect. 3.2.4), even though the rules allegedly abused in the case at hand were both of primary and secondary rank. Be that as it may, it should be pointed out that the discussion of abuse in *Lair* was almost entirely theoretical, for it was clear that Ms Lair had genuinely moved to Germany in order to seek employment and that her situation of intermittent unemployment was not the result of an attempt to abuse the German student assistance system, as feared by the three Member States (rather speciously, to be fair). Her situation was the result of normal working-life circumstances. It is not uncommon, especially for younger workers, to be job-hopping before settling in a more stable position. That seemed to be the case with Ms Lair, which has (even conceptually) little to do with the idea of abuse.

One last aspect deserves to be pointed out. In the *Lair* judgment, we can see the first signs of an approach that will mark the Court of Justice's case law on abuse in the field of free movement of persons, which will culminate in the well-known *Chen* ruling.[87] As we shall see, the Court will display a strong free mover-friendly attitude, rejecting the (often clumsy) attempts of the Member States to narrow down the primary and secondary rules governing the free movement of persons in the EU.

---

[83] Ibid., para 40–43.

[84] Ibid.

[85] See Regulation (EEC) No 1612/68 of the Council of 15 October 1968 on freedom of movement for workers within the Community, OJ L 257, 19 October 1968, pp. 2–12 (no longer in force).

[86] Ibid., para 42.

[87] See *infra*, Sect. 3.3.3.

3.2.8 *The "Greek Challenge" Cases*

Between May 1991 and March 2000, the Court of Justice handed down five judgments upon referral from Greek courts concerning similar factual and legal issues. This case law, which is collectively known as the "Greek challenge",[88] is not massively coherent, to say the least. All cases concerned the interpretation and application of the so-called Second Company Law Directive[89] to a series of Greek companies that experienced significant financial distress and entered, as a result, into a restructuring process supervised by Greek authorities under the relevant national legislation.

The first such case is *Karella*, in which two shareholders of a company under administration challenged, before a Greek court, the increase of capital of such company, which was decided unilaterally by the Greek authorities involved. According to Article 25(1) of the Directive, a capital increase was to be decided by the shareholders in a general meeting. The referring judge, therefore, asked for clarifications from the Court of Justice on whether the Greek rules that allowed a derogation from the ordinary company law rules in exceptional circumstances, such as collective liquidations or rejuvenation procedures of companies in distress, were compatible with EU law.[90] After finding that the relevant provisions of the Directive had direct effects,[91] the Court concluded that "Article 25 in conjunction with Article 41(1) of the Second Directive must be interpreted as meaning that they preclude national rules which, in order to ensure the survival and continued operation of undertakings which are of particular economic and social importance for society as a whole and are in exceptional circumstances by reason of their excessive debt burden, provide for the adoption by administrative act of a decision to increase the company capital".[92] Although the issue of abuse was not even brought up in this ruling, its examination is essential for the understanding of the following cases that eventually led to the "Greek challenge".

The second episode of the saga came only one year later. In *Kerafina*, the factual and legal circumstances were essentially identical to *Karella*. Unsurprisingly, the Court's ruling is extremely short and comes down to reaffirming the conclusions already reached in the relevant precedent. In fact, the cases are so similar that the Court merely copy-pasted the operative part of *Karella*.[93] However, the judgment is

---

[88] See De la Feria 2008, p. 404.

[89] See Second Council Directive 77/91/EEC of 13 December 1976 on coordination of safeguards which, for the protection of the interests of members and others, are required by Member States of companies within the meaning of the second paragraph of Article 58 of the Treaty, in respect of the formation of public limited liability companies and the maintenance and alteration of their capital, with a view to making such safeguards equivalent, OJ L 26, 31 January 1977, pp. 1–13 (no longer in force).

[90] CJEU, *Karella*, Judgment of the Court, 30 May 1991, joined cases C-19/90 and C-20/90, ECLI:EU:C:1991:229, paras 1–12.

[91] Ibid., paras 17–23.

[92] Ibid., para 36.

[93] CJEU, *Kerafina*, Judgment of the Court, 12 November 1992, joined cases C-134/91 and C-135/91, ECLI:EU:C:1992:434, para 18.

worth mentioning because it represented the first sign of what will become an outright defiance of the Court of Justice's position and authority. In other words, it is the first worrisome sign of the "Greek challenge". On the one hand, the Greek authorities openly argued that the Court's previous ruling was incorrect, requesting explicitly a *revirement de jurisprudence*.[94] On the other hand, the referral of a question in an identical situation and in relation to a decision of the Court that left little room for doubts was clearly indicative of discontent on the part of domestic judges.

The third ruling belonging to the "Greek challenge" is *Pafitis*. This is the first case of the saga where the issue of abuse was explicitly discussed. The factual and legal issues are once again quite similar to the previous episodes: the dispute focused on the capital increase of a company adopted in contrast to the provisions of the relevant Directive. The substantial difference, however, was that in the main proceedings pending before the Greek court, the defendant, that is, the company whose capital increase had been challenged, raised an objection concerning the abusive exercise of rights. The rights allegedly abused were those deriving from the Directive, which entitled the plaintiffs in the main proceedings to challenge the validity of a capital increase adopted contrary to its provisions. As AG Tesauro noted in his Opinion, "the national court has reserved judgment as to the merits"[95] of the objection. In other words, the Greek judge found it relevant to tell the Court of Justice that such an exception was looming on the dispute and that "exclusive jurisdiction to adjudicate on that point"[96] belonged to the referring judge. The Greek challenge had formally been issued, and AG Tesauro was eager to accept it (much less so was the Court, as we shall see).

More specifically, the Advocate General deemed it "inevitable that the Court should rule on the point since what is at stake is the primacy of [EU] law over domestic law and the effectiveness of the preliminary rulings given by the Court",[97] which was "precisely what happened in the *Kerafina* judgment".[98] Indeed, according to AG Tesauro, in that case the referring court had disregarded the Court of Justice's ruling by upholding an objection concerning abuse of rights based on Greek law. This time, the same outcome had been announced in the order for reference in a vaguely threatening tone. As we have seen in Chap. 2, in the Greek legal order, abuse of rights is enshrined in Article 281 of the Civil Code, which was precisely the provision brandished by the referring court in *Pafitis*. In the interpretation suggested by the Greek judge, abuse of rights of Greek law also applied to rights deriving from Union law by preventing their "abusive" exercise.

AG Tesauro started off by recognising that the abusive exercise of a right was censured in all Member States, albeit with some differences. However, in the case at hand, "the plaintiffs [...] merely wish to secure observance of the right which is at the

[94] Ibid., para 14–15.

[95] CJEU, *Pafitis*, Opinion of Advocate General Tesauro, 9 November 1995, case C-441/93, ECLI:EU:C:1995:368, para 11.

[96] Ibid., para 27.

[97] Ibid., para 28.

[98] Ibid.

heart of that provision"[99] of the Directive. The objective of the relevant provision was to protect shareholders from restructuring a company. The plaintiffs were exercising their rights to obtain such protection. To deny this protection on the ground that they were abusing their rights was "tantamount to censuring not the *abusive exercise* of the right but rather *any exercise of it*".[100] The Advocate General was convinced that this was a matter of crucial importance. He was convinced that a foundational stone of the EU legal order, that is, the principle of primacy, was at stake. Coherently, he suggested "the Court *make it absolutely clear* that legislation which allows a national court to prohibit the exercise of a right conferred by a provision of [Union] law by describing it as abusive cannot be applied".[101] He would have been disappointed by the Court's (again) terse consideration of the issue.

The Luxembourg Court essentially brushed off the issue in a few lines. We have seen above that the referring court declared itself to be exclusively competent to adjudicate on the issue of abuse of rights. To the Court of Justice, this meant that "since the national court has submitted no question on the matter, it is unnecessary to rule".[102] Contrary to what AG Tesauro believed, the question was not relevant (for the interpretation of EU law) in the eyes of the Court. However, it conceded that "the uniform application and full effect of [Union] law would be undermined if a shareholder relying on Article 25(1) of the Second Directive were deemed to be abusing his rights merely because he was a minority shareholder of a company subject to reorganization measures or had benefited from the reorganization of the company".[103] The key message indirectly sent to the Greek court was that (domestic) abuse of rights could not be applied, whereby the uniform application and effectiveness of the EU law were at stake. Or, to reframe it in positive terms, (domestic) abuse of rights could be applied provided that the uniform application and effectiveness of EU law were not in jeopardy. In the fourth episode of the saga, the Court would have to address the issue more straightforwardly.

The next episode, namely *Kefalas*, had to do with pretty much the same issue as the previous three episodes. This time, however, the referring court explicitly asked the Court of Justice whether a domestic judge could "apply a provision of national law (in this case Article 281 of the Greek Civil Code) in order to assess whether a right granted by the [Union] provisions at issue is being exercised abusively by the party possessing it".[104] The Court began by stating that EU law could not be "relied on for abusive or fraudulent ends",[105] recalling its case-law on the matter, such as *Van Binsbergen*, *Leclerc* and *Lair*. From this, the Court drew the conclusion that, as

[99] Ibid., para 31.

[100] Ibid., emphasis in the original.

[101] Ibid., para 34 (emphasis added).

[102] CJEU, *Pafitis*, Judgment of the Court, 12 March 1996, case C-441/93, ECLI:EU:C:1996:92, para 68.

[103] Ibid., para 70.

[104] CJEU, *Kefalas*, Judgment of the Court, 12 May 1998, case C-367/96, ECLI:EU:C:1998:222, para 18.

[105] Ibid., para 20.

a matter of principle, the application of a provision such as Article 281 of the Greek Civil Code "for the purposes of assessing whether the exercise of a right arising from a provision of [EU] law is abusive cannot be regarded as contrary to the [Union] legal order".[106] The Court left the assessment of the specific factual circumstances of the case to the national court, but it pointed out that the application of such a national rule could not affect the uniform application and full effectiveness of EU law, as stated in *Pafitis*. The Luxembourg Court then offered some guidance to the referring court as to whether, in a situation such as that at stake in the main proceedings, the exercise of the rights conferred by Article 25 of the Directive could be deemed abusive. This part of the decision seemed to side with AG Tesauro by suggesting that in the circumstances, the plaintiffs were merely using, not abusing, the rights granted by the Directive.[107] However, the Court was willing to concede more to the recurrent concerns of Greek judges. It added that EU law did not "preclude a national court, on the basis of sufficient telling evidence, from examining whether, by bringing an action under Article 25(1) of the Second Directive for a declaration that an increase in capital is invalid, a shareholder is seeking to derive, to the detriment of the company, an *improper advantage, manifestly contrary to the objective of that provision*".[108]

There was no evidence, in the cases referred to the Court of Justice, that shareholders were attempting to obtain an improper advantage contrary to the objective of the rights conferred to them. Rather, there was evidence of the opposite. It seemed plausible that shareholders were merely exercising their rights not to be excluded from making decisions affecting their share in the company, which was precisely the objective of Article 25 of the Directive. Nonetheless, the Court found it appropriate to make a far-reaching statement on the possibility of abusing the rights deriving from that provision. Furthermore, the Court also admitted that such abusive exercise of rights granted by EU secondary legislation could be countered by an instrument of domestic law (namely, abuse of rights based on Greek civil law) rather than by an instrument of EU law, such as, for example, a restrictive and teleologically oriented interpretation of the scope of EU law. That was, after all, the conclusion reached in *Cremer* and *Töpfer*, which also concerned rights derived from EU secondary legislation. It was perhaps the most reasonable and logical solution to the "Greek challenge" based on its previous case law. In fairness, it is difficult to see why the Court of Justice decided to go down a different road in *Kefalas*. As we shall see, later decisions on abuse of EU law would not further explain this position, which would, therefore, remain a sort of odd one out in the Court's case law.

The (poisoned) fruits of this ruling would materialise a few years later. *Diamantis* is the fifth and final episode of the saga. The dispute once again revolved around the challenge brought to two capital increases adopted in violation of Article 25 of the

[106] Ibid., para 21. According to Gestri 2003, p. 149, this statement should be interpreted as meaning that abuse of rights as foreseen in the Greek legal order had some foundation in EU law, which is why the Court allowed a national court to deny a right derived from EU law on the basis of a domestic provision.

[107] Ibid., paras 22–27.

[108] Ibid., para 28 (emphasis added).

Directive. This time, however, the plaintiff in the main proceedings, for reasons not explained in the ruling, had brought such a challenge before Greek courts five years and four years, respectively, after the initial approval of the first and second capital increase. Therefore, the referring court asked the ECJ whether Article 281 of the Greek Civil Code was applicable in the case at hand.[109]

After recalling its case law on the matter, particularly *Pafitis* and *Kefalas*, the Court addressed whether EU law precluded "the national court from verifying whether, in choosing to bring an action for a declaration that the alterations in capital were invalid, after periods of five years and four years had elapsed, the plaintiff in the main proceedings was seeking to derive [...] an improper advantage manifestly contrary to the objective of Article 25(1) of the Second Directive, thus constituting an abuse of his rights".[110] The Court went on to find "sufficient telling evidence of abuse of rights" (see above), which it did not find in the fact of "having instituted proceedings, even after a certain lapse of time, within the limitation period provided for under national law for such actions".[111] In other words, the plaintiff was compliant with domestic procedural law relating to limitation periods. However, since in that lapse of time "several operations took place", such as purchases, sales, mergers, etc., it was "indisputable that the invalidity of those alterations would inevitably affect the rights of *bona fide* third parties".[112] The most obvious logical consequence of this statement would have been that EU law did not preclude national law from safeguarding *bona fide* rights of third parties while recognising that the plaintiff in the main proceedings was doing no more than exercising his rights under the Directive. The assessment of how to safeguard the rights of third parties could be left to the domestic judge to sort out on the basis of national law. Instead, the Court decided to take a different path. It found that the uniform application and effectiveness of EU law did not preclude the referring court from verifying whether the remedy chosen by the plaintiff would "cause such serious damage to the legitimate interests of others that it appears manifestly disproportionate",[113] and therefore abusive.

From a practical point of view, the outcome of the main dispute would not have massively changed had the ECJ stated that Mr Diamantis was merely exercising his rights but that the rights acquired by third parties in those five years would not be affected. In practical terms, it is plausible that the only solution available to the domestic judge was to uphold the validity of, say, a sales contract with a third party while granting some form of remedial compensation to Mr Diamantis. However, it is one thing to say that one is entitled to compensation because her rights (under the Directive) have been breached. It is an entirely different thing to say that she has

---

109 CJEU, *Diamantis*, Judgment of the Court, 23 March 2000, case C-373/97, ECLI:EU:C:2000:150, paras 14–30. However, since the company of which he was a shareholder was undergoing a major restructuring, it is reasonable to assume that Mr Diamantis was waiting to see how events would unfold.

110 Ibid., para 38.

111 Ibid., para 39.

112 Ibid., para 40 (emphasis in the original).

113 Ibid., para 43.

exercised her rights abusively but might still, in spite of this, be entitled to a different remedy.

In conclusion of this lengthy examination of the "Greek challenge", it is possible to affirm that the main lesson we can learn from it is that the abusive exercise of rights deriving from EU secondary law can, in principle, be censured on the basis of abuse of rights foreseen by the domestic law of the Member States.[114] As we shall see, this line of cases would remain an isolated exception against the broader context of the ECJ's case law on abuse of law.[115] Had the Court already developed a fully-fledged doctrine of abuse of EU law, the outcome of *Diamantis* and the other Greek challenge cases might have been very different. With the benefit of hindsight, it seems reasonable to affirm that the conduct of the plaintiffs in these cases did not satisfy the two constitutive elements of abuse as developed in *Emsland-Stärke* and subsequent cases.

3.2.9 Merging the Findings of **Van Binsbergen** *and* **Leclerc***: The* **Veronica** *Ruling*

In *Veronica*, the Court of Justice had the opportunity to go back to the possibility of using improperly (better: of abusing) the freedom to provide services, which it already dealt with in *Van Binsbergen*. Since that foundational ruling, however, much had happened in the Court's case law. *Veronica* provided the chance to extend the reasoning developed in *Lecler* to the freedom to provide services while building on the foundations laid down in *Van Binsbergen*.

Veronica was a broadcasting organisation that contributed to setting up a commercial station broadcasting to the Netherlands in Luxembourg, named RTL-Véronique, and also provided material and financial support for it. The programmes of RTL-Véronique were relayed to the Netherlands by cable. Dutch authorities found Veronica's conduct to be in breach of Dutch media law (*Mediawet*), and the referring court sought clarification from the Court of Justice on whether the provisions in question constituted a restriction to the free movement of capital and the freedom to provide services.[116]

The ECJ started off by recalling its previous case law where it recognised that the *Mediawet* was "designed to establish a pluralistic and non-commercial broadcasting

---

[114] According to Tridimas 2006, p. 29, this decision is part of a tendency of the Court of Justice, which sometimes "has been content to allow national courts to rely on general principles recognized by the law of Member States". This deference, according to this prominent author, "may be seen as an application of judicial subsidiarity in the field of remedies and legal protection".

[115] An isolated exception to which a decisive contribution was given by the "stubbornness of the Greek courts", as noted by Gestri 2003, p. 156 ("*l'insistenza dei giudici greci*", in the original Italian text).

[116] CJEU, *Veronica*, Judgment of the Court, 3 February 1993, case C-148/91, ECLI:EU:C:1993:45, paras 1–6.

system and thus forms part of a cultural policy intended to safeguard, in the audiovisual sector, the freedom of expression of the various (in particular social, cultural, religious and philosophical) components existing in the Netherlands".[117] Those were public interests that a Member State could legitimately pursue.[118] The Court here employed language typical of (lawful) justifications for restrictions on fundamental freedoms, yet without expressly labelling the Dutch provisions in question as restrictions. It went on to recall the principle stated in *Van Binsbergen*, according to which a Member State could not "be denied the right to take measures to prevent the exercise by a person whose activity is entirely or principally directed towards its territory of the freedoms guaranteed by the Treaty for the purpose of avoiding the professional rules of conduct which would be applicable to him if he were established within that State".[119] The national rules in question, aimed at preventing the evasion of national legislation concerning the pluralistic and non-commercial content of TV programmes that were otherwise applicable to broadcasting organisations established in the Netherlands, could not be regarded as precluded by the Treaty.[120]

Although the Court did not explicitly talk about abuse or abusive practices, it is clear that it considered as not legitimate an activity aimed at evading national law on broadcasting rights, in much the same way it found unacceptable the exportation and immediate re-importation of books for the sole purpose of circumventing national legislation on fixed prices occurred in *Leclerc*. From *Van Binsbergen*, the ECJ borrowed the criterion that allowed it to distinguish a genuine cross-border supply of service from a disguised establishment, that is, the fact that the activity was entirely or principally directed towards the concerned Member State's territory.

After the dubious construction emerged from the Greek cases, *Veronica* represented a coherent confirmation of the principle that the measures adopted by the Member States to prevent fundamental freedoms from being used to circumvent national rules constituted restrictions justified by legitimate public interests. This case law would be confirmed in later rulings concerning similar issues, such as *TV10*.[121]

3.2.10 The Role of Harmonisation and Proportionality: The Kraus *Judgment*

Mr Kraus was a German national who obtained a Master of Laws (LL.M.) at the University of Edinburgh and returned to Germany with the intention of using his post-graduate academic title in his home country. German law provided that in order to use foreign academic titles, it was necessary to apply for an authorisation to be

[117] Ibid., para 9.

[118] Ibid., para 10.

[119] Ibid., para 12.

[120] Ibid., paras 13–15.

[121] CJEU, *TV10 SA*, Judgment of the Court, 5 October 1994, case C-23/93, ECLI:EU:C:1994:362.

given by the competent ministry of the relevant *Land*, which Mr Kraus refused to do. He then brought the matter before a German court, which asked the ECJ whether the rules in question constituted a restriction to the free movement of persons under EU law.[122]

In short, the Court of Justice confirmed its case law that Member States are allowed in similar cases to impose (justified) restrictions on fundamental freedoms, yet it added some qualifications. It affirmed that Union law did not "preclude a Member State from adopting, *in the absence of harmonization*, measures designed to prevent the opportunities created under the Treaty from being *abused* in a manner contrary to the legitimate interests of the State".[123] Such legitimate interest, in the case at hand, was to "protect a public which will not necessarily be alerted to *abuse of academic titles* which have not been awarded according to the rules laid down in the country in which the holder of the title intends to make use of it".[124] Put differently, the abuse of foreign academic titles constituted an abusive exercise of the free movement of persons. However, the Court added that national measures of this kind were to fulfil a number of conditions in order to comply with the principle of proportionality, and it provided some guidance in this direction.[125]

For the purpose of this book, the *Kraus* ruling is important because it added two significant qualifications to a case law that had become well-established after *Van Binsbergen*, *Leclerc* and *Veronica*.[126] The ECJ confirmed the principles formulated in those cases, yet further affirmed that: (a) restrictions justified by the objectively verifiable need to prevent abuse had nonetheless to be proportionate, which the Court had not said in those previous cases, and (b) although in an *obiter dictum*, the principles established in *Kraus* applied only *in the absence of harmonisation*. As we shall see in later cases (Sect. 3.3.7), the Court's position on using titles and qualifications in harmonised fields would be quite different.

3.2.11 The Prequel to **Emsland-Stärke: Boterlux**

We have already said above that the field of export subsidies has been particularly susceptible to abusive practices. After *Töpfer* and *Cremer*, they came up again in *Boterlux*, in which the Court of Justice laid the foundations that eventually led to *Emsland-Stärke*. For this reason, the former ruling can be considered a sort of prequel to the latter.

Boterlux was a company governed by Belgian law that exported butter to Switzerland for a number of years, for which it obtained a refund grant paid by Belgium.

[122] CJEU, *Dieter Kraus*, Judgment of the Court, 31 March 1993, case C-19/92, ECLI:EU:C:1993:125, paras 1–11.

[123] Ibid., para 34 (emphasis added).

[124] Ibid., para 35 (emphasis added).

[125] Ibid., para 37–41.

[126] For an overall assessment of the ruling see Smith 1994, pp. 67 ff.

After finding out that the butter was re-imported into the Union, namely to Italy, Belgian authorities refused to pay the grant on the ground that the exporter had not produced evidence that the butter had been put into free circulation in Switzerland. Re-importation to Italy was not disputed, but Boterlux argued that it played no part in that fraudulent practice. It claimed it was not involved in the re-importation. The Belgian court, before which the issue was brought, referred questions to the ECJ, seeking clarification on whether the export refund was due in the case at hand.[127]

The Court of Justice focused on the so-called anti-fraud provision foreseen in Article 4(1) of Regulation 1041/67,[128] which allowed the Member States to require additional proof that the exported product had been imported into a third country. The ECJ relied on the preamble to that Regulation to affirm that the aim of the anti-fraud provision was to "prevent abuses".[129] Hence, additional supporting documents could be required if there was suspicion or proof that abuses had been committed, as was the case in the circumstances underlying the main dispute.[130] The Court then went on to examine whether the exporter could still be entitled to export subsidies in view of its non-participation in what the Court referred to as fraudulent re-importation into the Union. It found, however, that an exporter could be exempted only in a case of *force majeure*, which included only "abnormal and unforeseeable circumstances beyond the control of the trader concerned, whose consequences could not have been avoided in spite of the exercise of all due care".[131] Such was not fraudulent re-importation, which represented an ordinary commercial risk in agricultural export business that could be avoided, or at least reduced, by means of *ad hoc* contractual measures.[132] Given the circumstances, the exporter "*loses* his right to a refund".[133]

A number of takeaways from this ruling can be pointed out. First, the Court's position was particularly strict. So far, the Court had dealt with exporters that willingly tried to exploit the rules to their advantage, as was clearly the case in *Cremer* and even more so in *Töpfer*. This time, it was different, considering Boterlux's lack of involvement in the re-importation. Nonetheless, the Court decided to take a firm hand in dealing with fishy situations in the field of export subsidies. This was possibly explained by the ECJ's willingness to combat a phenomenon that was probably widespread at the time. Second, the interchangeability between abuse and fraud was reiterated. Once again, the Court did not distinguish these two concepts. In this respect, it should be noted that *Boterlux* was arguably a case of fraud rather than

127 CJEU, *Boterlux SPRL*, Judgment of the Court, 9 August 1994, case C-347/93, ECLI:EU:C:1994:314, paras 1–7.

128 See Regulation no 1041/67/EEC of the Commission of 21 December 1967 on detailed rules for the application of export refunds on products subject to a single price system, OJ 314, 23 December 1967, pp. 9–16 (no longer in force).

129 *Boterlux SPRL*, para 25.

130 Ibid., para 27–29.

131 Ibid., para 34.

132 Ibid., para 35–36.

133 Ibid., para 37 (emphasis added).

abuse. The Court itself recognised that the butter was "re-exported under false documents".[134] As will shall see below and in Chap. 4, a misrepresentation of reality is arguably the main feature of *fraus legis*. In turn, the forging of false documents is perhaps the quintessential form of misrepresenting reality.[135] Third, differently from *Cremer* and *Töpfer*, the Court did not say explicitly that the abusive (*rectius*: fraudulent) practice in question was not covered by the relevant secondary legislation. Therefore, it could be doubted whether the Court used the same anti-abuse strategy of its previous case law, that is, restricting the scope of EU secondary law so that abusive practices fell outside it. If one looks under the surface, however, it seems that the Luxembourg Court employed exactly that same strategy. By stating that in the circumstances of the case, the exporter *lost* her right to a refund, the Court implicitly said that an exporter who employs fraudulent means (in this case, an exporter who failed to prevent fraud) places herself outside the coverage of EU secondary law.

Before moving on to the next section, the *Roquette Frères* ruling also deserves a quick mention.[136] The issue at stake was similar to *Boterlux* but with a substantial difference that would prove decisive. The dispute concerned the export of glucose syrup to Austria, a third country at that time. One of the plaintiff's customers in Austria had used the syrup to manufacture penicillin, some of which was re-imported into the Union in this form. The question was, therefore, whether Roquette Frères was entitled to the export refund despite the fact that the syrup was not consumed in the unaltered state on the Austrian market.[137] The Court of Justice was straightforward in excluding an abuse of the rules. It held that "[a]buse in the sense of the re-introduction into the Community of the product previously exported cannot exist where the product has undergone substantial and irreversible processing, as a result of which it has ceased to exist as such and a new product, coming under a different tariff heading, has been created".[138] The Court's reasoning was clear and difficult not to agree with. The principle emerging from this finding is that in the field of export subsidies, processing a product for which a refund is due eliminates any possibility of abuse. Furthermore, it should be emphasised that *Roquette Frères* was a case of (potential) abuse and not (potential) fraud, for no purposeful alteration of reality was involved. Coherently, the Court did not even mention fraud in its ruling. It is interesting to note that when the Court deals with an issue of fraud, abuse is often (but not always: see, for example, the *Könecke* decision above, Sect. 3.2.5) mentioned alongside it. The opposite is not true. The latter is not mentioned in a case clearly concerning

---

[134] Ibid., para 28.

[135] Another early case concerning false documents in which abuse and fraud are treated in a similar manner is *Brennet AG v Paletta*, which concerned a forged medical certificate. See CJEU, *Brennet AG v Paletta*, Judgment of the Court, 2 May 1996, case C-206/94, ECLI:EU:C:1996:182.

[136] CJEU, *Roquette Frères SA*, Judgment of the Court, 17 October 2000, case C-114/99, ECLI:EU:C:2000:568, not to be confused with the somewhat more famous CJEU, *SA Roquette Frères*, Judgment of the Court, 29 October 1980, case 138/79, ECLI:EU:C:1980:249, concerning the role of the European Parliament in law-making, on which see the comment of Leopold 1982, pp. 454–459.

[137] *Roquette Frères SA*, paras 7–9.

[138] Ibid., para 19.

abuse and not fraud. One can, therefore, wonder whether, in the ECJ's view, fraud almost invariably entails an abuse of the rules, while an abuse does not automatically translate into fraud. We will go back to this question below and in Chap. 4.

3.2.12 *How to Apply an Express Anti-abuse Clause and the Emergence of the Concept of "Valid Commercial Reasons": The* **Leur-Bloem** *Decision*

The provision dealt with by the Court of Justice in *Leur-Bloem* was not formally an anti-abuse clause but rather an anti-tax fraud and anti-tax evasion clause. However, given the conceptual and practical proximity between the concepts of abuse and evasion in the field of tax matters,[139] it is appropriate to examine the *Leur-Bloem* ruling.

The dispute revolved around the application of tax benefits foreseen by Council Directive 90/434/EEC to a transaction qualified by the plaintiff as a merger by exchange of shares.[140] Dutch authorities deemed the transaction not to be a merger under the Directive and refused to grant the benefits in question. Ms Leur-Bloem challenged the decision before a Dutch court, which referred the question to the ECJ.[141]

After finding that the transaction in question did indeed come under the scope of the Directive, the Court of Justice turned to examine whether the anti-tax evasion clause of the Directive could be invoked in order to refuse the tax benefits requested. To do so, it was necessary to ascertain whether the transaction in question had "tax evasion or tax avoidance as its principal objective or as one of its principal objectives".[142] Although the Directive contained no indication of how to conduct such an assessment, which was therefore left to the Member States, the ECJ provided some guidance on interpreting the relevant anti-abuse clause. It clarified that the provision in question required the Member States to conduct a general examination of the operation on a case-by-case assessment basis. This examination had to be subject to judicial review. It admitted that it was possible for the Member States to avail themselves of presumptions. For example, the Court stated that the fact that an operation was not carried out for valid commercial reasons could constitute a presumption of tax evasion or tax avoidance. However, the presumption had to be rebuttable. Furthermore, in order to comply with the principle of proportionality, the

---

[139] This issue will be further explored in Sect. 3.3.4 as well as in Chap. 4.

[140] See Council Directive 90/434/EEC of 23 July 1990 on the common system of taxation applicable to mergers, divisions, transfers of assets and exchanges of shares concerning companies of different Member States, OJ L 225, 20 August 1990, pp. 1–5 (no longer in force).

[141] CJEU, *A. Leur-Bloem*, Judgment of the Court, 17 July 1997, case C-28/95, ECLI:EU:C:1997:369.

[142] See Article 11(1)(a) of the Directive.

Member States could not automatically exclude certain categories of operations.[143] As for the meaning of "valid commercial reasons" under the Directive, the Court stated that it meant the relevant transaction had to attain "more than [...] a purely fiscal advantage such as horizontal off-setting of losses".[144]

It is difficult to overestimate the significance of *Leur-Bloem* for the topic of this book.[145] It is the first of a barrage of decisions concerning tax matters that, like export subsidies, would prove a prolific field for abuse of EU law. First of all, this ruling made clear that Member States were entitled to combat abusive tax behaviours by resorting to preventive measures, including (rebuttable) presumptions. The Member States could not use pre-determined criteria, leading to the automatic exclusion of certain transactions, and the measures had always to be amenable to judicial review. These findings were clearly indicative of the Court's concern about narrowing down the possibility for the Member States to unilaterally deny benefits granted by EU law to the detriment of its uniform application and full effectiveness. Secondly, *Leur-Bloem* marked the rise of the concept of valid commercial transactions, which would play a pivotal role in the case law concerning tax-related abuses of the law.

3.2.13 *When the Need to Combat Abuse Is Abused: The Misplaced Invocation of the Need to Prevent Tax Avoidance in* Imperial Chemical Industries

We have seen in the conclusion of the previous section that the Court in *Leur-Bloem* was concerned about narrowing down the interpretation of an anti-abuse clause that allowed the Member States to deny advantages deriving from EU law. It was the first manifestation of the awareness that the Member States could potentially abuse or at least overly rely on such a possibility. Precisely, this scenario materialised one year later, but the ECJ was prepared to deal with it.

Imperial Chemical Industries (hereinafter: *ICI*) concerned the refusal of a tax benefit to a holding established in the UK on the basis that the majority of its subsidiaries were not corporate residents in the UK. The tax benefit would apply if those subsidiaries were incorporated in the UK. ICI challenged the decision, arguing that it breached the freedom of establishment.[146] The Court had no doubt that a national measure granting a tax relief "only to companies controlling, wholly or

[143] See *Leur-Bloem*, para 48(b).

[144] Ibid., para 48(c).

[145] For a general comment of the decision see Hoenjet 1997, pp. 206 ff.

[146] CJEU, *Imperial Chemical Industries plc*, Judgment of the Court, 16 July 1998, case C-264/96, ECLI:EU:C:1998:370, paras 7–12.

mainly, subsidiaries whose seats are in the national territory"[147] constituted a restriction. It, therefore, examined "whether there [was] any justification for such inequality of treatment under the Treaty's provisions on freedom of establishment".[148]

The UK relied essentially on two grounds to justify the measure. First, it argued that it was designed to reduce the risk of tax avoidance arising from the possibility of channelling charges from foreign subsidiaries to the UK with the sole purpose of obtaining the requested tax benefits. Second, the legislation in question aimed at preventing a reduction in tax revenue. The Court of Justice noted that "the legislation at issue in the main proceedings [did] not have the specific purpose of preventing *wholly artificial arrangements*, set up to circumvent United Kingdom tax legislation".[149] It applied horizontally to all groups with subsidiaries established outside the United Kingdom. This was precisely the kind of automatic exclusion the Court had meant to rule out in *Leur-Bloem*. Therefore, the UK could not validly rely on this justification. As for the second ground put forward by the Member State in question, the ECJ simply noted that "diminution of tax revenue occurring in this way is not one of the grounds [explicitly mentioned in] the Treaty and cannot be regarded as a matter of overriding general interest which may be relied upon in order to justify unequal treatment".[150]

For the purpose of this book, the ruling commented on in this section is significant for a threefold reason.[151] First, it confirmed the ECJ's concern about anti-avoidance measures enacted by the Member States. It is another stepping stone in the case law concerning tax law that will eventually culminate in the rulings examined in Sect. 3.3.4. Second, it marked the emergence of the concept of "wholly artificial arrangements". These are the transactions that the Member States are allowed to combat by denying, among other things, the concession of tax benefits. As we shall see below, clarifying what constitutes a wholly artificial transaction will prove a contentious point in the Court of Justice case law on these matters. In *ICI*, the Court gave no direct indications. The only indirect one came from the fact that it considered the transactions at stake in the main proceedings as not being wholly artificial. Another useful indication could perhaps be derived from a combined reading of *Leur-Bloem* and *ICI*. Reading the two judgments conjunctively, it was possible to conclude that a wholly artificial arrangement was one devoid of valid commercial reasons. As we shall see, the Court would have to return to this concept. Finally, the *ICI* decision is important because it represented, if anything, a confirmation that anti-avoidance in tax matters is, at least in principle, a valid justification for restrictions. Whether they actually cut it depends on their compliance with the requirements set out in *Leur-Bloem* and subsequent case law.

---

[147] Ibid., para 23.

[148] Ibid., para 24.

[149] Ibid., para 26 (emphasis added).

[150] Ibid., para 28.

[151] For a general comment of the ruling, see Van den Hurk 1999, p. 211 ff.

3.2.14 *An Internal Market Is an Internal Market: The Endorsement of Regulatory Arbitrage in* Centros

Centros is a much-celebrated ruling that is foundational to the freedom of establishment of companies in EU law. Unsurprisingly, it has attracted much attention from the scholarship. In this section, however, the decision in question will only be analysed insofar as it is relevant for the purpose of this book. For the analysis of other aspects of it, the reader is referred to the abundant scholarly production.[152]

Centros Ltd was a private limited company registered in England and Wales by Mr and Mrs Bryde, two Danish nationals residing in Denmark. A few months after its formation, during which Centros Ltd never traded in the UK, Mr and Mrs Bryde requested Danish authorities to register a branch of Centros Ltd in Denmark, which they refused to do on the ground that it was not a British company seeking secondary establishment in Denmark. It was, so they argued, a Danish company that was created in the UK for the sole purpose of circumventing national rules concerning the paying-up of minimum capital, which was not required under British law. The Brydes challenged the refusal before a Danish court, which stayed proceedings and asked the Court of Justice whether the decision of Danish authorities was contrary to the freedom of establishment.[153]

In brief, the ECJ took a quite liberal, pro-market posture that we have already mentioned when the *Segers* ruling was discussed (see above, Sect. 3.2.7). Recalling precisely the findings in *Segers*, the Court pointed out that it was "immaterial that the company was formed in the first Member State only for the purpose of establishing itself in the second, where its main, or indeed entire, business [was] to be conducted".[154] What is more, it noted that the purpose "of avoiding Danish legislation requiring that a minimum amount of share capital be paid up has not been denied either in the written observations or at the hearing",[155] that is, the plaintiffs had openly admitted their intention to circumvent Danish law. That did not render the rules on establishment inapplicable. As long as a company is validly established in accordance with the rules of a Member State, that company is entitled to benefit from the Treaty rules on free movement. Consequently, just like in *Leur-Bloem* and *ICI*, the decisive question was whether a "Member State may adopt measures in order to prevent attempts by certain of its nationals to evade domestic legislation by having recourse to the possibilities offered by the Treaty".[156] In other words, it was a matter of (potential) abuse of the freedom of establishment.

[152] Among many, see Ballarino 2003, pp. 373–402; Cabral and Cunha 2000, pp. 157–164; Ebke 2001, pp. 623–660; Edwards 2000, pp. 147–155; Fortunato 2000, pp. 83–90; Gelter 2017, pp. 309–337; Gestri 2000, pp. 71–112; Lauterfeld 2001, pp. 79–88; Munari and Terrile 2001, pp. 1–38; Roth 2000, pp. 143–151.

[153] CJEU, *Centros Ltd*, Judgment of the Court, 9 March 1999, case C-212/97, ECLI:EU:C:1999:126, paras 1–13.

[154] Ibid., para 17.

[155] Ibid., para 18.

[156] Ibid.

Denmark had no doubt that the plaintiffs' action "constitute[d] abuse of the freedom of establishment".[157] The Court of Justice recalled almost its entire case law in which it recognised the right of the Member States to take measures aimed at preventing their nationals from improperly circumventing national laws by taking advantage of provisions of EU law, including *Van Binsbergen*, *Veronica*, *Lecler*, *Lair* and *Kefalas*. However, when combating abusive or fraudulent conduct, the Member States had to take into consideration the objectives pursued by the EU law provisions admittedly being abused.[158] From this perspective, the Court of Justice emphasised that the right to "form a company in accordance with the law of a Member State and to set up branches in other Member States is inherent in the exercise, in a single market, of the freedom of establishment guaranteed by the Treaty".[159] In other words, in the context of the single market, the very purpose of the rules on establishment is precisely to make possible what the plaintiffs in the main proceedings had done. To be sure, the rights in question include the possibility to choose "to form [a company] in the Member State whose rules of company law seem to him the least restrictive and to set up branches in other Member States".[160] Therefore, taking advantage of that possibility could not "*in itself*, constitute an abuse of the right of establishment".[161]

The use of the expression "in itself" left the door open to still reach the opposite conclusion, namely, that the plaintiffs had indeed abused the freedom of establishment. In fact, the Court went on to assess whether "the national practice in question might not be justified for the reasons put forward by the Danish authorities".[162] The ECJ scrutinised those reasons by applying the usual test used to assess the lawfulness of restrictions to free movement, which included four requirements. More precisely, national measures had to "be applied in a non-discriminatory manner; [...] be justified by imperative requirements in the general interest; [...] be suitable for securing the attainment of the objective which they pursue; [...] not go beyond what is necessary in order to attain it".[163] In short, they had to be justified and proportionate, which the ECJ thought was not the case in *Centros*.

Just like *Leur-Bloem*, it is difficult to overestimate the importance of *Centros* for the topic of this book. In this ruling, the Court of Justice recognised again that fundamental freedoms can be abused and that Member States can take measures to prevent their nationals from doing so. However, those measures have to be objectively justified and strictly proportionate.[164] Furthermore, by virtue of the Court's boldly liberal approach to the freedom of establishment, *Centros* confirmed an impression that had

---

157 Ibid., para 23.

158 Ibid., paras 24–25.

159 Ibid., para 27.

160 Ibid.

161 Ibid. (emphasis added).

162 Ibid., para 31.

163 Ibid., para 34.

164 However, see the critical remarks made by Tridimas 2009, pp. 13 ff., who pointed out, first, that the application of proportionality in the case at hand was not entirely coherent with the Court's usual approach and, second, that *Centros* left many questions unanswered, especially when it comes

already emerged in *Segers*, namely, that as long as this one particular fundamental freedom was concerned, justifying anti-abuse measures would prove decidedly challenging. As long as the right to choose the Member State with the most suitable legal framework to organise one's business was affirmed, the ECJ formally endorsed so-called regulatory arbitrage in EU company law, at least to some extent.[165] Finally, *Centros* highlighted that the purpose pursued by EU provisions is central to determining whether they are being abused. This aspect would come back quite strongly in later judgments, starting from the next one in line, which marks the beginning of a new era referred to above as the second phase of the Court of Justice's case law on abuse. We shall now proceed to its examination.

3.3 The Second Phase

3.3.1 Developing a Test for Abuse: Emsland-Stärke

Emsland-Stärke was a veritable watershed moment in the evolution of the ECJ's case law on abuse of EU law. In this ruling, the Luxembourg Court coined a test that would assist national authorities in assessing whether abuse existed in a given case. From the previous analysis, we know that this ruling was not a bolt from the blue. The build-up to it included the early *Cremer* and *Töpfer* and the later *Boterlux* and *Roquette Frères*. However, *Emsland-Stärke*, which was followed within a few years by a handful of equally landmark rulings such as *Chen*, *Halifax* and *Cadbury-Schweppes*, brought the discussion on abuse of Union law to a different level, as demonstrated by the deluge of scholarly writings devoted to this topic that appeared in the following 10 years or so.[166]

Emsland-Stärke was a German undertaking that exported products based on potato starch and wheat starch to Switzerland. The recipients were two Swiss undertakings established at the same address in Lucerne, Switzerland, managed and represented by the same persons. German authorities found out that the exported consignments were immediately transported back to Germany and Italy unaltered. Subsequently, they stopped granting the export refunds and demanded repayment of the amount that was considered unduly paid. Emsland-Stärke challenged the decision before a German court, arguing that the customs formalities for release for home use had been completed in Switzerland, as evidenced by the production of a customs entry certificate. The company claimed not to be aware of what the purchasers intended to do with the consignments and that there was no intent to deceive on their part. The German court stayed proceedings and referred the dispute to the Court of Justice.[167]

---

to what kind of limitations would be acceptable for the Court in like circumstances. The case law analysed in Sect. 3.3.4 will partly clarify these aspects.

[165] See Eidenmüller et al. 2019, p. 400.

[166] Richelle et al. 2025.

[167] See *Emsland-Stärke*, paras 2–19.

The ECJ's answer could be inferred from its previous case law. Let us try to imagine how the reasoning could have unfolded based on a combined reading of the relevant precedents. The Court could opine that, since the exported goods were not processed (*Roquette-Frères*), and the re-importation was not due to *force majeure* (*Boterlux*), the aim of the rules, which was admittedly to incentivise export to third countries, had not been achieved (*Cremer* and *Töpfer*), given that the exported products were effectively not put into free circulation on the Swiss market if only to process them and manufacture a new product. This could be a perfectly logical answer based on existing case law. However, it would not offer a clear-cut solution to the dispute pending before the German court. In *Emsland-Stärke,* there was a fundamental difference compared to the relevant precedents. In fact, German authorities demanded repayment of the amounts already obtained by the exporter, which the Belgian authorities did not in *Boterlux*. In addition, the Court was confronted with a strong argument from the Commission, which invited it to rule that "[b]y virtue of *the legal principle of abuse of rights in force in [Union] law*, financial advantages are not to be granted or, in some cases, are to be withdrawn retrospectively if it is shown that the commercial operations at issue were for the purpose of obtaining an advantage which is incompatible with the objectives of the applicable [...] rules in that the conditions for obtaining that advantage were created artificially".[168] From the Court's perspective, it is easy to see that the invitation to rule on the existence of such a legal principle could not pass unattended. Therefore, the existing case law was not sufficient. The Court had to come up with more than a re-statement of its previous decisions.

Nonetheless, the Court started off with *Cremer*, stating that EU law "must in no case be extended to cover abuses on the part of a trader".[169] In this way, it made it clear that if abuse existed, it fell outside the scope of the relevant rules. The ECJ was set to develop a test for abuse, which consisted of two constitutive elements. It held that abuse required "first, a combination of objective circumstances in which, despite formal observance of the conditions laid down by the [Union] rules, the purpose of those rules has not been achieved".[170] This was not entirely innovative. We already knew from the previous case law that the aim pursued by EU law is relevant in determining abuse. The Court, however, added a second requirement, namely "a subjective element consisting in the intention to obtain an advantage from the Community rules by creating artificially the conditions laid down for obtaining it. The existence of that subjective element can be established, inter alia, by evidence of collusion between the [Union] exporter receiving the refunds and the importer of the goods in the non-member country".[171] The subjective element was a veritable novelty. It is true that the intention of the parties involved had already played a significant role in the case law on abuse. One should think of cases such as *Van Binsbergen*, *Leclerc* and *Leur-Bloem*. However, *Emsland-Stärke* elevated the intention of the party involved to the

---

[168] Ibid., para 43 (emphasis added).

[169] Ibid., para 51.

[170] Ibid., para 52.

[171] Ibid., para 53.

rank of a constitutive element of abuse. To be sure, it was not purely the intention that needed to be assessed in order to establish abuse. The Court already added two qualifications. First, the intention in itself was not sufficient. It was a very specific one: it was the intention to act by artificially creating the conditions for the application of EU law. Second, the subjective intention was somewhat objectified: it was necessary to prove it by means of objective evidence, such as collusion between the Union exporter and the third-country importer. The existence of those two elements was for the national court to establish.[172]

As we shall see, the Court of Justice would have to return to these constitutive elements several times. Particularly, the construal of the subjective element, which would prove far more contentious and problematic than the objective one, would keep the Court busy on a number of occasions.[173] However, it was clear that *Emsland-Stärke* was a first attempt to systematise abuse, though the Court of Justice stopped short of characterising it as a legal principle of the Union legal order, as suggested by the Commission.[174] The time for this additional step would come at a later stage.

3.3.2 *The Strengthening of the Court's Free Mover-Friendly Attitude in Relation to Persons: The Irrelevance of the Worker's Motives in* Akrich

When commenting on the *Lair* ruling, it was pointed out that the said ruling was the first sign of what would become a general trend in the Court's case law, which would settle upon interpretations generally favourable to the persons exercising free movement and unfavourable to the Member States seeking to restrict the freedom in question. *Akrich* was a demonstration of this and an important stepping stone in the build-up of *Chen*, which we will address in the next section.

Mr Akrich was a third-country national who entered the UK on a tourist visa but remained in the country after its expiry. Within a few years, he was convicted of various crimes, such as attempted theft and using false IDs. After being deported and returning to the UK several times, he eventually married a British citizen, but his leave to remain as her spouse was rejected. In the meantime, Mrs Akrich took up employment in Dublin in the banking sector, while Mr Akrich joined her in Ireland and did whatever work was available. More than a year later, Mrs Akrich returned to the UK, where she was offered a new job. Mr Akrich applied to stay as the spouse

[172] Ibid., para 54.

[173] See Sørensen 2006, p. 454 ff.

[174] More generally, when *Emsland-Stärke* was handed down, it was not at all clear whether the abuse test developed in this ruling "was limited to the field of agricultural levies or whether it could be extrapolated to other areas of the EU legal order", as noted by Lenaerts 2015a, p. 333. As we shall see, the Court will clarify this aspect.

of an EU citizen who had settled in the UK. The application was rejected, and the matter ended up in Luxembourg after the national court referred it to the ECJ.[175]

It was not disputed that Mr and Mrs Akrich had planned a strategic stay in Ireland to benefit from EU law.[176] During interviews held at the British Embassy in Dublin, Mr and Mrs Akrich had clearly stated that "they intended to return to the United Kingdom because [they] had heard about EU rights, staying six months and then going back to the UK. She [that is, Mrs Akrich] said that she had been given that information by solicitors and others in the same situation".[177] The information was indeed correct: a free mover returning to her home Member State is entitled to rely on the rights granted to free movers by EU law against that State. Hence, those rights existed. The point was, therefore, whether there was an abuse of those rights in the case at hand.

The Court's answer was straightforward. It held that "the motives which may have prompted a worker of a Member State to seek employment in another Member State are of no account as regards his right to enter and reside in the territory of the latter State provided that he there pursues or wishes to pursue an effective and genuine activity".[178] In other words, as far as the free movement of workers was concerned, what mattered was the nature of the activity pursued by the free mover. If it was effective and genuine employment, the freedom in question was applicable, with all the consequences flowing therefrom. No matter the motives underlying the worker's decision to seek work in another Member State. The only exception would be marriages of convenience, which the ECJ expressly called an "abuse [of] the facilities afforded by [Union] law".[179]

In its previous case law, the Court of Justice had already demonstrated that it was well aware that the fundamental freedoms could be abusively exploited by careful legal planning of a given activity. In *Van Binsbergen* and *Leclerc*, the ECJ recognised this possibility in relation to the freedom to provide services and the free movement of goods, respectively. It also recognised the same possibility in relation to rights deriving from EU secondary legislation. One can think of *Leur-Bloem* and *Emsland-Stärke*, among others. As we have seen, in all these cases, the party's intention had played an increasingly important role. It is, therefore, appropriate to wonder what the difference was between those cases and *Akrich*. The decisive factor appears to be the purpose of the EU rules in question. In the cases mentioned, there was always some degree of artificiality involved in the activity or transaction designed by the private party. In *Van Binsbergen*, the service was provided entirely or principally towards the territory of another Member State. This artificial arrangement suggested that the applicable freedom was establishment and not services. That is because the purpose of the freedom to provide services is to allow providers across the EU to

[175] CJEU, *Hacene Akrich*, Judgment of the Court, 23 September 2003, case C-109/01, ECLI:EU:C:2003:491, paras 29–45.

[176] See above, Sect. 3.2.2.

[177] *Hacene Akrich*, para 36.

[178] Ibid., para 55.

[179] Ibid., para 57.

"*temporarily* pursue [their] activity" in another Member State.[180] Although the Court did not talk about the purpose of EU law in *Van Binsbergen* (it was, after all, the very first decision on abuse of Union law), it did mention the temporary nature of service when it defined the meaning of this concept.[181] In *Leur-Bloem*, the transaction was artificial because it was not based on valid commercial reasons. Since the purpose of the rules was not to grant purely fiscal advantages but rather to "introduce tax rules which are neutral from the point of view of competition in order to allow enterprises to adapt themselves to the requirements of the common market, to increase their productivity and to improve their competitive strength at the international level",[182] the transaction was inconsistent with it (in reality, the ECJ left this assessment to the referring court).

When it comes to the free movement of workers, the purpose of the freedom in question was famously clarified in *Levin*, where the Court held that "that freedom is to entail the abolition of any discrimination based on nationality between workers of the Member States as regards employment, remuneration and other conditions of work and it is to include the right [...] to accept offers of employment actually made, to move freely within the territory of the Member States for this purpose, to stay in a Member State for the purpose of employment and to remain there after the termination of that employment".[183] In no way do the rules in question require the creation of a long-term, let alone permanent, connection between the worker and the host Member State; in fact, seasonal workers are also plainly included.[184] The only limit is the effective and genuine nature of the employment. In much the same way as a seasonal worker, Mrs Akrich had taken up temporary employment in Ireland. Her motives were irrelevant because in no way did they run counter to the purpose of the rules on the free movement of workers. Therefore, there can be no abuse unless the employment is not effective or genuine. This reading of the *Akrich* ruling is coherent with the development in *Emsland-Stärke*. The Court decided in the latter that abuse of Union law has two constitutive elements, the first of which is an objective one and is related to the achievement of the purpose of the rules admittedly being abused. If the purpose of the rules has been attained, as in *Akrich*, the two-tiered abuse test fails on the first one.[185]

---

[180] See Article 57(2) TFEU (emphasis added).

[181] See *Van Binsbergen*, para 8.

[182] See *Leur-Bloem*, para 45.

[183] Centros para 7.

[184] Ibid., para 14.

[185] But see the considerations made by Ionescu 2012, pp. 177–182, who, while also recognising that the Court has a generally more permissive approach when it comes to conducts carried out by natural persons, criticised the ruling for depriving national immigration decisions of effectiveness.

3.3.3 The Further Strengthening of the Court's Free Mover-Friendly Attitude in Relation to Persons: The Irrelevance of the Motives in Chen

Chen was a landmark ruling in many respects, as demonstrated by the veritable deluge of comments devoted to it, many of which were from authors of great prominence.[186] For the purpose of this book, it is a confirmation of the Court's case law and possibly a strengthening of its pro-free movement posture in the field of free movement of persons, which, in turn, narrows down the possibilities that abuse is found in the context of this freedom.

Mrs Chen was a Chinese national married to a Chinese businessman who, for the purpose of his work, frequently travelled to the EU, particularly to the UK. When Mrs Chen was six months pregnant, she went to Belfast, where she gave birth to Catherine three months later. Irish law at that time provided that any person born on the island of Ireland acquired Irish citizenship if she was not entitled to citizenship of any other country. Catherine was, therefore, issued an Irish passport under those rules. Mrs Chen and her daughter then moved to Cardiff. Catherine, being an Irish national, was entitled to enter and reside in the UK without a permit. However, as is natural for a child of her age, she depended entirely on her mother. Therefore, Mrs Chen applied for a long-term residence permit in the UK, which was rejected by British immigration authorities. She challenged the rejection before a national court, which turned to the Court of Justice for clarification concerning a number of EU law questions.[187] We will focus on the alleged abuse of EU rights perpetrated by Mrs Chen.

It was not disputed that Mrs Chen purposefully gave birth to Catherine in Northern Ireland for her to acquire Irish nationality and, with it, the right of both to live and reside in the UK. In other words, just like in *Akrich*, the ECJ was effectively confronted with a strategic stay in Ireland with the aim of benefitting from EU law. Unsurprisingly, or perhaps surprisingly, given that the UK had already succumbed on this point in the *Akrich* case, the British authorities argued that there was an abuse of EU rights. Relying on one single ruling, which, for some reason, was *Centros*, and ignoring more compelling precedents, including the one in which a test for abuse was coined, they suggested that the ECJ's "settled case-law [confirmed] that Member States are entitled to take measures to prevent individuals from improperly taking advantage of provisions of [Union] law or from attempting, under cover of the rights created by the Treaty, illegally to circumvent national legislation. That rule [...] is in conformity with *the principle that rights must not be abused*".[188] This was the last one among the multiple arguments advanced by the UK, and it is reasonable to think that British authorities were themselves unconvinced by it. It was possibly an

---

[186] See Barnard 2005, pp. 560–563; Bergamini 2006, pp. 347–368; Kochenov and Lindeboom 2017, pp. 201–223; Tryfonidou 2005, pp. 527–541.

[187] CJEU, *Kunqian Catherine Zhu and Man Lavette Chen*, Judgment of the Court, 19 October 2004, case C-200/02, ECLI:EU:C:2004:639, paras 7–15.

[188] Ibid., para 34 (emphasis added).

exercise in throwing everything at the wall and seeing what sticks, a strategy often used in litigation.

British authorities were not wrong to argue that such a principle existed, although the Court had not yet called it a principle. However, of all the decisions surveyed in this chapter, *Centros* was arguably the single least suitable one on which to ground an argument based on the principle that rights in the field of free movement of persons must not be abused. The Court of Justice rejected this argument without even mentioning abuse. It did so by relying on international law, under which "it is for each Member State, having due regard to [Union] law, to lay down the conditions for the acquisition and loss of nationality".[189] On that basis, the Court stated that it was not "permissible for a Member State to restrict the effects of the grant of the nationality of another Member State by imposing an additional condition for recognition of that nationality with a view to the exercise of the fundamental freedoms provided for in the Treaty".[190]

In *Chen*, the Court of Justice reverted to the terse style we have found in other rulings. In such cases, what the Court did not say is often more meaningful than what it said explicitly. Imagining a court saying what it did not actually say, most likely on purpose, is often a risky exercise. Still, let us try to spell out the Court's (unspoken) reasoning on abuse. In the case at hand, there was not even an issue of whether abuse existed or not. Catherine was not abusing a right deriving from EU law. She was merely using it, being the Irish citizen that she was. The problem, if there was a problem at all, was that she was Irish. Or, put differently, it was how she acquired Irish nationality, from which she derived EU rights. But EU law (and the ECJ) had little to do with it. It was an issue entirely governed by Irish law. Hence, the argument based on abuse of EU rights was not even worth refuting, which is exactly what the Court did.[191]

As was once written by a prominent scholar, Opinions of the Advocate Generals are (especially) "invaluable for understanding the Court's often terse decisions".[192] AG Tizzano devoted the whole section E of his learned Opinion, meaningfully titled "abuse of law", to the topic of this book.[193] By referring to *Emsland-Stärke*, he applied the two-tiered test therein developed, essentially stopping at the first tier, which concerned the attainment of the purpose of the rules relied on. Coherently, he wondered whether Catherine, "by invoking the [Union] provision which grants the right in question, is betraying its spirit and scope".[194] He went on to state that the purpose of the right of residence is "to eliminate any restriction on the

[189] Ibid., para 37.

[190] Ibid., para 39.

[191] See the considerations made by Costello 2011, pp. 335–336, who also praised the Court's refusal to see Chen through the prism of abuse.

[192] Neville Brown 1994b, p. 1355.

[193] CJEU, *Kunqian Catherine Zhu and Man Lavette Chen*, Opinion of Advocate General Tizzano, 18 May 2004, case C-200/02, ECLI:EU:C:2004:307, paras 108–129.

[194] Ibid., para 114.

movement and residence of [Union] nationals".[195] Therefore, there was in his view "nothing 'abusive' about taking action, in compliance with the law, to ensure that the child, when born, satisfies the conditions for acquiring the nationality of a Member State",[196] from which the child would derive rights granted by EU law. AG Tizzano recognised that "the criterion used by the Irish legislation for granting nationality [...] lends itself to the emergence of situations like the one at issue in this case".[197] He also conceded that "the criterion could have been moderated by the addition of a condition of settled residence of the parent within the territory of the island of Ireland",[198] which was not the case. AG Tizzano concluded his Opinion on this matter with a very eloquent statement, which is worth reproducing word for word: "if the United Kingdom's argument were accepted, suspicions of abuse could be raised in almost all cases of *intentional* acquisition of nationality of a Member State. And, paradoxically, that could lead to a situation in which the enjoyment of rights deriving from citizenship of the Union was subject to the condition ... that such citizenship had to have been acquired involuntarily".[199]

Masterfully drafted, this Opinion was at once a remarkable short essay on abuse of law and a plea to be wary of the Member States relying on it lest we find ourselves in paradoxical situations. Additionally, it correctly highlighted that the crux of the matter was the Irish law on citizenship. As we have seen, in this respect, he was followed by the Court of Justice. As is well-known, the Irish government proposed a new law on citizenship, which was approved in a referendum in 2004, proving AG Tizzano and the Court of Justice right.[200]

3.3.4 *Abuse of (Union) Law Meets Tax Evasion: The Court's Rulings in* **Marks and Spencer, Halifax, Cadbury Schweppes** *and* **Kofoed**

In the mid-2000s, the Court of Justice handed down a quartet of rulings on tax evasion that spurred a wave of (mostly unenthusiastic) reactions from tax lawyers.[201] For the purpose of this book, *Marks & Spencer*, *Halifax*, *Cadbury Schweppes* and *Kofoed* highlighted that there is a clear *trait d'union* between tax evasion and abuse of law in the EU legal order. As is often the case with the ECJ's case law on abuse, these decisions were not bolts from the blue. They were preceded by a number of relevant

---

[195] Ibid., para 119.

[196] Ibid., para 120.

[197] Ibid., para 124.

[198] Ibid., para 125.

[199] Ibid., para 127 (emphasis in the original).

[200] See Handoll 2010, pp. 8–10.

[201] See, among many, De La Feria 2005, pp. 394–401; Crosby 2006, pp. 37–48; Douma and Engelen 2006, pp. 429–440; Vinther and Werlauff 2006, pp. 383–387; Amand 2008, pp. 189–200; Weber 2013, pp. 313–328.

precedents that gradually prepared the floor for these groundbreaking judgments. Before turning to their analysis, it is appropriate to take a step back and examine how we got to that juncture.

To begin with, it bears noting that the close interconnection between tax evasion and abuse of law had emerged in three rulings already discussed in this chapter, namely *Leur-Bloem*, *ICI* and *Centros*. As we have seen above, in all these cases, the Member States denied (or in any case attempted to deny) benefits deriving from EU law based on the need to combat tax avoidance or evasion. From that line of case law, we learned that the Member States could validly invoke these reasons provided that their measures have the effect of censuring only wholly artificial transactions devoid of valid commercial reasons, provided the measures were proportionate. After these decisions and before the quartet to which this section is devoted, the Court of Justice dealt with similar issues in two additional minor cases (to be sure: minor in terms of their importance for the purpose of this book).

In short, in *Lankhorst-Hohorst,* the German tax authorities denied certain tax benefits to a German undertaking on an intercompany loan based on the fact that the loan was taken from its parent company incorporated in the Netherlands. German authorities argued, among other things, that the measure was justified on the risk of tax evasion, to which the Court could easily reply, based on existing case law, that the "legislation at issue [...] does not have the specific purpose of preventing wholly artificial arrangements, designed to circumvent German tax legislation, from attracting a tax benefit, but applies generally to any situation in which the parent company has its seat, for whatever reason, outside the Federal Republic of Germany".[202] That was a mere re-statement of the principle already affirmed in *ICI*.

Similarly, *Hughes de Lasteyrie du Saillant* concerned French legislation imposing an unfavourable tax treatment on natural persons who held significant shares of companies subject to French corporate tax but transferred their residence outside France. French authorities justified the measure with the aim of preventing tax avoidance, to which the ECJ could again easily reply that the legislation at issue "is not specifically designed to exclude from a tax advantage purely artificial arrangements aimed at circumventing French tax law, but is aimed generally at any situation in which a taxpayer with substantial holdings in a company subject to corporation tax transfers his tax residence outside France for any reason whatever".[203]

It is against this background that *Marks & Spencer* was referred to the Court of Justice. The case is the EU law ramification of the well-known business story of one of the leading British retailers. Marks & Spencer opened subsidiaries in several EU countries between 1975 and 1990. In the mid-1990s, it was increasingly incurring losses, which brought it to the decision of divesting its Continental European activities. By 2001, it had ceased trading in other EU Member States. For the accounting periods of 1998, 1999, 2000, and 2001, Marks & Spencer claimed group tax relief

---

[202] CJEU, *Lankhorst-Hohorst GmbH*, Judgment of the Court, 12 December 2002, case C-324/00, ECLI:EU:C:2002:749, para 37.

[203] CJEU, *Hughes de Lasteyrie du Saillant*, Judgment of the Court, 11 March 2004, case C-9/02, ECLI:EU:C:2004:138, para 50.

in accordance with British tax law in an attempt to deduct from its taxable profits in the UK the losses incurred by its Belgian, German and French subsidiaries. The claim was rejected and appealed by the company. Therefore, the Court of Justice was asked to assess whether the national legislation in question was at variance with the freedom of establishment.[204]

The Luxembourg Court had an easy task in declaring that the measures at issue constituted "a restriction on freedom of establishment within the meaning of Articles 43 EC and 48 EC, in that it applies different treatment for tax purposes to losses incurred by a resident subsidiary and losses incurred by a non-resident subsidiary".[205] As a result, it was a matter of whether those measures were justified and proportionate. The British authorities put forward a number of justifications. In line with the purpose of this book, we will only focus on the need to prevent tax avoidance. The ECJ recognised that "the possibility of transferring the losses incurred by a non-resident company to a resident company entails the risk that within a group of companies losses will be transferred to companies established in the Member States which apply the highest rates of taxation and in which the tax value of the losses is therefore the highest".[206] For this reason, the Court held that the "restrictive provisions such as those at issue in the main proceedings pursue legitimate objectives which are compatible with the Treaty and constitute overriding reasons in the public interest and that they are apt to ensure the attainment of those objectives".[207] The restrictions were therefore justified, but it remained to be seen whether they were also proportionate. The Court found that the measures went beyond what was necessary to achieve the objectives pursued in so far as they did not allow the resident company to receive the tax relief where there was no possibility for its non-resident subsidiary to obtain a similar tax benefit in the host Member State.[208]

The Court of Justice could have stopped there. Instead, it decided to add two important qualifications. Number one, it added that the "Member States are free to adopt or to maintain in force rules having the specific purpose of precluding from a tax benefit wholly artificial arrangements whose purpose is to circumvent or escape national tax law".[209] This statement could appear not strictly necessary to settle the dispute pending before the referring court. It was clear that Marks & Spencer's losses were actual and that no other artificial transaction seemed to be at stake. However, if one looked under the surface the picture changed. The dispute revolved around the possibility of preventing the company from either (a) deducting the losses twice or, most importantly, (b) transferring the losses to the Member State with the highest taxation rate by means of artificial intergroup transactions. Hence, the Court's first qualification made perfect sense: it made it clear that national measures

---

[204] CJEU, *Marks & Spencer plc*, Judgment of the Court, 13 December 2005, case C-446/03, ECLI:EU:C:2005:763, paras 18–26.

[205] Ibid., para 34.

[206] Ibid., para 49.

[207] Ibid., para 51.

[208] Ibid., paras 53–56.

[209] Ibid., para 57.

were admissible only to the extent that they targeted wholly artificial arrangements, such as transactions whose sole purpose was to transfer losses to the Member State with the highest tax rate. Number two, the ECJ stated that "in so far as it may be possible to identify other, less restrictive measures, such measures in any event require harmonisation rules adopted by the Community legislature".[210] It is not easy to understand the meaning of this statement. The most likely explanation is that, just like it did once many years before in *Knoors*, the Court of Justice was reminding everyone that issues such as those at stake in *Marks & Spencer* could be avoided, or at least greatly reduced, by harmonising the Member States legislation in the field of taxation. But this is a politically and legally difficult process, which is still ongoing to a large extent.[211]

The second judgment of the quartet is the much-celebrated *Halifax*, whose factual circumstances are quite intricate and very difficult for non-tax experts to grasp entirely. Here is a simplified summary of what happened in (hopefully) plain language. Halifax, a UK-based bank, engaged in a series of complex transactions through a web of subsidiaries involving construction and property development with the purpose of reclaiming VAT. These transactions were designed to create input tax deductions, which Halifax could then recover despite the fact that the underlying economic activity (which was, in essence, the construction of call centres) was largely exempt from VAT and would not usually allow for such deductions. The UK tax authorities challenged these arrangements, arguing that they were artificial and constituted an abuse of rights.[212]

For the purpose of this book, it is worth noting that the very existence of abuse of rights in the EU legal order was debated before the Court of Justice. The plaintiffs in the main proceedings argued that EU law did not "contain any theory of abuse of rights which the tax authorities of a Member State can invoke against individuals".[213] Conversely, the "United Kingdom Government considers that the principle of abuse of rights is *a general principle* of [Union] law and prevents a taxable person from deducting VAT under Article 17 of the Sixth Directive and any applicable national legislation implementing that article where it is apparent from the application for deduction that the objectives of VAT, laid down by the Sixth Directive, are not being attained and that the taxable person is artificially creating conditions to justify the application for deduction".[214] Slightly more nuanced positions favourable to

[210] Ibid., para 58.

[211] In that direction go the rules adopted by the EU in 2016. See Council Directive (EU) 2016/1164 of 12 July 2016 laying down rules against tax avoidance practices that directly affect the functioning of the internal market, OJ L 193, 19 July 2016, which feature a number of anti-abuse measures, including a general anti-abuse rule at Article 6. But also the yet-to-be-approved Proposal for a Council Directive on a Common Consolidated Corporate Tax Base (CCCTB), COM/2016/0683 final.

[212] CJEU, *Halifax plc, Leeds Permanent Development Services Ltd and County Wide Property Investments Ltd*, Judgment of the Court, 21 February 2006, case C-255/02, ECLI:EU:C:2006:121, paras 12–43.

[213] Ibid., para 62.

[214] Ibid., para 63 (emphasis added).

the existence of such principle were submitted by France and Ireland, while the Commission, perhaps surprisingly, having been the first to explicitly argue in favour of its existence back in *Emsland-Stärke* (see above Sect. 3.3.1), supported the UK's conclusion that the artificial transactions were to be disregarded without grounding it on the principle of abuse of rights.[215]

By referring to its case law, the Court of Justice recalled that EU legislation could not "be extended to cover abusive practices by economic operators, that is to say transactions carried out not in the context of normal commercial operations, but solely for the purpose of wrongfully obtaining advantages provided for by [Union] law".[216] With this statement, the Court clarified that abuse (better: abusive practices) was outside the scope of EU secondary law. Juxtaposed to it is the first recognition of abuse of law as a legal principle, for the Court added that the "*principle* of prohibiting abusive practices also applies to the sphere of VAT".[217] Put differently, the Court declared that there was a principle of prohibition of abusive practices in the EU legal order.

If it was legitimate to prevent tax evasion, avoidance and abuse, the crux of the matter in *Halifax* was whether the transactions carried out by the plaintiffs were abusive. This, in turn, entailed an assessment of what constituted an abusive practice in the field of tax matters, and in particular of VAT. To answer that question, the Court resorted to the abuse test developed in its previous case law, but with a twist. It is helpful to recall that in *Emsland-Stärke,* the ECJ held that abuse consisted of (a) a combination of objective circumstances in which, despite formal observance of the conditions laid down by Union rules, the purpose of those rules had not been achieved, and (b) a subjective element consisting in the intention to obtain an advantage from the [Union] rules by creating artificially the conditions laid down for obtaining it. Consequently, the Court found that "in the sphere of VAT, an abusive practice can be found to exist only if, first, the transactions concerned, notwithstanding formal application of the conditions laid down by the relevant provisions of the Sixth Directive and the national legislation transposing it, result in the accrual of a tax advantage the grant of which would be contrary to the purpose of those provisions".[218] This was entirely in line with *Emsland-Stärke*'s first element. However when it comes to the second constitutive element, that is, the subjective one, the Court stated that "it must also be apparent from a number of objective factors that the essential aim of the transactions concerned is to obtain a tax advantage [whereas] the prohibition of abuse is not relevant where the economic activity carried out may have some explanation other than the mere attainment of tax advantages".[219]

The Court continued by stating that the actual assessment of whether an abusive practice existed in the case at hand was eventually for the national court to do. However, it issued some guidance to that end. As regards the first element, the

215 Ibid., para 64–66.

216 Ibid., para 69.

217 Ibid., para 70 (emphasis added).

218 Ibid., para 74.

219 Ibid., para 75.

ECJ held that the purpose of the rules on VAT in question was to ensure complete neutrality of taxation of economic activities provided they were subject to VAT. To allow VAT deductions in relation to transactions that would normally not be subject to VAT, as was the case in *Halifax*, was therefore contrary to that purpose. Hence, the ECJ seemed to suggest to the referring court that the first tier of the abuse test was satisfied.[220] As regards the second element of abuse, the Court stated that in order to ascertain whether the aim of the transactions was to obtain a tax advantage, the referring court could take into account the purely artificial nature of it, as well as any links of a legal, economic and/or personal nature between the economic operators involved.[221]

The Court of Justice made yet another crucial finding in *Halifax*. It held that if the transactions are found to be abusive by the national court, they "must be redefined so as to re-establish the situation that would have prevailed in the absence of the transactions constituting that abusive practice", with the consequence that "the tax authorities are entitled to demand, with retroactive effect, repayment of the amounts deducted in relation to each transaction whenever they find that the right to deduct has been exercised abusively".[222]

The relevance of *Halifax* for the topic of this book cannot be overestimated. Number one, the Court extended its case law on abusive practices to tax matters for the first time. So far, it had only been able to apply it to export subsidies and the (abusive) reliance on fundamental freedoms. As we shall see below, the number of EU law fields to which this case law will be extended would grow gradually, as is natural for a general principle of EU law. Number two, the Court of Justice refined its approach to the second constitutive element of abuse. In *Emsland-Stärke,* it had talked about a subjective element consisting of the intention to obtain an advantage from EU law (by artificially creating the conditions to do so). In Halifax, the *person's intention* was replaced by *the essential aim of the transactions*, further objectifying the subjective element. As was rightly pointed out by the current President of the ECJ, this recalibration was likely "explained by the criticisms put forward by some scholars and Advocates General before the Court of Justice delivered its judgment".[223] AG Maduro was particularly convincing on this point. He opined that "it is not [the] intention that is decisive for the assessment of the abuse. It is instead the activity itself, objectively considered. In that regard, suffice it to imagine, by way of example, a case where A confines himself without further reflection to following the advice of B and to carrying out an activity for which there is no explanation other than securing a tax advantage for A. The fact that A did not have any subjective intention of abusing [Union] law will certainly not be material for the assessment of the abuse. What

220 Ibid., paras 76–80.

221 Ibid., para 81.

222 Ibid., paras 94–95.

223 See Lenaerts 2015a, pp. 335–336.

matters is not the actual state of mind of A, but the fact that the activity, objectively speaking, has no other explanation but to secure a tax advantage".[224]

The third reason why *Halifax* should genuinely be considered a landmark ruling for the purpose of this book is the circumstance that the Court, for the first time, employed the term "principle", *in extenso* principle of prohibition of abusive practices, although for now, it stopped short of qualifying it as "general". The fabrication of a general principle of EU law was, however, clearly in the making.

The third component of the quartet of rulings relevant to this section is *Cadbury-Schweppes*, which was a case of strategic corporate structuring aimed at reducing the group's overall tax liability. Cadbury-Schweppes was a UK-based multinational corporation that set up two subsidiaries in Ireland, where the corporate tax rate was significantly lower than in the UK. These subsidiaries allowed Cadbury Schweppes to reduce its overall tax liability. The UK tax authorities applied the UK's controlled foreign company (CFC) rules, which were designed to prevent profit shifting to low-tax jurisdictions by taxing the profits of foreign subsidiaries as if they were profits of the UK parent company. Cadbury Schweppes challenged this, arguing that the application of the CFC rules infringed on its freedom of establishment under EU law.[225]

The Court of Justice started off by reaffirming its strong liberal approach towards this freedom. It ruled that "the fact that the company was established in a Member State for the purpose of benefiting from more favourable legislation does not in itself suffice to constitute abuse of that freedom".[226] The UK legislation at issue created a difference in the treatment of resident companies on the basis of their control of holdings established in another Member State, which the ECJ could easily declare a restriction on the freedom of establishment.[227] Subsequently, it went on to verify whether it was justified by the need to prevent circumvention of national law on corporate tax and whether it was proportionate.

As usual, that assessment had to be made taking account of the objective pursued by the freedom of establishment, which was to allow a national of a Member State to pursue an economic activity in another Member State for, in principle, an indefinite period through a secondary establishment. Therefore, a restriction aimed at preventing abusive practices must pursue the specific objective of preventing "conduct involving the creation of wholly artificial arrangements which do not reflect economic reality, with a view to escaping the tax normally due on the profits generated by activities carried out on national territory".[228] The Court found that the CFC rules complied with this requirement, for they only applied to transactions that had

---

[224] CJEU, *Halifax plc, Leeds Permanent Development Services Ltd and County Wide Property Investments Ltd*, Opinion of Advocate General Maduro, 7 April 2005, case C-255/02, ECLI:EU:C:2005:200, para 70.

[225] CJEU, *Cadbury Schweppes plc*, Judgment of the Court, 12 September 2006, case C-196/04, ECLI:EU:C:2006:544, paras 13–28.

[226] Ibid., para 37.

[227] Ibid., paras 43–46.

[228] Ibid., para 55.

no other purpose than to escape national tax law.[229] The ECJ then turned to the assessment of "whether that legislation goes beyond what is necessary to achieve that purpose",[230] which is another way of saying whether it is proportionate. It was at this stage of its reasoning that the Court of Justice applied the test for abuse developed in *Emsland-Stärke* and, at that time, already tested in different contexts. To find whether the CFC rules only targeted wholly artificial arrangements, it was necessary to assess whether there were, "in addition to a subjective element consisting in the intention to obtain a tax advantage, objective circumstances showing that, despite formal observance of the conditions laid down by [Union] law, the objective pursued by freedom of establishment [...] has not been achieved".[231] Coherently, such an assessment, which was eventually left to the referring court, had to focus on whether the foreign subsidiary was not just a letterbox but rather reflected an economic reality that could suggest the carrying out of genuine economic activities in the territory of the host Member State in line with the purpose of the freedom of establishment.[232]

The Court's findings in *Cadbury-Schweppes* are not massively coherent with its previous case law. To begin with, it is unclear why it has applied the abuse test developed in *Emsland-Stärke* at the stage of the proportionality assessment of the restriction at issue. The purpose of the abuse test is to detect the existence of abusive situations. If abuse is found, the national measure designed to combat abuse is to be assessed under the proportionality principle, which has its own assessment test.[233] In addition, the first and the second elements of abuse, as coined in *Emsland-Stärke,* overlapped at least to some extent in *Cadbury-Schweppes.* It should be recalled that in *Emsland-Stärke,* the subjective element consisted of the intention to obtain an advantage from the Union rules by artificially creating the conditions laid down for obtaining it. The objectification operated by *Halifax* turned that requirement into an analysis of the aim of the transaction, which could be demonstrated by its purely artificial nature. In *Cadbury-Schweppes*, the artificial nature of the subsidiary, which was supposed to be assessed in relation to the second constitutive element, was instead used to demonstrate the existence of the first element of abuse, that is, non-compliance with the purpose of the freedom of establishment. Finally, it might not be easy to understand, at least at first sight, why the Court found the Danish restrictions in *Centros* incompatible with the purpose of the freedom of establishment and the British restrictions in *Cadbury-Schweppes* compatible with it. If, however, one looks under the surface, there seems to be a fundamental difference between these two rulings. In *Centros*, the Danish authorities were effectively attempting to deny the very right of establishment of Centros. In *Cadbury-Schweppes*, the right to create subsidiaries in Ireland was not disputed. The controversy did not revolve around their right to exist as Irish corporate bodies. It had to do with them being used

---

[229] Ibid., para 59.

[230] Ibid., para 60.

[231] Ibid., para 64.

[232] Ibid., paras 65–75.

[233] On the principle of proportionality, among many, see the ample analysis of Harbo 2010, p. 158 ff, as well as Tridimas 2018, p. 243 ff.

as a means to artificially reduce the tax liability of a company having its primary establishment in the UK. Hence the difference. Reading *Centros* in retrospect, it is reasonable to believe that had the Danish authorities attempted to impose on Centros a less restrictive measure than denying its right to register in Denmark (such as, for example, imposing the total or partial paying-up of the minimum capital requirement or some kind of tax guarantee), the outcome of the dispute may have been different.

The *Kofoed* ruling is the last component of the quartet. It also involved a complex arrangement to reduce the tax liability of two Danish taxpayers. More specifically, Mr Kofoed and Mr Toft were the only shareholders of Cosmopolit Holding ApS, a company incorporated in Denmark. They acquired the shares of Dooralong Ltd, a company incorporated in Ireland, which consisted of only two shares, of which the plaintiffs owned one each. After the acquisition by Mr Kofoed and Mr Toft, Dooralong increased its share capital. They then exchanged all the shares they held in Cosmopolit for all the new shares in Dooralong. At the end of this intricate series of transactions, Mr Kofoed and Mr Toft held the total share of Dooralong and no share of Cosmopolit, whose total share capital was, in fact, held by Dooralong. Following this exchange, Dooralong collected a significant dividend from Cosmopolit and subsequently distributed a large dividend to Mr Kofoed and Mr Toft. Mr Kofoed declared the share exchange as tax-exempt, but the Danish tax authorities disagreed, arguing that the dividend exceeded the 10% cash payment threshold, disqualifying the exchange from the exemption. Mr Kofoed challenged the tax authorities' decision, leading to the national court referring a question to the ECJ. The Court was asked whether the arrangement fell within the meaning of exchange of shares under Article 2(d) of Directive 90/434.[234]

After finding that the exchange of shares did indeed come under the scope of the Directive and was therefore not subject to tax, the Court focused on the argument put forward by the referring court and the Danish government that it "was not carried out for any commercial reason whatsoever but solely for the purpose of achieving tax savings, [constituting a] possible abuse of rights".[235] The ECJ noted from the outset that the Directive featured an explicit anti-abuse clause in Article 11, which allowed the Member States to refuse the benefits to operations not carried out for valid commercial reasons. This provision, the Court added, reflected "the *general* [Union] law principle that abuse of rights is prohibited".[236] There was a problem, though. Danish legislation had no provision that specifically transposed this rule of the Directive. Therefore, the Court of Justice spent the remainder of the decision on the (lack of inversely vertical) direct effects of the Directive, finding that, in those circumstances, it was for the national court to "ascertain whether there is, in Danish law, a provision or general principle prohibiting abuse of rights or other provisions on tax evasion or tax avoidance which might be interpreted in accordance with Article 11(1)(a) of Directive 90/434 and thereby justify taxation of the exchange of shares

[234] CJEU, *Hans Markus Kofoed*, Judgment of the Court, 5 July 2007, case C-321/05, ECLI:EU:C:2007:408, paras 14–22.

[235] Ibid., para 36.

[236] Ibid., para 38 (emphasis added).

in question".[237] In other words, faced with the impossibility of directly applying the Directive to the detriment of the individual concerned, the ECJ invited the national court to explore the possibility of preventing abuse of rights by resorting to the consistent interpretation of domestic law.

Similarly to the other three rulings of the quarter, *Kofoed* was groundbreaking but also slightly contradictory. On the one hand, the Court of Justice, for the first time, affirmed the existence of a *general* principle of Union law that abuse of rights is prohibited. This can effectively be considered the very first explicit recognition of abuse of Union law (abuse of rights, in this case) as a general legal principle. As a general principle, one would typically expect it to have a gap-filling role where no other provisions are applicable.[238] Here, however, lay the contradiction of *Kofoed*. If abuse of law was a general principle, it should have applied to a situation where there was a gap in the domestic legislation in the absence of inversely vertical direct effects of the Directive. But the Court of Justice was not ready to go that far. It focused on the lack of a provision implementing the specific anti-abuse clause of the Directive. Hence, the *Kofoed* judgment did not clear all doubts concerning the legal nature of the principle of abuse of Union law (better: the general principle that abuse of rights is prohibited). As we shall see, these doubts will be unequivocally clarified in the subsequent case law, culminating with *Cussens*.

This conclusion paves the way for examining the remaining judgments belonging to the second phase of the Court of Justice's case law on abuse of Union law. Between *Kofoed* and *Cussens*, in fact, the ECJ would be mainly focused on adjusting its approach relative to the existing case law before actually bringing the evolution of the principle in question to its final stage. The next few cases that will be analysed are, therefore, essentially a fine-tuning exercise. This gradual adjustment will be carried out through rulings that can be organised into four main groups, which will be examined in an equivalent number of sections: (a) (more) cases concerning tax evasion, (b) cases concerning the recognition of professional qualifications, (c) (more) cases concerning free movement of persons, with a focus on EU citizenship, and d) single cases concerning a variety of topics. We shall start from the first group, which is by far the most numerous.

3.3.5 More Cases of Tax Evasion and Abuse

In the string of cases that will be examined in this section, the Court of Justice was slightly ambivalent and contradictory. The first ruling of this group is *Part Service*, in which the applicability of the principles developed in *Halifax* was tested in a different case of potential tax evasion.

Part Service Srl (formerly Italservice Srl) and IFIM Leasing Sas, both part of the same financial group, engaged in leasing transactions for motor vehicles in 1987.

[237] Ibid., para 46.

[238] See Tridimas 2006, pp. 17–19.

IFIM leased vehicles to customers with an option to purchase, requiring a surety and unlimited security. Italservice insured the vehicles, provided financial guarantees, and received advance payments from customers, which reduced the total lease payments. Italservice paid IFIM on behalf of customers. IFIM, acting as an intermediary, received additional remuneration from Italservice, on which VAT was levied. Italservice's revenues were instead invoiced without VAT. The Italian tax authorities considered the separate contracts as a single contract designed to reduce the taxable amount, issuing a VAT adjustment notice with penalties. Italservice contested this, claiming that the contractual structure was not adopted with the aim of tax evasion but for valid commercial reasons. Italservice appealed the decision, and the issue was brought to litigation.[239] The dispute went all the way to the *Suprema Corte di Cassazione*, which was "of the view that the decision to be taken requires resolution of the question whether the actions of the relevant parties, having regard to their reciprocal links, can be considered to be an abuse of rights or of legal form according to the definition given by [Union] case-law, notably in Case C-255/02 *Halifax and Others*".[240] In particular, the referring court sought clarifications on the interpretation of the second element of abuse, which in *Halifax* consisted of a transaction carried out with the essential purpose, or sole aim, of obtaining a tax advantage without any other economic justification.[241]

The Court of Justice, in essence, took the chance of this preliminary ruling to extend the scope of what constituted abuse under Union law by interpreting its second constitutive element extensively. It held that the relevant finding in *Halifax* was not a necessary condition for the existence of an abusive practice. It only meant that the minimum threshold for classifying the practice as abusive in that case had been passed. Therefore, the Court concluded that "there can be a finding of an abusive practice when the accrual of a tax advantage constitutes the principal aim of the transaction or transactions at issue".[242] It is not necessary that it is the only aim. The principle deriving from this statement is that, at least in the field of VAT, a transaction that pursues multiple aims, including valid commercial ones, remains an abusive practice to the extent that its main purpose is the unduly obtainment of a tax advantage, "notwithstanding the possible existence, in addition, of economic objectives arising from, for example, marketing, organisation or guarantee considerations".[243]

While this development might be considered a fairly logical one, the ECJ seemed to change its mind only a few months later in another Italian case concerning VAT adjustments. *Ampliscientifica* involved Ampliscientifica Srl, which was partly owned by Amplifin SpA. Italian tax authorities challenged the latter's VAT assessments for 1990 and 1991, arguing that it did not meet the requirement that the parent company

---

[239] CJEU, *Ministero dell'Economia e delle Finanze v Part Service Srl*, Judgment of the Court, 21 February 2008, case C-425/06, ECLI:EU:C:2008:108, paras 8–23.

[240] Ibid., para 24.

[241] Ibid., paras 28–32.

[242] Ibid., para 45.

[243] Ibid., para 62.

(Amplifin) must have held more than 50% of the subsidiary's share capital (Ampliscientifica) since the start of the previous calendar year. This led Italian authorities to issue additional VAT adjustments, which Amplifin and Ampliscientifica challenged. Therefore, the Court of Justice was again asked to rule on the application of the abuse test.[244]

In a few terse statements, the ECJ referred to *Halifax*, and not to *Part Service*, to find that the aim of the principle of abuse of rights is to "prohibit wholly artificial arrangements which do not reflect economic reality and are set up with *the sole aim* of obtaining a tax advantage".[245] Taken at its face value, *Ampliscientifica* seemed to be a return to a less extensive interpretation of the second element. However, the reason for which the Court added that even transactions not solely justified by tax motives may constitute abuse is likely the same as in *Halifax*. As we have seen, in that case, the transactions involved had no justification but to obtain a tax advantage. The Court clarified in *Part Service* that, in such a case, it was sufficient to note that the minimum threshold for abuse had been passed. Adding any other qualifications would be superfluous. In *Ampliscientifica*, it seems likely that the Court assumed to be in the same scenario. Hence, the ambivalence of *Ampliscientifica* had possibly more to do with style than substance. The Court was concise and laconic, as it is quite often. Hence the uncertainties.

The following case rivals Halifax in terms of its factual complexities. *RBS Deutschland* concerned RBSD, a German company providing banking and leasing services, which was part of the Royal Bank of Scotland Group but had no place of establishment in the UK. It was, however, registered in the UK for VAT purposes. RBSD purchased motor cars in the UK from Vinci Fleet Services (VFS), a subsidiary of Vinci plc, and then leased these cars to Vinci under different contractual arrangements. Under UK law, the transactions were treated as supplies of services made in Germany and were not subject to VAT in the UK, whereas German law treated them as supplies of goods made in the UK, thus not subject to VAT in Germany. RBSD sought to deduct the input VAT paid on purchasing the cars, but the British tax authorities refused, arguing that the transactions aimed to exploit differences in VAT treatment between the UK and Germany, constituting an abusive practice. RBSD appealed, and the dispute was referred to Luxembourg on a request from the Scottish court before which it was pending.[246]

The Court recalled *Halifax* and applied the abuse test along the same lines. When focusing on the second element, it held that it was fulfilled if "the *essential aim* of the transactions concerned [was] *solely* to obtain that tax advantage".[247] With this statement, the ECJ seemed to confirm the return to a narrower scope, in line

[244] CJEU, *Ampliscientifica Srl and Amplifin SpA v Ministero dell'Economia e delle Finanze and Agenzia delle Entrate*, Judgment of the Court, 22 May 2008, case C-162/07, ECLI:EU:C:2008:301, paras 17–23.

[245] Ibid., para 28.

[246] CJEU, *The Commissioners for Her Majesty's Revenue & Customs v RBS Deutschland Holdings GmbH*, Judgment of the Court, 22 December 2010, case C-227/09, ECLI:EU:C:2010:810, paras 12–27.

[247] Ibid., para 49 (emphasis added).

with *Ampliscientifica* and contrary to *Part Service*. The most relevant part of *RBS Deutschland*, however, was not this one particular finding. It was the conclusion that followed. The Luxembourg Court noted that it was common ground that the transactions at issue in the *RBS Deutschland* ruling were not artificial in nature. They were instead normal commercial operations. They may have been structured so as to minimise the tax burdens of the companies involved, but they remained part and parcel of genuine economic activity.[248] It concluded by recalling a statement it had already made in *Halifax*, namely, that "where it is possible for the taxable person to choose from among a number of transactions, he may choose to structure his business in such a way as to limit his tax liability".[249] The difference is that in the *Halifax* ruling, this statement had been made only in principle, while in *RBS Deutschland*, it was decisive for the outcome of the dispute.

With this conclusion, the Court of Justice put a strong emphasis on the liberal economic principle that tax motives are legal motives.[250] The ECJ made it clear that the aim of limiting the tax burden of a transaction was, in principle, totally admissible and lawful, provided that it was in the context of a genuine economic operation. To achieve this result by exploring the possibilities offered by the common market was also lawful, and perhaps inherent to the very idea of a common market. For the purpose of this book, one may wonder whether this assessment concerns the first or the second constitutive element of abuse. In *RBS Deutschland*, the Court made these considerations when assessing the artificial nature of the transactions. Hence, in relation to the second element. However, it is reasonable to believe that the first constitutive element would also be affected by the finding that a transaction is genuinely commercial, for it would be absurd to affirm that the purpose of the rules on VAT is not achieved in connection with normal commercial operations.

The next ruling of this group of tax evasion cases is *Foggia*. Foggia Sociedade Gestora de Participações Sociais SA (Foggia SGPS), was a Portuguese holding company, which merged with three other holding companies within the same group in 2003. Foggia SGPS sought approval from the Ministry of Finance to transfer tax losses incurred by the acquired companies and deduct them from its revenues. The Ministry granted the transfer for two companies but denied it for one company named Riguadiana, citing a lack of commercial interest in this operation. Foggia SGPS challenged the refusal, leading to legal proceedings that were referred to the Court of Justice. The dispute revolved around the interpretation and application of the anti-abuse clause foreseen in Article 11 of Council Directive 90/434/EEC, which

---

[248] In other words, an entirely lawful corporate decision, as pointed out by Lettieri 2014, p. 129 ff.

[249] Ibid., para 54.

[250] One of the most famous judicial recognitions of this principle can be found in the classic British case law concerning tax evasion and avoidance, as exemplified by the ruling handed down in *Inland Revenue Commissioners v. Duke of Westminster* [1936] A.C. 1, 19 TC 490. In that decision, Lord Tomlin famously stated that "[e]very man is entitled, if he can, to order his affairs so that the tax attaching under the appropriate Acts is less than it otherwise would be. If he succeeds in ordering them so as to secure this result, then, however unappreciative the Commissioners of Inland Revenue or his fellow tax-payers may be of his ingenuity, he cannot be compelled to pay an increased tax". See *Inland Revenue Commissioners v. Duke of Westminster*, paras 19–20.

is the same that was at issue in *Kofoed*. The ECJ had to clarify whether, in the circumstances of the case at hand, the merging between Foggia and Riguadiana was to be regarded as an operation carried out for valid commercial reasons in accordance with the said Article 11.[251]

For the purpose of this book, the Court's answer is relevant for two reasons. Firstly, it clarified that "the cost savings resulting from the reduction of administrative and management costs [...] is inherent in any operation of merger by acquisition as this implies, by definition, a simplification of the structure of the group".[252] This circumstance alone could not constitute a valid commercial reason within the meaning of Article 11. Secondly, for the second time after *Kofoed*, and this time in more explicit terms, the Court of Justice stated that Article 11 reflected "*the general principle of EU law* that abuse of rights is prohibited".[253] If abuse was found by the national court after a thorough assessment of the circumstances of the dispute, that general principle mandated a restrictive interpretation of the secondary rules in question, for they could not "be extended to cover abusive practices".[254] This was, so far, effectively the most straightforward recognition of abuse as a general principle of EU law.

The next ruling consists of three joined cases that we will collectively refer to as *Italmoda* for the sake of brevity. The cases concerned three Dutch companies engaged in intra-Union supplies of various goods, which bypassed VAT declarations in the Netherlands by adopting a complex contractual structure. The Dutch tax authorities found a number of irregularities and took measures against the companies, which challenged these decisions. The questions referred to the Court of Justice focused on whether EU law required national authorities to deny VAT exemptions, deductions, or refunds when the taxpayer is involved in VAT evasion, even if national law did not explicitly provide for such refusals.[255]

The Court started off by referring to its case law on abuse of EU law in the field of tax evasion, recalling that individuals could not rely on EU law for abusive or fraudulent ends. The main problem in this case was the (alleged) lack of rules in the national legal order aimed at preventing abuse or fraud, specifically in the field of VAT. At least, this was the view of the referring court, with which the Dutch government disagreed, arguing that abuse and fraud prevention was a general principle of law.[256] If the national court were right, the ECJ would be faced with a situation akin to that in *Kofoed*. That is, the lack of inversely vertical direct effects of a directive, which, in the *Kofoed* ruling, the Court sorted out by recalling the national court of the duty of consistent interpretation. In *Italmoda*, it reiterated the existence of such

---

[251] CJEU, *Foggia—Sociedade Gestora de Participações Sociais SA v Secretário de Estado dos Assuntos Fiscais*, Judgment of the Court, 10 November 2011, case C-126/10, ECLI:EU:C:2011:718, paras 8–15.

[252] Ibid., para 48.

[253] Ibid., para 50 (emphasis added).

[254] Ibid.

[255] CJEU, *Staatssecretaris van Financiën v Schoenimport 'Italmoda' Mariano Previti vof and Others*, Judgment of the Court, 18 December 2014, joined cases C-131/13, C-163/13 and C-164/13, ECLI:EU:C:2014:2455, paras 9–15.

[256] Whether of Dutch or Union law was not clear. See *Italmoda*, para 51.

duty, but it added an important qualification. It found that "should it transpire [...] that, in this case, national law contains no such rules which may be interpreted in accordance with the requirements of EU law, it cannot nevertheless be inferred from this that the national authorities and courts would, in circumstances such as those at issue in the main proceedings, be prevented from satisfying those requirements and, accordingly, refusing a benefit derived from a right laid down by the Sixth Directive in the event of fraud".[257] As for the argument made by Italmoda that a directive cannot of itself impose detrimental effects directly on individuals, the Court answered that the refusal of the plaintiff's right in the case at hand was not the consequence of a direct application of the directive, but rather of the "the principle that rules of EU law cannot be relied on for abusive or fraudulent ends".[258]

Thanks to this finding, *Italmoda* should certainly be considered a landmark ruling for the topic of this book. Leaving aside the fact that it most likely concerned a case of fraud rather than abuse (an assessment which, in any case, was for the national court to do), this ruling clarified, if only indirectly, what had remained unspoken in *Kofoed*. Namely, in the absence of an anti-abuse clause in EU secondary legislation or in national law, the prohibition of abuse of EU law has the typical gap-filling function of a general principle of EU law. This aspect will be clarified in even more explicit terms by later case law.

The examination of this decision concludes the survey of the case law concerning tax evasion and abuse handed down in the pre-*Cussens* era. In the following section, we will deal with cases regarding the free movement of persons, with a special focus on citizenship rights.

3.3.6 Abuse of Law (or Lack Thereof) in the Field of Free Movement of Persons

As we have seen above, over the years, the Court of Justice has dealt with a handful of cases relating to the (alleged) abuse of the free movement of persons. Some of them, such as *Chen*, have attracted a lot of attention due to their broader social implications, which go well beyond the technicalities of EU law. In this section, we will survey a few more rulings focused on the free movement of persons, in which the general trend that has already emerged in previous cases has been strengthened.

Let us start with the *Metock* ruling. It concerned a number of third-country nationals who married EU citizens of different nationalities in Ireland and, as a result, applied for residence cards. All the requests were denied on the ground that the plaintiffs in the main proceedings had not lawfully resided in Ireland before the marriage. It should be noted that their spouses, being nationals of EU countries other than Ireland, were all free movers lawfully residing in Ireland. Moreover, the plaintiffs had one thing in common: before marrying an EU citizen in Ireland, they all

[257] Ibid., para 54.

[258] Ibid., para 56.

applied for asylum in that country and had their applications rejected. Therefore, one could speculate that they were attempting to obtain through the marriage with an EU citizen what they had been denied under the rules governing asylum, that is, a valid residence card in Ireland. However, as declared by the referring court, it appeared that none of the marriages in question was a marriage of convenience. Therefore, the Court of Justice was called upon to assess whether the imposition of a minimum lawful residence requirement on the part of Ireland was compatible with the so-called Citizenship Directive,[259] which had come into force in the meantime.[260]

The ECJ settled on a literal interpretation of the Directive, holding that "as regards family members of a Union citizen, no provision of Directive 2004/38 makes the application of the directive conditional on their having previously resided in a Member State".[261] This statement alone would suffice to rule out the lawfulness of a prior residence requirement unilaterally imposed by a Member State on top of the conditions set out in the Directive. However, the Court also decided to address the issue of the (potential) abuse of the relevant rules. Perhaps it felt compelled to respond to the politically sensitive argument put forward by Ireland and several other intervening governments,[262] based on which "in a context typified by strong pressure of migration […] [a]n interpretation of Directive 2004/38 prohibiting a host Member State from requiring prior lawful residence in another Member State would undermine the ability of the Member States to control immigration".[263]

As is well-known, the Citizenship Directive features a general anti-abuse clause in Article 35, meaningfully titled "abuse of rights". It states that "Member States may adopt the necessary measures to refuse, terminate or withdraw any right conferred by this Directive in the case of abuse of rights or fraud, such as marriages of convenience". The Court recalled that under the Directive, "it is not all nationals of non-member countries who derive rights of entry into and residence in a Member State from Directive 2004/38, but only those who are family members, within the meaning of point 2 of Article 2 of that directive, of a Union citizen who has exercised his right of freedom of movement by becoming established in a Member State other than the Member State of which he is a national".[264] This statement seemed to be putting the Member States' concerns in the right perspective: there was no reason to fear "a great increase in the number of persons able to benefit from a right of residence in the Community", as claimed by the intervening governments.[265] To benefit from

---

[259] CJEU, *Blaise Baheten Metock and Others v Minister for Justice, Equality and Law Reform*, Judgment of the Court, 25 July 2008, case C-127/08, ECLI:EU:C:2008:449, paras 12–47.

[260] See Directive 2004/38/EC of the European Parliament and of the Council of 29 April 2004 on the right of citizens of the Union and their family members to move and reside freely within the territory of the Member States amending Regulation (EEC) No 1612/68 and repealing Directives 64/221/EEC, 68/360/EEC, 72/194/EEC, 73/148/EEC, 75/34/EEC, 75/35/EEC, 90/364/EEC, 90/365/EEC and 93/96/EEC, OJ L 158, 30 April 2004, pp. 77–123.

[261] *Metock*, para 49.

[262] Apart from Ireland, no less than 10 Member States intervened.

[263] *Metock*, para 71.

[264] Ibid., para 73.

[265] Ibid., para 72.

the Directive, it was insufficient to marry EU citizens. It was necessary that such citizens exercised free movement in accordance with the Treaty. At any rate, the Court concluded, the Member States are not prevented from adopting "the necessary measures to refuse, terminate or withdraw any right conferred by that directive in the case of abuse of rights or fraud", in accordance with Article 35.[266] In short, the ECJ seemed to say that the rules contained all the legal safeguards necessary to prevent individuals from exploiting them abusively.

The decision in *Metock* was a confirmation of the previous case law and of the Court's extensive interpretation of the rules on the free movement of persons. It was also a confirmation of the tendency of the Member States to come up with rather specious arguments when it comes to (restricting) this freedom. The ECJ was elegantly dismissive of these arguments, which were set aside based on a simple literal interpretation of the Directive.[267]

At any rate, the adequacy of the legal safeguards the Court referred to in *Metock* was tested in *O.* It concerned a case of two third-country nationals who, to say the least, attempted to stretch the boundaries of the rules to their very limits. The plaintiffs in the main proceedings married two Dutch citizens who lived in the Netherlands. Since they were unable to obtain a residence card from the marriage with an EU citizen who had not exercised free movement, they orchestrated a scheme consisting of registering with their spouses at an address located in another EU Member State without actually residing there. It was, in fact, clear from the record submitted by the referring court that, despite formal registration in a host Member State, they only spent occasional stays there, such as weekends and holidays. The national court, therefore, sought clarifications from the ECJ on whether such an occasional residence in another Member State was sufficient under the Citizenship Directive.[268]

The Court held that it was "genuine residence in the host Member State of the Union citizen and of the family member who is a third-country national [...] which creates, on the Union citizen's return to his Member State of origin, a derived right of residence".[269] While the genuineness of the residence was ultimately for the national court to determine, the ECJ recalled that "the scope of Union law cannot be extended to cover abuses".[270] It continued by referring to the abuse test as developed in *Emsland-Stärke*. When mentioning the second constitutive element, it returned to the language used in that ruling, holding that it consisted of "the *intention* to obtain an advantage from the European Union rules by artificially creating the conditions laid down for obtaining it".[271] Finally, even if the national court established that the

[266] Ibid., para 75.

[267] But see the considerations made by Costello 2009, pp. 621–622, pointing out that the decision in question left unanswered whether the Court's reasoning could be extended to atypical family members.

[268] CJEU, *O. v Minister voor Immigratie, Integratie en Asiel and Minister voor Immigratie, Integratie en Asiel v B*, Judgment of the Court, 12 March 2014, case C-456/12, ECLI:EU:C:2014:135, paras 14–32.

[269] Ibid., para 56.

[270] Ibid., para 58.

[271] Ibid. (emphasis added).

settlement in the host Member State was genuine and not abusive, "short periods of residence such as weekends or holidays spent in a Member State other than that of which the citizen in question is a national, even when considered together, fall within the scope of Article 6",[272] which does not give rise to a right of residence.

For the purpose of this book, the *O* ruling is relevant for the following two reasons. Number one, the legal safeguards of the system to which the Court referred in *Metock* held. Faced with a situation that, if not abusive, was, at the very least, a creative attempt to exploit legal loopholes, the interpretation proffered by the ECJ confirmed that the Union legal order was equipped with the required antibodies. Number two, the second constitutive element of abuse, whose definition had already given some headaches, was confirmed to be more problematic than the first. While the latter was defined in exactly the same manner irrespective of the domain of EU law and remained unchanged over time, the former had to be modulated in different ways almost on a case-by-case basis. It must be recalled that, in other fields, the aim of the transaction (essential or principal, as the case may be) had replaced the reference to the intention of the alleged abuser. As we have seen, the replacement served the purpose of objectifying the subjective element. The fact that the Court, in the field of free movement of persons, chose to return to the concept of *intention* can hardly be regarded as an accident. There are several options that come to mind to objectively replace the use of the term "intention". The ECJ could have referred, for example, to the "essential aim of the arrangement". If such aim was not to genuinely settle in the host Member State but to artificially create the conditions to obtain the right to reside in the home Member State, then the second condition for abuse could be deemed fulfilled. It could work like this, but the Court chose otherwise. In later cases, we will see that it will continue to refer to the intention of the parties from time to time.

The next relevant case is *McCarthy*, in which the arguments put forward by the concerned Member State, namely the UK, won the Champions Cup of speciousness. Mr McCarthy, a British and Irish national, lived with his child and his wife, a Colombian national, in Marbella (Spain). They had a house in the UK, to which they travelled regularly. Ms McCarthy Rodriguez held a residence card issued by Spain under Article 10 of the Citizenship Directive, a document called "Residence card of a family member of a Union citizen". Under Article 5 of the Directive, this document was enough for her to enjoy free movement within the Union. It was not enough to enter the UK, though, which required her to hold, in addition to the Article 10 residence card, an EEA family permit. This additional document required a personal application to be submitted at the UK diplomatic mission in Spain every six months, which for Ms Rodriguez effectively meant travelling from Marbella to Madrid on a regular basis. Airlines often denied her boarding when she tried to travel only with her residence card, following UK guidance to discourage carriers from transporting third-country nationals without a UK-issued residence card or valid travel document, such as the EEA family permit.

The UK argued the measure was necessary under Article 35 of the Citizenship Directive, to combat a systemic problem of abuse of rights and fraud by third-country

---

[272] Ibid., para 59.

nationals. Article 10 residence cards, so argued the UK, were admittedly susceptible to forgery because they did not meet appropriate security standards, except those issued by Germany and Estonia. The British government then speculated that these two countries would be exempted from the UK legislation in the future (yes, they really pleaded that). The referring court agreed that residence cards were ripe for exploitation in the context of illegal immigration and that there was a palpable risk that a significant proportion of those engaged in the business of sham marriages would use fake residence cards for their illicit activities. Hence the referral to the ECJ.[273]

The Court of Justice made it clear that the measures adopted by the Member States under Article 35 of the Citizenship Directive had to "be based on an individual examination of the particular case".[274] Not even a Member State that "is faced, as the United Kingdom considers itself to be, with a high number of cases of abuse of rights or fraud committed by third-country nationals resorting to sham marriages or using falsified residence cards can [...] justify the adoption of a measure, such as that at issue in the main proceedings, founded on considerations of general prevention, to the exclusion of any specific assessment of the conduct of the person concerned himself".[275] If such a measure were allowed, belonging to a particular group of persons would automatically trigger the suspect of abuse or fraud, and the same would be true if "recognition [...] were limited to persons who are in possession of residence cards issued by certain Member States, as the United Kingdom has envisaged".[276] This was something that could not be allowed by the Court of Justice, and, frankly, quite obviously so.

The contribution of *McCarthy* to the understanding of abuse of Union law was clear. Firstly, it confirmed once again the many ways in which the Member States tried to ride on abuse of law to narrow down the fundamental freedoms, particularly the free movement of persons. Secondly, it confirmed that the Court of Justice was ready to counter these attempts firmly. Thirdly, as far as citizens' rights were concerned, it was clearly emerging that Article 35 of the Directive was difficult to invoke outside of cases relating to marriages of convenience or sham marriages, as the UK court put it in *McCarthy*. Fourthly, the judgment made clear that in the field of citizenship rights, the Member States cannot combat abuse through general presumptions of abusiveness. This is different from what the Court had stated in relation to tax evasion (see *Leur-Bloem*, Sect. 3.2.12), where the use of rebuttable presumptions was admitted to a limited extent.

Having completed the analysis of cases relating to the free movement of persons, we can now turn to the next group of cases, which concerns an area that so far

[273] CJEU, *The Queen, on the application of Sean Ambrose McCarthy and Others v Secretary of State for the Home Department*, Judgment of the Court, 18 December 2014, case C-202/13, ECLI:EU:C:2014:2450, paras 20–28.

[274] Ibid., para 52.

[275] Ibid., para 55.

[276] Ibid., para 56.

has remained almost entirely unexplored, bar in the *Knoors* and *Kraus* rulings (see above). Namely, (real or imaginary) abuses connected with the recognition of titles and qualifications acquired abroad.

3.3.7 Abuse of Union Law and the Recognition of Foreign Titles and Qualifications

In the string of cases that will be analysed in this section, the Court of Justice dealt with issues revolving around the recognition of titles and professional qualifications across the Member States, a field which, despite being largely harmonised, has often given rise to difficulties due to the regulatory differences (still) existing between the Member States.[277]

In *Commission v. Spain*, the European Commission brought an infringement procedure against Spain for not recognising professional engineering qualifications obtained in Italy. In brief, Spanish law distinguished between "official diplomas" that allowed access to regulated professions and "own diplomas" awarded by universities that did not grant such access. The infringement procedure originated from several complaints submitted to the Commission by a number of individuals who held Spanish "own diplomas" obtained at the University of Alicante, which had a framework cooperation agreement in place with the Polytechnic University of Marche, Italy. On the basis of this agreement, the Italian university recognised for the benefit of the complainants the equivalence between the Spanish diplomas and the Italian university diploma of civil engineer (*laurea in ingegneria civile*), which granted them access to the Italian State exam conferring on them the entitlement to pursue the profession of civil engineer in that Member State. The complainants passed the Italian State exam, thus becoming civil engineers entitled to practice in this country. Subsequently, they requested the Spanish Ministry of Equipment and Transport the recognition of the professional qualifications of civil engineer obtained in Italy to be able to pursue their profession in Spain. The Ministry rejected those applications based on the fact that all the university education and training received by the complainants had been provided in Spain. The Commission took the view that the Spanish legislation was at variance with the secondary legislation on mutual recognition of diplomas and brought an infringement procedure.[278]

For the purpose of this book, it is important to emphasise that the Spanish authorities made an argument based on the principle of prohibition of abuse of EU law, invoking the Court's case law "according to which [Union] law cannot be relied on for abusive or fraudulent ends".[279] After all, the complainants held a Spanish

[277] For an overview of the relevant issues, with a special focus on health professions, see van Riemsdijk 2013, p. 47 ff.

[278] CJEU, *Commission of the European Communities v Kingdom of Spain*, Judgment of the Court, 23 October 2008, case C-286/06, ECLI:EU:C:2008:586, paras 41–49.

[279] Ibid., para 52.

academic ("own diploma") title that would not normally give them access to the profession of civil engineer in Spain, for which they needed an "official diploma". They obtained the title of civil engineer in Italy by exploiting the regulatory differences between these two Member States and then sought recognition in Spain of the title so obtained in Italy—a title they would have never acquired in Spain based on their education. Given these circumstances, the argument that the claimants had found a way to circumvent the Spanish law was not entirely indefensible.

The Court of Justice recognised, as a matter of principle, that Member States could deny the benefits deriving from Union law in case of abusive or fraudulent practices. It did so by referring to the *Centros* ruling.[280] It then made a statement that is very similar to the Court's main finding in *Centros*. It held that "the fact that a national of a Member State who wishes to pursue a regulated profession chooses to take up that profession in his preferred Member State cannot *of itself* constitute an abuse of the general system of recognition [...]. The rights of nationals of a Member State to choose the Member State in which they wish to acquire their professional qualifications is inherent in the exercise, in a single market, of the fundamental freedoms guaranteed by the [...] Treaty".[281]

Although, this time, the ECJ did not say so explicitly, the statement above clearly implied the acceptance of regulatory arbitrage as an inevitable feature of the common market. In *Centros*, taking advantage of more favourable rules concerning the establishment of companies was not *in itself* an abuse. In much the same way, in *Commission v. Spain,* taking advantage of more favourable rules on access to the profession of civil engineer was not *in itself* a problem. The two judgments are consistent with each other and in line with the Court's liberal approach to the exercise of economic freedoms in the single market. The message the Court sent with *Commission v. Spain* was that the prohibition of abuse of law could not be used to counter practices that are inherent in the single market, no matter how fishy they may look from the perspective of the authorities of a Member State.

The following *Cavallera* case concerned the same profession. It involved the same two countries, but this time, an Italian national obtained a qualification in Spain and attempted to use it in Italy. More specifically, Mr Cavallera obtained a mechanical engineering qualification from the University of Turin. He then sought homologation of his title in Spain, where he applied and received recognition of his Italian qualification by the Spanish Ministry for Education and Sciences as equivalent to a Spanish industrial technical engineer qualification. Afterwards, Mr Cavallera sought recognition of his Spanish certificate in Italy to enrol in the Italian Register of Engineers, which was granted by the Italian Ministry of Justice. The *Consiglio Nazionale degli Ingegneri* (National Board of Engineers) challenged this decision, arguing it circumvented Italian law, under which it was necessary to pass a State

[280] Ibid., para 70.

[281] Ibid., para 72 (emphasis added).

exam to practice the profession of engineer. The national court had doubts over the interpretation of EU law and referred the matter to the Court of Justice.[282]

The ECJ noted that the "Spanish homologation does not provide evidence of any additional qualification".[283] It was a mere recognition of the education acquired in Italy by Mr Cavallera. Under those circumstances, it would be contrary to the purpose of the secondary legislation in question to allow someone who has not received any additional training or qualification in the host Member State to gain access to the profession in the home Member State after a mere homologation abroad of the original academic title.[284] At first sight, this may appear as a contradiction compared to what the Court stated in *Commission v. Spain*. However, at closer scrutiny, there was one fundamental difference between the two cases, which the Court emphasised in its decision. In fact, in the case at hand, it was "common ground that Mr Cavallera has not worked outside Italy and that he has not followed any course of study or taken any examinations under the Spanish education system".[285] There lay the decisive element: in *Commission v. Spain*, the complainants had all taken and successfully passed the Italian State exam to be admitted to the profession of civil engineer. Mr Cavallera had done nothing else than recognising his Italian diploma in Spain. Hence, the different conclusion.

For the purpose of this book, it bears noting that in *Cavallera*, there was no explicit mention of abuse of Union law, which remained somehow in the background. However, it was clear that the arrangement carried out by Mr Cavallera was indeed abusive in the sense envisaged by the Spanish authorities in *Commission v. Spain*. Technically speaking, the Court censured it by resorting to the usual interpretive strategy, which consists of placing abusive practices outside the scope of application of the relevant secondary legislation.

The last case concerning the recognition of qualifications is *Torresi*. It involved Mr Angelo Alberto Torresi and Mr Pierfrancesco Torresi, who obtained their law degrees in Italy and subsequently obtained law degrees in Spain, registering as lawyers in Spain at the *Ilustre Colegio de Abogados de Santa Cruz de Tenerife*. Shortly after that registration, they applied for registration in the special section of the lawyers' register relating to lawyers holding a professional title issued in a Member State other than the Italian Republic and established in the Italian Republic ('lawyers qualified abroad'), which is a special register Italy keeps to comply with Directive 98/5 on so-called established lawyers.[286] Their request landed on the desk of the Italian BAR (named *Consiglio Nazionale Forense*, hereinafter: CNF), which the ECJ considers a

[282] CJEU, *Consiglio Nazionale degli Ingegneri v Ministero della Giustizia and Marco Cavallera*, Judgment of the Court, 29 January 2009, case C-311/06, ECLI:EU:C:2009:37, paras 33–43.

[283] Ibid., para 56.

[284] Ibid., para 57.

[285] Ibid., para 36.

[286] See Directive 98/5/EC of the European Parliament and of the Council of 16 February 1998 to facilitate practice of the profession of lawyer on a permanent basis in a Member State other than that in which the qualification was obtained, OJ L 77, 14 March 1998, pp. 36–43. On this matter, see Vitale 2009, pp. 541 ff.

national jurisdiction under Article 267 TFEU since the famous *Gebhard* ruling.[287] The CNF asked the Court to rule on whether, in light of the general principle that prohibits any abuse of rights, registration of lawyers in a case where Italian nationals have abused EU law could be validly refused.[288]

From the outset, it is worth noting the strong position of the referring court. From the phrasing of the questions referred, it was clear that the CNF was not asking the ECJ whether there was an abuse of EU law in the case in point. It was assumed that such an abuse existed. The question was whether faced with abusive conduct, national authorities were still obliged to approve registration. The Court, however, was equipped to deal with this case irrespective of the strong (but wrong) beliefs of the CNF. After all, the answer to the questions raised was in the rules, as interpreted in decisions such as *Commission v. Spain*. And in fact, the Court went down that road.

As usual, the ECJ recalled that Member States are, in principle, allowed to take measures to combat abuse. It also reiterated that a finding of abuse requires an objective and a subjective element, which this time was defined as the "intention to obtain an improper advantage from the EU rules by artificially creating the conditions laid down for obtaining it",[289] confirming that when it comes to persons, reference to the intention of the action is to be preferred over reference to the aim of the arrangement. However, it (re)affirmed that "the fact that the national of a Member State has chosen to acquire a professional qualification in a Member State other than that in which he resides in order to benefit there from more favourable legislation is not, in itself [...] sufficient ground to conclude that there is an abuse of rights".[290] We have already seen this principle stated in *Commission v. Spain*, and before that, *mutatis mutandis*, in *Centros*. The *Torresi* ruling confirmed the (by then) established principle that the idea of a common market entails the possibility that market actors—such as companies, workers, artisans, professionals, you name it—may choose the normative environment that best suits their needs. If the idea is to trade in Denmark but establishing a company is easier in the UK than in Denmark, it is possible and perhaps logical, but most importantly, lawful, to choose the UK as the place of primary establishment and Denmark as the place of secondary establishment. If the idea is to become a practising lawyer but obtaining the title is easier in Spain than in Italy, it is possible and perhaps logical, but most importantly, lawful, to choose Spain to obtain the relevant professional title and Italy as the place of establishment. In this state of affairs, which is rooted in the very idea of a free market, the prohibition of abuse of law is triggered only in exceptional situations, that is, when the arrangement

---

[287] CJEU, *Reinhard Gebhard v Consiglio dell'Ordine degli Avvocati e Procuratori di Milano*, Judgment of the Court, 30 November 1995, case C-55/94, ECLI:EU:C:1995:411.

[288] CJEU, *Angelo Alberto Torresi and Pierfrancesco Torresi v Consiglio dell'Ordine degli Avvocati di Macerata*, Judgment of the Court, 17 July 2014, joined cases C-58/13 and C-59/13, ECLI:EU:C:2014:2088.

[289] Ibid., para 46.

[290] Ibid., para 50.

is so deviant that it does not deserve any legal protection whatsoever. The assessment of that deviance is carried out through the abuse test created by the Court of Justice.

One may wonder what the difference is between *Cavallera* and *Torresi*. In my view, the difference is quite clear. Mr Cavallera had not acquired any education, training or professional experience in Spain. He merely obtained the homologation of his Italian degree. In other words, as was pertinently argued by AG Maduro, Mr Cavallera's situation was "in fact purely domestic but [...] has by artificial means been brought within the scope of [Union] law".[291] In *Torresi*, the plaintiffs in the main proceedings had enrolled in a Spanish university and obtained a Spanish law degree. Based on this degree, they acquired the entitlement to practice law as *abogados* in Spain. They were, in other words, as much *abogados* as any other person who graduated in Spain and practised law in that country. It is undeniable that the well-known phenomenon of Italian professionals, especially legal professionals, who acquire their qualifications outside Italy for the sole purpose of circumventing the national system and without a real intention to genuinely establish themselves in the host Member State has some degree of artificiality. For years, this has been facilitated by private agencies selling the whole package to interested persons: they would take care of the paperwork, organise trips to the host Member State to take exams, if necessary, or provide IT assistance for courses and exams that are often (and increasingly) offered online, provide help with the registration with a *Colegio de Abogados* in Spain, with the forwarding of documents to the Italian BAR, and so forth.[292]

However, that is yet another inevitable consequence of a free market. So long as the Member States' legislations are not fully harmonised and regulatory arbitrage is admitted, the emergence of intermediaries facilitating it is only a logical consequence of that state of affairs and hardly a surprising one. Let us use this example to clarify. Joe Bloggs is a postdoc who lives and works in his home Member State (State A). He marries Mrs Miggins, a third-country national he met during a research stay abroad. Mrs Miggins has no right to reside in State A. Therefore, they intend to relocate to another EU Member State (State B) for the sole purpose of having Mrs Miggins obtain residence rights under the Citizenship Directive upon return to State A. It should be noted that this was more or less the situation at issue in *Akrich* (see Sect. 3.3.2). If they need help, it is sufficient for Mr Bloggs and Mrs Miggins to make a simple search on the internet (even simpler nowadays with the use of IA) to find agents, companies, lawyers, and so forth that can provide (for a profit) practical assistance, logistical assistance, administrative assistance, legal assistance—you name it. All this is entirely lawful, no matter how fishy it may look to somebody. The fact that the same phenomenon occurs in relation to professional qualifications is, therefore, hardly anomalous, especially if one considers the many (and often intricate) regulatory differences existing between Member States. It is the perfect situation for intermediaries to offer their services and thrive. It is true

[291] CJEU, *Consiglio Nazionale degli Ingegneri v Ministero della Giustizia and Marco Cavallera*, Opinion of Advocate General Poiares Maduro, 28 February 2008, case C-331/06, ECLI:EU:C:2008:130, para 56.

[292] See Colavitti 2013, pp. 1048–1049.

that legal professionals like Mr Torresi never intended to establish themselves as lawyers in Spain. However, the fact that they effectively exercised free movement and obtained education in a host Member State cannot be disregarded solely because, for example, they studied law in Spain at a university where courses and exams were partially or totally offered online or because they were assisted by a private agency.[293] The problem, if there was a problem at all, did not lie in the EU rules. It lay in the Member State's rules that were being exploited by Torresi and the like. In fact, those rules were changed at the national level,[294] just like the Irish law on citizenship, which was changed after *Chen*.

The examination of the *Torresi* ruling concludes the saga concerning the recognition of diplomas and professional qualifications. Although not abundant, this case law contributed significantly to a better understanding of the general principle of prohibition of abuse of Union law. In particular, it strengthened the idea that in the single market, natural and legal persons have the right to make normative choices based on the suitability of the rules to their individual situation. In the common market of the European Union, the law is an additional factor that market actors, when making strategic decisions about, for example, where to establish a company, can weigh against other factors, such as costs, language, quality of life, efficiency of the administration, and so forth. Abuse of Union law can be used to censure purely artificial arrangements in exceptional cases. It cannot, however, be invoked to deny dynamics that, whether one likes it or not, are structural features of a common market.

In the following section, we will deal with the last string of cases of this second phase of the case law before moving on to the third and final phase inaugurated by *Cussens*.

3.3.8 *Three Remaining Cases:* Slancheva, Kratzer *and* Polbud

The three rulings that will be examined in this section concern very different topics. We will start with *Slancheva*, in which abuse was invoked in a field that had not yet come under the Court's scrutiny.

The case involved Slancheva sila EOOD (hereinafter: Slancheva) and the Bulgarian agency responsible for agricultural issues. Slancheva applied for funding under the European Agricultural Fund for Rural Development (EAFRD) for a photovoltaic power plant. The EAFRD had a maximum financing limit of EUR 200,000 per project. The application was submitted by the company's agent, Mr. Mitsov, and the company's sole member and manager, Ms. Mitsova, who were married. The Bulgarian agency rejected the application, stating that the conditions for obtaining aid had been artificially created to gain an advantage contrary to the objectives of

---

[293] But see Mastroianni and Arena 2015, pp. 381–383, who offered thoughtful arguments in support of the opposite conclusion.

[294] See Di Federico 2014, p. 554 ff.

the aid scheme. More specifically, Slancheva and other related entities submitted multiple applications for financing under the same EAFRD support scheme, each for constructing a photovoltaic power plant. Those projects were formally independent but closely linked geographically and operationally. Therefore, the Bulgarian authorities suspected that the project had been artificially fragmented in order to circumvent the maximum financing limit. Slancheva contested the rejection, leading to proceedings before the Administrative Court of Sofia and the preliminary question before the ECJ.[295]

The Court of Justice recalled its established case law on the two constitutive elements of abuse of Union law. For the purpose of this book, it is worth emphasising what the Court said in relation to the subjective element. It held that the "financing cannot be refused for a project where the investment in question may have some explanation other than the mere payment under the EAFRD support scheme".[296] As we know, the subjective element consists of the intention to obtain an advantage from EU law. If it was demonstrated that the plaintiffs in the main proceedings did not have *solely* the intention of obtaining such advantage (in the case at hand, the requested EU funds) but also had some other explanation, such as, one may assume, effectively develop a solar power plant, an abuse of Union law did not exist.

The *Slancheva* ruling was not really innovative compared to the existing case law. It largely reaffirmed what the Court had already said in previous decisions. However, the ECJ seemed to be concerned with the idea of narrowing down the possibilities to invoke abuse, which is an approach in line with the tendency that emerged in the decisions concerning the recognition of professional qualifications seen above.

The *Kratzer* case concerned a completely different matter, but it is equally interesting for the purpose of this book. A German company named R+V advertised trainee positions for graduates in economics, mathematical economics, business informatics, and law. Applicants were required to have a recent, very good university degree and relevant practical vocational experience. For the legal field, passing both state examinations and having employment law or medical knowledge was required. Mr Kratzer applied for the legal trainee position, emphasising his qualifications, management experience, and expertise in employment and medical law. However, R+V rejected his application. Following the rejection, Mr Kratzer demanded EUR 14,000 in compensation for age discrimination from R+V and an additional EUR 3,500 for sex discrimination after learning that the trainee positions were awarded to women only. The dispute went all the way up to the top employment law jurisdiction, namely the Federal Labour Court, which believed the plaintiff sought to obtain the

[295] CJEU, *Slancheva sila EOOD v Izpalnitelen direktor na Darzhaven fond «Zemedelie» Razplashtatelna agentsia*, Judgment of the Court, 12 September 2013, case C-434/12, ECLI:EU:C:2013:546, paras 11–22.

[296] Ibid., para 42.

status of an applicant for the sole purpose of claiming compensation for discrimination under the relevant EU secondary legislation. It, therefore, asked the ECJ to clarify whether such legislation was applicable.[297]

The Court started off by holding that a "factual situation with characteristics such as those described in the abovementioned decision is, in principle, outside the scope of Directives 2000/78 and 2006/54".[298] That was because "a person making an application for a post in circumstances such as those described [...] clearly is not seeking to obtain the post for which he formally applies. That person cannot, therefore, rely on the protection offered by Directives 2000/78 and 2006/54. A contrary interpretation would be incompatible with the objective pursued by those directives, which is to ensure equal treatment 'in employment and occupation'".[299] The reasoning is clear: since Mr Kratzer was not effectively seeking employment but only creating an *escamotage* to be in a position to claim compensation, he could not rely on the legislation in question. From the perspective of abuse of law, this was an indication that the objective element existed: despite the formal observance of the directives, Mr Kratzer's conduct was at variance with their purpose.

The rest of the ruling is a sort of summary of the ECJ's case law on abuse of Union law. The Court recalled the two constitutive elements, defining the second as a situation where the essential aim of the transaction is to obtain an undue advantage, provided there is no other economic explanation.[300] It then held that "if it appears objectively, first, that despite formal compliance with the conditions laid down in Directives 2000/78 and 2006/54 the objective pursued by those directives has not been achieved and, second, that Mr Kratzer applied artificially for a post with the essential aim of not actually taking up that post but of relying on the protection offered by those directives with a view to obtaining an undue advantage, which is for the national court to determine, it would then have to be considered that Mr Kratzer is relying abusively on that protection".[301] The Court's conclusion is so clear that no further explanation is needed.

The last case that will be analysed in this section is *Polbud*, part of the saga concerning the freedom of establishment of companies. Polbud was a Polish limited company that decided to transfer its registered office to Luxembourg without changing its actual place of business or management. Following this decision, Polbud requested to be removed from the Polish commercial register while establishing its new registered office in Luxembourg under the name of Consoil Geotechnik. Despite the transfer, Polbud's request for removal from the Polish commercial register was denied due to non-compliance with the Polish liquidation requirements. Polbud challenged this decision, arguing that the transfer of its registered office to Luxembourg should have brought to an end the liquidation procedure under Polish law. The Polish

[297] CJEU, *Nils-Johannes Kratzer v R+V Allgemeine Versicherung AG*, Judgment of the Court, 28 July 2016, case C-423/15, ECLI:EU:C:2016:604, paras 15–25.

[298] Ibid., para 30.

[299] Ibid., para 35.

[300] Ibid., paras 37–42.

[301] Ibid., para 43.

courts, however, maintained that the company had to fulfil the liquidation requirements under Polish law before it could be removed from the register. The Supreme Court of Poland referred questions to the ECJ regarding the compatibility of Polish law with the freedom of establishment.[302]

Unsurprisingly, the Court stated that the national legislation was a restriction of the freedom in question.[303] The problem was whether it could be justified on the objective of preventing abusive practices, as the Polish government argued. First, the Court recognised that it was "open to the Member States to adopt any appropriate measure for preventing or penalising *fraud*".[304] Second, it reiterated that "the fact that either the registered office or real head office of a company was established in accordance with the legislation of a Member State for the purpose of enjoying the benefit of more favourable legislation does not, in itself, constitute *abuse*".[305] Given that the Polish legislation gave rise to a presumption of abuse, the Court concluded it was not proportionate.[306]

The outcome of *Polbud* is squarely in line with the Court's relevant precedents. The emphasis on the possibility of taking advantage of more favourable legislation when making intra-EU strategic decisions is also a confirmation of existing case law, and so is the idea that general presumptions are not allowed (see *McCarthy*, Sect. 3.3.6). However, it is regrettable that the Court of Justice, in this ruling, returned to the semantic confusion generated by the interchangeable reference to fraud and abuse. In the last phase of the case law, as we shall see, the ECJ will return to this issue and clarify the differences between these two concepts.

This was the last ruling of the second phase of the Court's evolutionary case law on abuse of Union law. Starting from the next section, we will deal with cases belonging to the consolidation phase, which is the third and final stage of a journey that will eventually lead to establishing a fully-fledged general principle of EU law.

3.4 The Third Phase

3.4.1 Introduction

As already stated above, the third phase of the ECJ's case law on the principle of abuse of law started in 2017, when the Court handed down the landmark *Cussens* ruling. This third and final phase was referred to above as the consolidation stage. It is marked by three important developments. Number one, the nature of the prohibition of abuse of Union law as a general principle of EU law is unequivocally and repeatedly

---

[302] CJEU, *Polbud—Wykonawstwo sp. z o.o*, Judgment of the Court, 25 October 2017, case C-106/16, ECLI:EU:C:2017:804, paras 8–18.

[303] Ibid., paras 52–65.

[304] Ibid., para 61 (emphasis added).

[305] Ibid., para 62 (emphasis added).

[306] Ibid., para 64.

affirmed by the Court so as to leave absolutely no doubt about it. Number two, and consequently, abuse manifests itself in a variety of fields and situations that confirm its generalised applicability. In the case law analysed so far, actual or potential abuse occurred essentially in two typical situations. First, abuse was invoked in a situation where a natural or legal person relied on EU law, mostly primary law (or a combination of primary and secondary law), in order to circumvent national rules. Examples of this group of cases are *Van Binsbergen*, *Centros*, and *Torresi*.[307] Second, it was invoked in a situation where a natural or legal person attempted to unduly obtain an advantage deriving from EU secondary legislation by means of abuse or fraud in the context of a vertical relationship, that is, in a dispute between a private party and the competent authorities of the Member States. Examples of this group of cases are *Emsland-Stärke*, *Halifax* and *Foggia*. In the third phase, abuse will manifest itself repeatedly in horizontal situations, that is, in (domestic) disputes between two private parties in which EU law, mostly secondary law, plays a decisive role, confirming the general nature of the principle.[308] The third development that occurred in this final stage of the case law is connected with the second one, but it is worth pointing it out separately. In fact, among the new areas of EU law to which it is applied, asylum law stands out as a particularly interesting one, as we shall see below.

Having highlighted the main trends of this last group of cases, we can turn to the examination of the ECJ's decisions, which will be carried out case by case.

3.4.2 *The Beginning of a New Era: The Landmark* Cussens *Ruling*

Cussens was a case of tax evasion, which, like many tax evasion cases, involved an intricate web of transactions aimed at reducing tax liability. More specifically, the plaintiffs in the main proceedings owned a development site in Baltimore, Ireland, and constructed 15 holiday homes for sale. In March and April 2002, they entered into transactions with Shamrock Estates Limited, a company associated with them. A long lease of 20 years and one month was granted to Shamrock Estates, which leased the properties back to them on a two-year deal. On 3 April 2002, both leases were extinguished by mutual surrender, and full ownership reverted to the plaintiffs. In May 2002, they sold the properties to third parties. No VAT was payable on those sales, as the properties had been the subject of a first supply on which VAT was chargeable, that is, the long lease. However, national authorities charged additional VAT assessments,

[307] It should be noted that of these three examples, only in one case, namely *Van Binsbergen*, did the Court recognise that the fundamental freedom invoked had been relied on abusively. This is not a coincidence: as will be argued in Chap. 4, the invocation (typically on the part of the Member State involved) of the general principle of prohibition of abuse of Union law is more difficult in cases concerning the circumvention of national law through reliance on the fundamental freedoms. See Chap. 4, Sect. 4.3.

[308] The only case examined so far in which abuse was invoked in a horizontal dispute was in fact *Kratzer*.

arguing that the leases were artificially created to avoid VAT on subsequent sales. The plaintiffs challenged this decision, and in the judicial dispute that followed, the Irish courts applied the principle of abuse of Union law as developed in *Halifax*. The plaintiffs contested this, arguing that in the absence of national legislation transposing the principle that abusive practices are prohibited, that principle could not be deployed against them. Faced with this dilemma, the Supreme Court of Ireland referred the matter to the ECJ, which seized the opportunity to issue a landmark ruling.[309]

The Court of Justice started off by issuing what can be considered the most comprehensive systematisation to date of the principle of abuse of Union law, which the Court repeatedly referred to in this ruling as *the principle that abusive practices are prohibited*. Recalling early cases such as *Kefalas*, *Diamantis*, *Cremer* and *Emsland-Stärke*, it stated that the principle, based on settled case law, entailed that "first, EU law cannot be relied on for abusive or fraudulent ends [...] and, secondly, the application of EU legislation cannot be extended to cover abusive practices by economic operators".[310] Furthermore, it held that it was not "subject to a requirement of transposition",[311] meaning that, owing to its nature as a general principle of EU law, it could be applied irrespective of whether national law made provision for it.[312] It should be noted that this aspect had remained unclear in *Kofoed* but was partly clarified in *Italmoda*. After *Cussens*, there could no longer be doubts that the general principle prohibiting abuse of Union law applies in the absence of an anti-abuse clause in secondary legislation or national law. The Court then went on to list some of the areas of EU law in which the principle had been applied, citing company law, the common agricultural policy, and the sphere of VAT as examples.[313] It emphasised that "the principle that abusive practices are prohibited is applied to the rights and advantages provided for by EU law irrespective of whether those rights and advantages have their basis in the Treaties [...], in a regulation [...] or in a directive [...]" making it "apparent that that principle is not of the same nature as the rights and advantages to which it applies".[314] Based on these premises, the Court unequivocally concluded that "[t]he principle that abusive practices are prohibited [...] displays the general, comprehensive character which is naturally inherent in general principles of EU law [whose application] does not require a specific legal basis".[315]

The Court then made two important additional statements. First, it recalled that the interpretations given by it on the basis of Article 267 TFEU clarify the meaning and scope of EU law as it must be, or ought to have been, understood and applied from the date of its entry into force. This also applied to the principle of abuse of Union law and was not contrary to legal certainty. In the case at hand, it meant that

---

309 CJEU, *Edward Cussens and Others v T. G. Brosman*, Judgment of the Court, 22 November 2017, case C-251/16, ECLI:EU:C:2017:881, paras 12–24.

310 Ibid., para 27.

311 Ibid., para 28.

312 Put it different, it was directly applicable, as pointed out by De La Feria 2020, p. 143.

313 Ibid., para 29.

314 Ibid., para 30.

315 Ibid, paras 31–32.

it applied to the transactions carried out by the plaintiffs, which predated *Halifax*.[316] Second, it repeated that it was not necessary that "the accrual of a tax advantage is the only objective of the transactions at issue".[317] It was sufficient that "the accrual of a tax advantage constitutes the essential aim of the transactions at issue".[318]

Cussens truly was a landmark ruling. Its weight cannot be overestimated. The Court clarified that the principle of prohibition of abuse of Union law is a general principle of EU law that applies horizontally to all areas of EU law even in the absence of national legislation providing for it. The ruling truly delivered a comprehensive systematisation of the principle. In the following judgments, after the systematisation, the ECJ would have the opportunity to define some issues further and apply the principle to new areas.

3.4.3 The Differences Between Fraud and Abuse as They Emerged in the Altun *Ruling*

As we have seen, the Court of Justice has not yet distinguished fraud from abuse despite the two concepts having different legal meanings. We have also seen that every time it dealt with a fraud case, abuse was cited alongside it, while the opposite did not happen. Based on this, it was speculated that, in the Court's view, fraud always includes abuse, while abuse does not always include fraud, as if fraud is a specific manifestation of abuse. Or, put differently, as if fraud is in relation of species to genus with abuse in much the same way abuse of process is (see Sect. 3.2.3). In *Altun*, the Court returned to this issue and made some clarifications.

The case originated from an investigation carried out by the Belgian Social Security Inspectorate, which found that Absa, a Belgian construction company, employed almost no staff. Instead, it subcontracted work to Bulgarian firms that were posting workers to Belgium. These workers held E 101 or A 1 certificates issued by Bulgarian authorities, indicating compliance with social security regulations in that country. However, an investigation in Bulgaria revealed that the Bulgarian firms had no significant activity in Bulgaria. Consequently, the Belgian authorities requested the Bulgarian institution to review or withdraw the certificates. Still, the Bulgarians confirmed their validity for the purpose of posting workers, allegedly without taking into account the facts established by the Belgian authorities. Legal proceedings were brought in Belgium against Absa and its agents for employing unauthorised foreign workers and for failing to declare their employment to Belgian social security authorities. Initially, a Belgian court acquitted the defendants, but the Antwerp Court of Appeal later convicted them, asserting that the certificates were fraudulently obtained. The defendants appealed, leading the Belgian Court of Cassation to seek a preliminary ruling from the Court of Justice on whether a court in a Member State

[316] Ibid, paras 39–41.

[317] Ibid., para 53.

[318] Ibid.

other than the issuing one could annul or disregard an E 101 certificate provided it was established that it was fraudulently obtained.[319]

The Court first affirmed that "[t] he principle of prohibition of fraud and abuse of rights [...] is a general principle of EU law which individuals must comply with".[320] It went on to clarify the two constitutive elements of fraud, which also had to satisfy an objective and a subjective factor. It stated that the "objective factor consists in the fact that the conditions for obtaining and relying on an E 101 certificate, laid down in Title II of Regulation No 1408/71 [...] are not met".[321] Those conditions are two, as recalled by the ECJ earlier in the judgment: "[t]he first condition [...] requires the maintenance of a direct link between that undertaking and that worker during the period of the worker's posting. The second condition, which relates to the relationship between the undertaking and the Member State in which it is established, requires that the latter habitually carries out significant activities in the territory of that Member State".[322] In these lines, a fundamental difference between fraud and abuse emerged. As far as abuse is concerned, the objective element consists of the fact that despite the formal observance of the rules, their purpose has not been achieved. In *Altun*, there was no formal observance of the rules. The Bulgarian firms involved in the arrangement had no significant activities in Bulgaria, which meant that the second condition to obtain an E 101 certificate was not met. Hence, the objective element of fraud differs from the objective element of abuse. It consists of a misrepresentation of reality, for example, by means of a false statement. Or, as the Court put it, "by means of a representation of facts which did not reflect the reality of the situation".[323] From this perspective, it bears noting that in a later ruling concerning fraudulently obtained E 101 certificates, the Court clarified that the objective element could "result from a deliberate action, such as the misrepresentation of the real situation of the worker or of the undertaking employing that worker, or from a deliberate omission, such as the concealment of relevant information".[324]

As regards the subjective element, the Court held that it corresponded with the "intention of the parties concerned to evade or circumvent the conditions for the issue of that certificate, with a view to obtaining the advantage attached to it".[325] This is also different from the subjective element of abuse, which consists of the intention to obtain an advantage from EU rules by artificially creating the conditions for obtaining it (or, in some areas of EU law, by carrying out a transaction whose essential aim is to obtain an advantage deriving from EU law). When it comes to

---

[319] CJEU, *Criminal proceedings against Ömer Altun and Others*, Judgment of the Court, 6 February 2018, case C-359/16, ECLI:EU:C:2018:63, paras 12–24.

[320] Ibid., para 48.

[321] Ibid., para 51.

[322] Ibid., para 34.

[323] Ibid., para 58.

[324] CJEU, *Caisse de retraite du personnel navigant professionnel de l'aéronautique civile (CRPNPAC) v Vueling Airlines SA v Vueling Airlines SA and Jean-Luc Poignant*, Judgment of the Court, 2 April 2020, joined cases C-370/17 and C-37/18, ECLI:EU:C:2020:260, para 52.

[325] Ibid., para 52.

fraud, the parties involved were to have a very specific mental element, that is, the intent to evade or circumvent the rules, as the Court put it.

If it were established that the E 101 certificates had indeed been obtained fraudulently in the sense clarified above and that the authorities of the issuing Member State had failed to take into account the results of investigations such as those carried out by the Belgian authorities—which was for the referring court to verify in the light of the facts submitted to it—the ECJ concluded that such certificates could be disregarded by the authorities of the Member State to which the workers were posted.[326]

The *Altun* ruling is another landmark for the purpose of this book for at least two reasons. First, it confirmed an impression that had already emerged in previous cases concerning fraud, namely that fraud is a specific manifestation of abuse, to which the relevant case law applies, as well as a specific variation of the abuse test. Secondly, it clarified for the first time that abuse and fraud are not one and the same thing. They are somehow similar but different. Like fraternal twins, they share a lot of chromosomes, yet they look different.[327]

3.4.4 Setting the Boundaries of the General Principle of Prohibition of Abuse of Law: The Contribution of (a New Wave of) Tax Evasion Cases

We have seen above that in the mid-2000s, the Court of Justice handed down, within a relatively short timeframe, several landmark rulings concerning tax evasion that can be considered watershed moments for the principle of abuse of Union law, particularly *Halifax* and *Cadbury Schweppes*. By the end of the second decade, a bit of a *déjà vu* occurred when the ECJ handed down a number of equally landmark rulings in the field of tax evasion within a similarly short timeframe.[328] The first two judgments, namely *N Luxembourg 1* and *Skatteministeriet*,[329] are the most significant. We will start from them, and since their contents are largely similar, if not identical, we will only focus on the first one.

N Luxembourg 1 is a typical tax case that is difficult for non-tax experts to fully comprehend. In short and crude terms, it concerned a Luxembourg company and three Danish companies that challenged the SKAT's (Danish tax authority) decisions denying them exemption from corporation tax under Directive 2003/49 for interest

[326] Ibid., para 59–60.

[327] For a different reading of the ruling, see Leczykiewicz 2019, p. 705, and pp. 737 ff.

[328] For a generally critical take on the recent ECJ's case law on tax evasion, see Vanistendael 2020, p. 17 ff.

[329] CJEU, *N Luxembourg 1 and Others v Skatteministeriet*, Judgment of the Court, 26 February 2019, joined cases C-115/16, C-118/16, C-119/16 and C-229/16, ECLI:EU:C:2019:134; CJEU, *Skatteministeriet v T Danmark and Y Denmark Aps*, Judgment of the Court, 26 February 2019, joined cases C-116/16 and C-117/16, ECLI:EU:C:2019:135.

paid to entities in other Member States, arguing that these entities were mere conduit companies and not the beneficial owners of the interest. The issue involved complex financial structures set up by the group to benefit from Directive 2003/49, which requires the interest recipient to meet certain conditions. The national court referred various questions to the ECJ. We will focus on the applicability of abuse of rights.[330]

As became usual after the *Cussens* ruling, the Court of Justice started by recalling "that there is, in EU law, a general legal principle that EU law cannot be relied on for abusive or fraudulent ends".[331] According to settled case law, EU law does not cover fraudulent or abusive transactions. That is, they fall outside its scope.[332] Just like in *Cussens*, the Court went on to list areas of EU law where the principle is applicable, this time providing a much longer list than in the previous ruling. In the case at hand, it referred to, in this order, free movement of goods, freedom to provide services, public service contracts, freedom of establishment, company law, social security, transport, social policy, restrictive measures and VAT.[333] The Court then further and unequivocally reaffirmed that abuse of Union law, as a general principle, prevails over "domestic or agreement-based provisions required for the prevention of fraud or abuse".[334] In other words, the existence of a specific anti-abuse clause in domestic law cannot exclude the application of the general principle of EU law, provided that the "transactions [at issue] constitute an abuse of rights [that] fall[s] within the scope of EU law [...] and could prove incompatible with the objective pursued by [EU law]".[335]

The *N Luxembourg 1* ruling is particularly relevant for two additional reasons. First, in it, the Court of Justice provided arguably the most extensive guidance to the referring court on how to establish the existence of the constitutive elements of abuse, with a special focus on the subjective one, which was defined as "the intention to obtain an advantage from the EU rules by artificially creating the conditions laid down for obtaining it".[336] This is a formulation that the Court has rarely employed, after *Emsland-Stärke*, in cases involving legal persons whose "intention" is clearly

[330] See *N Luxembourg 1*, paras 27–79.

[331] Ibid., para 96.

[332] Ibid., para 97.

[333] Ibid., para 100.

[334] Ibid., para 104.

[335] Ibid.

[336] Ibid., para 124.

more challenging to establish.[337] In other words, the Court made an effort to typify as much as possible the subjective element in the field of tax evasion.

The second additional relevant finding concerns the burden of proof. First, the Court stated that it is for the national authorities to establish "the existence of elements constituting [...] an abusive practice while taking account of all the relevant factors".[338] This statement can hardly be considered surprising since we already know that the Member States are usually precluded from applying general presumptions in this domain. However, the Court recognised that in some cases, because of the complexities of the case, especially in tax matters, the Member States cannot be required to adduce a sort of *probatio diabolica*. More specifically, it held that where the "complexity of certain financial arrangements and the possibility that the intermediary companies involved in the arrangements are established outside the European Union, the national tax authority [...] cannot be required to furnish evidence that would be impossible for it to provide".[339] In the case in point, it meant that it was unnecessary to prove the identity of the actual beneficial owners of the payments. It was sufficient to prove the existence of artificial arrangements, even if the ultimate beneficiary would get lost in the complex web of corporate transactions and its identity was difficult, if not impossible, to disclose. In general, it might mean that the burden to prove abuse, while certainly resting on the national authorities, is somehow attenuated in cases of abuse whereby the arrangements at issue are particularly intricate.

One final aspect deserves to be pointed out. It should be recalled that firstly in *Halifax*, but more emphatically in *RBS Deutschland*, the Court of Justice held that, as a general rule, where it is possible for the taxpayer to choose from among a number of transactions, she is free to choose to structure her business in such a way as to limit her tax liability. We have also seen that this was the Court's version of the liberal economic principle according to which tax motives are lawful motives. The Court repeated this statement of principle in *N Luxembourg 1*, although in a negative formulation. It stated that "the *right* of taxpayers to take advantage of competition engaged in by the

[337] In short, the Court held that an arrangement could be deemed artificial if set up without economic reality and aimed primarily to obtain a tax advantage. Indications included conduit companies interposed to avoid tax on interest, rapid pass-through of interest to entities not meeting the conditions set out in the relevant secondary legislation, and the arrangement having a purely formal structure. Furthermore, entities resident outside the EU or investment funds do not generally meet the conditions established by the relevant directive. If interest had been paid directly to them, the concerned Member State could levy withholding tax. Moreover, artificiality could be indicated by conduit companies passing interest to third parties without retaining a significant taxable profit. The absence of actual economic activity could be inferred from management, balance sheet, costs, staff, and equipment analysis. Indications could also include contracts between companies leading to intragroup fund flows aimed at tax avoidance, primarily if carried out close to a major change of the relevant tax legislation. Economic use of interest by conduit companies is another indication. In summary, taxation must reflect economic reality. Transactions carried out without any economic and commercial justification other than benefiting from tax exemptions constituted an abuse of rights not covered by EU law. Ibid., paras 126–136.

[338] Ibid., para 142.

[339] Ibid., para 143.

Member States on account of the lack of harmonisation of taxation of income cannot be raised against the application of the general principle that abusive practices are prohibited [...] where the transaction at issue is purely artificial".[340] While denying, in the case at hand, that the entities involved could take advantage of more favourable tax legislation because of the purely artificial nature of the transactions they carried out, the Court affirmed, at least in principle, the existence of a *right* to regulatory arbitrage in the EU legal order. This confirmed, if a confirmation was necessary, the ECJ's strong liberal approach to the issue of abuse in the common market.[341]

The next ruling is *Kuršu zeme*, a case concerning the payment of VAT on intra-Union acquisitions of goods. Without going into too much detail regarding the dispute in the main proceedings, suffice it to say that the Latvian company concerned was found to be knowingly involved in a chain of sham transactions. Still, the Latvian authorities were unable to establish that it had unduly obtained a tax advantage from the transactions in question. The Courtof Justice was, therefore, requested to clarify whether, in such circumstances, the granting of VAT deductions could be refused based on the principle of abuse of law.[342]

After recalling the constitutive elements of abuse, the ECJ held that the sole existence of a chain of sham transactions was not, in itself, ground for concluding that the company had put in place an artificial transaction whose essential purpose was to deduct VAT unduly. In other words, if no actual tax advantage had been obtained, the subjective element of abuse was not there.[343] Consequently, since the "tax authority has adduced no evidence demonstrating the existence of an abusive practice, the taxable person cannot be refused the right of deduction".[344]

The main takeaway of this ruling was that for the second constitutive element of abuse to be established, it was insufficient to prove the existence of fake transactions *per se*. Those transactions, on top of being sham ones, were to be specifically aimed at obtaining an undue advantage deriving from EU law (in the case at hand, VAT deductions). Only with this additional qualification could abuse of Union law be relied on. However, this did not mean that the transactions were necessarily legitimate. It simply meant that the prohibition of abuse of law was not the right instrument to be deployed against them.

The following ruling is *KrakVet*, which concerned the payment of VAT in a case of cross-border supply of goods. KrakVet was a Polish company selling products for animals primarily through its website, catering to Hungarian customers. Although it

---

[340] Ibid., paras 108–109 (emphasis added).

[341] But see the different reading of the ruling provided, again, by Leczykiewicz 2019, p. 737 ff., who claimed that *N Luxembourg 1* is not a further development coherent with the gradual construction of a general principle of abuse of EU law, but rather a graceful retraction to a narrower proposition that eventually leads the author to conclude that this new general principle is merely "putative" because "it is not possible for EU law to impose such a 'general principle'" (see Leczykiewicz 2019, pp. 741–742).

[342] CJEU, *SIA „Kuršu zeme' v Valsts ieņēmumu dienests*, Judgment of the Court, 10 July 2019, case C-273/18, ECLI:EU:C:2019:588, paras 21–30.

[343] Ibid., paras 32–37.

[344] Ibid., para 38.

lacked a physical presence in Hungary, KrakVet offered its Hungarian customers the option to contract a Polish transport company for delivery. It also allowed them to choose alternative carriers or pick up goods directly from KrakVet's warehouse. Due to uncertainty regarding what Member State was responsible for collecting VAT, KrakVet sought clarification from Polish tax authorities, who determined that the place of supply for VAT purposes was Poland. However, Hungarian tax authorities inspected KrakVet's activities, after which they demanded the company to pay additional VAT, penalties, and fines. KrakVet appealed the decision, bringing a dispute before Hungarian courts. The Administrative and Labour Court of Budapest decided to stay proceedings and seek clarification from the ECJ on whether KrakVet's practice could be regarded as abusive. The Hungarian court suspected that KrakVet had put in place an artificial arrangement to ensure that the place of supply, under the relevant secondary legislation, was Poland, which had a lower VAT rate, rather than Hungary, where the goods were dispatched.[345]

For the purpose of this book, the Court's answer is relevant for two reasons. Number one, it seized the opportunity to reaffirm that "in the sphere of VAT [...] where the taxable person has a choice between two transactions, he is not obliged to choose the one which involves paying the higher amount of VAT but, on the contrary, may choose to structure his business so as to limit his tax liability".[346] Number two, it clarified that the existence of a connection between the supplier and the transport company was not the decisive element to conclude that the arrangement was wholly artificial. It was necessary to prove that "the transport company recommended by the supplier at issue in the main proceedings did not carry out a genuine economic activity".[347]

Just like in *Kuršu zeme*, in *KrakVet* the Court denied the possibility of relying on abuse of law by narrowing down the circumstances in which a transaction could be considered artificial for the purpose of obtaining a tax advantage. In *Kuršu zeme*, it found that the existence of sham transactions was insufficient in itself. *KrakVet* was not even a case of sham transactions. It was, if anything, a case of clever business structuring that allowed the company concerned to lawfully reduce its tax liability, a possibility recognised by the Court time and again. The flip side of this case law was that it (further) demonstrated the tendency of the Member States' authorities to exploit reliance on abuse of Union law in the attempt to constrain the application of EU law and impose their own restrictive interpretation of EU rules. Put it differently, their attempts to abuse the doctrine of abuse.

---

345 CJEU, *KrakVet Marek Batko sp. K. v Nemzeti Adó- és Vámhivatal Fellebbviteli Igazgatósága*, Judgment of the Court, 18 June 2020, case C-276/18, ECLI:EU:C:2020:485, paras 26–40.

346 Ibid., para 90.

347 Ibid., para 95.

3.4.5 *The Application of the Principle of Abuse of Union Law in Horizontal Disputes*

So far, all cases analysed concerned a vertical situation, consisting of a natural or legal person relying on (mostly primary) EU law *vis-à-vis* a Member State with a view to circumventing national law or on (mostly secondary) EU law vis-à-vis the Member States' authorities with a view to (unduly) obtaining an advantage directly granted by EU rules. Examples of the first type of case are the foundational *Van Binsbergen* and the more recent *Polbud*; examples of the second type are the tax evasion cases examined in the previous section. The only exception so far was the *Kratzer* ruling (see Sect. 3.3.8), where an individual attempted to (abusively) rely on EU law against a company. In this section, we will examine three recent rulings concerning cases in which abuse of Union law was raised in a horizontal dispute, that is, in a dispute between two private parties.

Ellinika Nafpigeia concerned a Greek company privatised in 2002 with a no-redundancy clause not to reduce its workforce until September 2008. In 2006, it created a subsidiary called ETYE to handle rolling stock contracts, to which it seconded some of its employees. ETYE experienced significant financial difficulties and was eventually declared insolvent in 2010. The plaintiffs in the main proceedings were Ellinika Nafpigeia's former employees who sought to obtain a judicial declaration that they continued to be bound to it by contracts of employment of indefinite duration, arguing that the transfer of business from Ellinika Nafpigeia to ETYE was immaterial since the latter was not an autonomous organisational entity. The Greek Court of Cassation doubted that the transferor, the transferee or both had carried out an abuse and referred the question to the ECJ.[348]

After recalling that EU law could not be extended to cover abusive or fraudulent transactions and that the benefits of EU law had to be denied if abuse was established,[349] the Court of Justice gave some guidance to the referring court concerning possible indications of abuse in the case at hand. Particularly, it held that "[a] grouping of factors of production which tends, from the time of the transfer, to give rise to an imbalance between production inputs and outputs, and which thus may well lead to production being stifled and, gradually but inevitably, to the activity transferred ceasing to exist, not only cannot be regarded as complying with the requirement of stability but could in particular betray an *abusive intent* of the economic operators at issue in order to escape the adverse financial consequences connected with the future liquidation of the entity transferred which would normally have fallen on the transferor and which the transferee is not in position to assume".[350] As a consequence, if the referring court found that the general principle of abuse of EU law applied to

[348] CJEU, *Ellinika Nafpigeia AE v Panagiotis Anagnostopoulos and Others*, Judgment of the Court, 13 June 2019, case C-664/17, ECLI:EU:C:2019:496, paras 18–33.

[349] Ibid., paras 50–51.

[350] Ibid., para 56 (emphasis added).

the transactions carried out by the transferor and the transferee, the benefits deriving from EU rules concerning the transfer of undertakings had to be refused.[351]

For the purpose of this book, the main lesson drawn from *Ellinika Nafpigeia*, confirming the *Krazter* ruling, is that abuse of Union law can be invoked in horizontal relations and lead to the benefits of Union law being denied in the context of a dispute between two private parties if it is established that one of them has committed an abuse of the rules.

Mircom was the case of a company that brought a dispute against Telenet before a court in Antwerp, demanding Telenet disclose customer identification data used to share films from Mircom's catalogue using the BitTorrent client sharing software. Mircom tracked thousands of dynamic IP addresses using FileWatchBT software. Telenet, supported by two other Belgian internet access providers named Proximus NV and Scarlet Belgium NV, opposed the action. The referring court questioned whether the practice of automatic seeding, coupled with the fact that the copyright holder (Mircom) did not exploit those rights but only claimed damages from alleged infringers (it was, in short, a so-called "copyright troll"), constituted an abuse of the relevant EU rules.[352]

Even though in the questions referred there was no explicit mention of abuse, the ECJ correctly identified the question concerning copyright trolling as a question concerning "the existence of a possible abuse of rights by Mircom".[353] However, the Court did not say much in this respect, except that it was for the referring court to establish whether Mircom's action did not amount to a genuine attempt to combat intellectual property rights infringements under the relevant directive but was rather a mere attempt to extract economic revenue from the users it tracked. To do that, the national court had to take into account Mircom's overall operating method, which included an assessment, *inter alia*, of whether it actually brought legal proceedings in the event of a refusal to reach an amicable solution.[354]

For the purpose of this book, the relevance of *Mircom* lay in the finding that the principle of prohibition of abuse of Union law could, at least in principle, be invoked in a horizontal dispute between private parties in a field where it had never arisen before, that of intellectual property rights, and that if abuse existed—this was the unspoken but clear consequence of the Court's statements—the relevant EU rules could not be relied on by a copyright troll.

The last horizontal dispute in which the issue of abuse was raised is *UK and Others v Volkswagen Bank and Others*—where UK are the initials of an individual and not the abbreviation for United Kingdom. The facts of the case are as follows. A number of consumers in Germany concluded a credit agreement for the purchase of a vehicle with several automobile brands through their financial divisions, as is standard practice in the car market. The agreements featured several vaguely phrased

---

[351] Ibid., para 58.

[352] CJEU, *Mircom International Content Management & Consulting (M.I.C.M.) Limited v Telenet BVBA*, Judgment of the Court, 17 June 2021, case C-597/19, ECLI:EU:C:2021:492, paras 29–37.

[353] Ibid., para 78.

[354] Ibid., paras 94–95.

provisions, such as those concerning the late-payment interest rate, the arrangements for adjusting the rate of late-payment interest, and the conditions for termination by the creditor. After making regular payments, the consumers withdrew from the agreements, seeking repayment of the instalments already paid and a down payment made upon returning the vehicle. The companies refused to grant the withdrawal, arguing that it was out of time. The national court before which the dispute was brought had doubts about the interpretation of the applicable EU rules and referred to the ECJ.[355]

Under the relevant secondary legislation, consumers normally have a 14-day period to withdraw from a credit agreement, which had clearly elapsed in the case at hand. The crux of the matter was whether the withdrawal period had at all begun to elapse in consideration of the lack of some of the information that was to be included mandatorily in the agreement. If the 14-day period did not formally begin, the question was whether the right to withdraw could still be denied based on the general principle of abuse of Union law, thus considering such late withdrawal an abuse of rights. After recalling its relevant case law and the two constitutive elements of abuse, the Court of Justice held that "where a trader has failed to provide a consumer with the [relevant mandatory] information [...] and the consumer decides to withdraw from the credit agreement after the 14-day period following its conclusion, that trader cannot complain that the consumer has abused his or her right of withdrawal, even if a considerable length of time has elapsed between conclusion of that agreement and withdrawal by the consumer".[356] Although the ECJ did not say it explicitly, from this statement, we can infer that the abuse test failed on the first tier. Since the very purpose of the relevant secondary legislation is to dissuade traders from incorrect practices, the penalising effect of a late withdrawal was not contrary to the purpose of the rules—quite the opposite.

For the purpose of this book, *UK and Others v Volkswagen Bank and Others* is yet another confirmation of the general applicability of the principle of prohibition of abuse of Union law, even though, in the case at hand, the conditions for its application had not been fulfilled.

3.4.6 The Emergence of a New Trend? Recent Cases Concerning Abuse and Asylum

So far, the issue of abuse of Union law has been raised in cases regarding migration and asylum, but only in connection with the free movement of persons, primarily citizenship rights. That changed in 2021 when the Court of Justice handed down the

---

[355] CJEU, *UK and Others v Volkswagen Bank GmbH and Others*, Judgment of the Court, 9 September 2021, joined cases C-33/20, C-155/20 and C-187/20, ECLI:EU:C:2021:736, paras 22–63.

[356] Ibid., para 126.

KS and Others ruling, which is the first of two cases that will be examined in this section. They are both concerned with the rules on asylum.

KS and Others had to do with two third-country nationals who applied for international protection in Ireland. The Irish Refugee Applications Commissioner decided to transfer their applications to the UK under the Dublin III Regulation. Both individuals appealed unsuccessfully and initiated judicial review proceedings. Meanwhile, their application for permission to access the labour market was refused, leading to further appeals, all of which were dismissed. The referring court, therefore, wondered whether the delay caused by manifestly unfounded judicial action taken by the individuals concerned to challenge the relevant decisions constituted an abuse of rights.[357]

After recalling the two constitutive elements of abuse, the Court of Justice referred to its finding in *McCarthy,* holding that even if a Member State is faced with a high number of abuses and frauds, as the UK alleged in that case, it could not adopt measures of general prevention to combat abuse. To state otherwise "would mean that the mere fact of belonging to a particular group of persons would allow the Member States to refuse to recognise a right expressly conferred by EU law",[358] which the Court could not allow. Hence, no general presumption of abuse could be applied to individuals who activated the legal remedies foreseen by the law to challenge rejection decisions in the field of asylum.

A similar issue emerged in *Commission v. Hungary*. The case was an infringement procedure concerning, among other things, a provision of the Hungarian criminal code criminalising the organising activity of facilitating the lodging of an asylum procedure. According to the Commission, its wording was too vague and imprecise, affecting not only intentionally abusive or misleading activities but also lawful humanitarian assistance to asylum seekers. Hungary contested the Commission's view.[359]

After recalling, as usual, its case law on abuse of Union law, the Court of Justice noted that the criminal code criminalised whatever assistance was given, provided the individual who gave assistance was aware that the asylum seeker would not obtain refugee status under Hungarian law. That included assistance given with no intention to mislead the authorities. Such activity, concluded the Court, could not "be regarded as a fraudulent or abusive practice within the meaning of the case-law"[360] concerning the general principle of abuse of Union law. In other words, assistance given for the purpose of preparing an asylum application could not be considered

[357] CJEU, *KS and Others v The International Protection Appeals Tribunal and Others*, Judgment of the Court, 14 January 2021, joined cases C-322/19 and C-385/19, ECLI:EU:C:2021:11, paras 23–40.

[358] Ibid., para 92.

[359] CJEU, *European Commission v Hungary*, Judgment of the Court, 16 November 2021, case C-821/19, ECLI:EU:C:2021:930, paras 43–69.

[360] Ibid., para 117.

abuse under Union law even if the chances to obtain refugee status are slim or non-existent, provided that such assistance is not given with the intention of misleading the authorities.

With these two cases, the Court of Justice confirmed that the Member States can take measures to combat abuse in the field of asylum procedures. *KS and Others* is essentially an extension of the McCarthy case law to this field and yet another confirmation that the Member States cannot resort to general presumptive rules not based on an individualised, case-by-case assessment. *Commission v. Hungary*, on its part, is a healthy confirmation that the Member State's attempts to abuse the principle of abuse of do not make the cut (but also a confirmation of their tendency to give it a try).

3.4.7 Going Back to the Origins: Abuse of Law and the Free Movement of Goods

As we have seen above, one of the first judgments in which the Court stated that the fundamental freedoms could be abused was *Leclerc* (see Sect. 3.2.6), which concerned the free movement of goods. In that case, the Court held (if only implicitly) that the Member States could validly justify a restriction to this freedom on the need to combat abuse. In the *Companhia de Distribuição Integral Logística Portugal (CDILP)* ruling, the ECJ returned to this matter.

The case concerned CDILP, a tobacco retailer in Madeira, which declared its average monthly cigarette consumption from September 2009 to August 2010. On September 22, 2010, the Funchal customs office set a monthly limit of 1,644,005 cigarettes for CDILP. CDILP's request to exceed this limit was denied on January 7, 2011. CDILP declared a release of cigarettes exceeding the limit, incurring an additional excise duty. CDILP's challenge to the additional duty was dismissed by the Administrative and Tax Court, resulting in its appeal to the *Supremo Tribunal Administrativo*, arguing that the relevant Portuguese law was a restriction contrary to Article 34 TFEU and could not be justified under Article 36 TFEU. The national court decided to stay proceedings and refer the matter to the ECJ.[361]

Unsurprisingly, the Court found that the measure in question was a restriction to free movement of goods within the meaning of Article 34 TFEU. It then turned to assess whether such restriction could be justified. It observed that the measure was aimed at avoiding a situation in which, at a time when the rate of excise duty which will be applicable to cigarettes the following year is already known, the traders release them for consumption in order to build up large stocks of cigarettes on which excise duty is payable at a lower rate than that which would be applicable in the following year. The Court found that "the release for consumption in excessive quantities of

[361] CJEU, *CDILP – Companhia de Distribuição Integral Logística Portugal, SA v Autoridade Tributária e Aduaneira*, Judgment of the Court, 21 December 2023, case C-96/22, ECLI:EU:C:2023:1025, paras 15–29.

packets of cigarettes at the end of the year in anticipation of an increase in excise duty may constitute a form of abuse that the Member States are entitled to prevent by the appropriate measures".[362] Therefore, it concluded that the legislation was "appropriate for attaining the objectives of protecting public health and combating tax avoidance or abusive practices".[363]

CDILP did not innovate with respect to what the Court had already affirmed in its previous case law. It confirmed that when it comes to fundamental freedoms, the need to combat abuse is a valid reason to justify restrictions adopted by the Member States. The most interesting aspect of this ruling is that the ECJ's reasoning appeared much more linear and clearer compared to earlier ones, such as *Leclerc*. This is not at all surprising. Once it has been established unequivocally and conclusively that the prohibition of abuse of Union law is a general principle of the legal order, it is only logical that the Court of Justice is in a better place than it was in the pre-*Cussens* or, even more so, pre-*Emsland-Stärke* era.

3.4.8 Abuse of Union Law and the Insurance of Motor Vehicles: The Matmut *Ruling*

In the recent *Matmut* ruling, the issue of abuse of Union law arose in a new field, namely the secondary legislation concerning the insurance of motor vehicles. This case is at once an interesting development and a partial step back for the doctrine of abuse of Union law.

In 2012, PQ entered into a motor insurance contract with Matmut, a French insurer. He declared himself the sole driver of the insured vehicle, admittedly in order to obtain a lower premium. In 2013, the vehicle, driven by TN under the influence of alcohol, caused a road accident which injured PQ, who was a passenger in the insured vehicle. TN was criminally convicted for causing unintentional injuries while driving under the influence. Matmut obtained the annulment of the insurance contract based on the fact that PQ made an intentionally false statement about the usual driver's identity. On appeal, it was established that the nullity could not be invoked against PQ as a victim, even though he was the policyholder and had made the false statement. This finding was based on EU law and, more specifically, on the provisions of the so-called Motor Vehicle Insurance Directive (MVID).[364] The question was brought to the French *Cour de Cassation*, which asked the ECJ whether EU law allows insurance

[362] Ibid., para 39.

[363] Ibid., para 45.

[364] See Directive 2009/103/EC of the European Parliament and of the Council of 16 September 2009 relating to insurance against civil liability in respect of the use of motor vehicles, and the enforcement of the obligation to insure against such liability (Codified version), OJ L 263, 7 October 2009, pp. 11–31.

nullity to be enforced against a victim-policyholder who intentionally misrepresented facts when signing the insurance contract.[365]

This case is relevant for this book because both AG Szpunar and the ECJ discussed the issue of abuse of rights, even though the referring court had not raised the question. We will go back to the relevant part of the Advocate General's conclusions in Chap. 4.[366] In this section, we will focus on the Court's reasoning. The ECJ found that MVID allowed the invocation of a nullified contract against a victim only in the exceptional case that such a victim had "voluntarily entered [the] vehicle knowing that it had been stolen".[367] In all other cases, the relevant legislation did not release the insurer from its obligation to compensate.[368] After reaching this conclusion, the Court turned to examine whether the circumstance that the victim-policyholder had made false statements could be relevant under the doctrine of abuse of rights. The ECJ noted that MVID contained no express anti-abuse provision.[369] The absence of such a provision was not the end of the story, though, given that, in EU law, there is a "general legal principle that EU law cannot be relied on for abusive or fraudulent ends [which] must be complied with by individuals".[370] It recalled the well-established two constituent elements of abuse and provided guidance to the referring court on their application to the present case. The ECJ first concluded that the objective of MVID, which was to guarantee the protection of the victims of road accidents across the Union, had clearly been achieved. Thus, the existence of the first constitutive element of abuse was excluded.[371] Secondly, since the intention of the victim-policyholder was not to artificially obtain an advantage granted by EU law (in this case, the protection of MVID) but rather to obtain more favourable conditions from the insurer, the existence of the subjective element was also excluded.[372]

For the purpose of this book, two main considerations can be drawn from the *Matmut* ruling. First, it confirmed that the principle of prohibition of abuse of Union law is susceptible to being applied to horizontal disputes between private parties in all areas of EU law. Second, the already-mentioned confusion between abuse and fraud was regrettably reiterated. *Matmut* had to do with false statements made by the policyholder. Based on the case law examined above, this would suggest that it was a case of potential fraud rather than potential abuse. However, the ECJ applied the standard anti-abuse test, not an adaptation of it as it did, for example, in *Altun*.

---

[365] CJEU, *Mutuelle assurance des travailleurs mutualistes (Matmut) v TN and Others*, Judgment of the Court, 19 September 2024, case C-236/23, ECLI:EU:C:2024:761, paras 9–25.

[366] See Chap. 4, Sect. 4.3.

[367] See *Matmut*, para 46.

[368] Ibid., para 47.

[369] Ibid., para 50.

[370] Ibid., paras 51–52.

[371] Ibid., para 57.

[372] Ibid., paras 58–60.

AG Szpunar did the same in his conclusions.[373] This is lamentable, as will be further explained in Chap. 4.

3.5 Conclusions (a Postponement)

At the end of this rather long journey through the meandering case law of the Court of Justice on abuse of Union law, the terrain appears ready to lay down some foundations. This will be done in Chap. 4, where I will trace the boundaries of the principle of prohibition of abuse of Union law by providing a systematic appraisal of the rulings commented upon in this chapter.

The main features of the principle have clearly emerged in this chapter. In the next one, I will try to connect the dots through the relevant rulings and systematise (what currently looks like) a disordered picture. One consideration, however, can already be made here. In an article published in 2015, the current President of the Court wrote that in order to understand its case law, it is necessary to take a holistic approach to it, reading all the interconnected parts as a whole. In this way, what can, at first sight, look like an unorderly patchwork appears instead entirely logical. Koen Lenaerts was referring to the case law on citizenship rights. More specifically, he wrote that "[i]n order to fully apprehend the approach of the Court of Justice in an area of EU law, a critical observer should also read the relevant case predating as well as postdating that case […] A joint reading of *Rottmann*, *Ruiz Zambrano*, *McCarthy*, *Dereci*, *Lida*, *O and S*, *Ymeraga* and *Alokpa* shows that the legal reasoning of the ECJ is far from being laconic or cryptic. The sequence of these cases demonstrates that the new approach set out in Ruiz Zambrano has been built up progressively, i.e., on a 'stone-by-stone' basis".[374] It seems to me that the exact same words apply to the case law on the general principle of abuse of Union law, which was indeed, slowly but coherently, built up by the Court of Justice stone after stone.

References

Amand C (2008) Prohibition of Abusive Practices in European VAT: Court Aid to National Legislation Bugs? Intertax 36:189–200.

Arnull A (2011) What is a General Principle of EU Law? In: De la Feria R, Vogenauer S (eds) Prohibition of Abuse of Law. A New General Principle of EU Law? Hart Publishing, Oxford/Portland, pp. 7–23.

Ballarino T (2003) Les règles de conflit sur les sociétés commerciales à l'épreuve du droit communautaire d'établissement. Remarques sur deux arrêts récents de la Cour de justice des Communautés européennes. Revue critique de droit international privé 2:373–402.

Barnard C (2005) Of Students and Babies. The Cambridge Law Journal 64:560–563.

[373] CJEU, *Mutuelle assurance des travailleurs mutualistes (Matmut) v TN and Others*, Opinion of Advocate General Szpunar, 27 June 2024, case C-236/23, ECLI:EU:C:2024:560, paras 72–80.

[374] See Lenaerts 2015b, p. 9.

Bergamini E (2006) Il difficile equilibrio fra riconoscimento del diritto alla libera circolazione, rispetto della vita familiare e abuso del diritto. Il diritto dell'Unione Europea 11:347–368.
Bone RG (1997) Modeling Frivolous Suits. University of Pennsylvania Law Review 145:519–605.
Butler G, Sørensen KE (2022) The Prohibition of Abuse of EU Law: a Special General Principle. In: Ziegler K, Neuvonen PJ, Moreno-Lax V (eds) Research Handbook on General Principles in EU Law. Edward Elgar, Cheltenham, pp. 402–422.
Cabral P, Cunha P (2000) "Presumed Innocent": Companies and the Exercise of the Right of Establishment under Community Law. European Law Review 2:157–164.
Carbone SM (2011) Brevi riflessioni sull'abuso del diritto comunitario: commercio internazionale e esercizio delle libertà individuali. Diritto del commercio internazionale 25:67–83.
Cerioni L (2010) The "Abuse of Rights" in EU Company Law and EU Tax Law: A Re-reading of the ECJ Case Law and the Quest for a Unitary Notion. European Business Law Review 21:783–813.
Colavitti G (2013) Accesso alla professione forense e libertà di concorrenza: gli *abogados* italiani tra abuso del diritto europeo e libertà di stabilimento. La nuova giurisprudenza civile commentata 29:1047–1058.
Costello C (2009) *Metock*: Free Movement and "Normal Family Life" in the Union. Common Market Law Review 46:587–662.
Costello C (2011) Citizenship of the Union: Above Abuse? In: In: De La Feria R, Vogenauer S (eds) Prohibition of abuse of law: a new general principle of EU law? Hart, Oxford/Portland, pp. 321–353.
Crosby S (2006) Abuse and Intention in EU VAT Law: Gradual Adoption of a *Mens Rea* Test? Journal of European Criminal Law 1:37–48.
De La Feria R (2005) 'Game Over' for Aggressive VAT Planning?: RAL v. Commissioners of Customs & Excise. British Tax Review 4:394–401.
De la Feria R (2008) Prohibition of Abuse of (Community) Law: The Creation of a New General Principle of EC Law through Tax. Common Market Law Review 45:395–442.
De la Feria R (2020) On Prohibition of Abuse of Law as a General Principle of EU Law. EC Tax Review 29:142–146.
Di Federico G (2014) La libera circolazione degli avvocati nell'Unione europea, tra abuso del diritto e identità nazionale. Il caso degli *abogados* dinanzi alla Corte di giustizia. Diritto comunitario e degli scambi internazionali 53:553–572.
Douma S, Engelen F (2006) Halifax Plc and Others v. Commissioners of Customs & Excise: The ECJ Applies the Abuse of Rights Doctrine in VAT Cases. British Tax Review 5:429–440.
Ebke WF (2001) Centros - Some Realities and Some Mysteries. American Journal of Comparative Law 4: 623–660.
Edwards V (2000) Case-Law of the European Court of Justice on Freedom of Establishment after Centros. European Business Organization Law Review 1:147–155.
Eidenmüller H, Enriques L, Helleringer G, van Zwieten K (2019) Centros at 20: Regulatory Arbitrage and Beyond—An Introduction. European Business Organization Law Review 20:399–405.
Fortunato S (2000) La libertà di stabilimento delle società in una recente sentenza della Corte di giustizia: il caso CENTROS. Il Diritto dell'Unione europea 5:83–90.
Gelter M (2017) Centros, the Freedom of Establishment for Companies and the Court's Accidental Vision for Corporate Law. In: Nicola F, Davies B (eds) EU Law Stories. Contextual and Critical Histories of European Jurisprudence. Cambridge University Press, Cambridge, pp. 309–337.
Gestri M (2000) Mutuo riconoscimento delle società comunitarie, norme di conflitto nazionali e frode alla legge: il caso "Centros". Rivista di diritto internazionale 83:71–112.
Gestri M (2003) Abuso del diritto e frode alla legge nell'ordinamento comunitario. Giuffrè, Milan.
Handoll J (2010) EUDO Citizenship Observatory. Country Report: Ireland. Available here: https://cadmus.eui.eu/bitstream/handle/1814/19618/ReportIreland_2010_22.pdf?sequence=1&isAllowed=y.
Harbo TI (2010) The Function of the Proportionality Principle in EU Law. European Law Journal 16:158–185.

Hoenjet F (1997) The Leur-Bloem Judgement: the Jurisdiction of the European Court of Justice and the Interpretation of the Anti-Abuse Clause in the Merger Directive. EC Tax Review 6:206–215.
Ionescu RN (2012) L'abus de droit en droit de l'Unione européenne. Bruylant, Brussels.
Kamanabrou S (2018) Abuse of Law in the Context of EU Law. European Law Review 43:534–548.
Kjellgren A (2002) On the Border of Abuse: The Jurisprudence of the European Court of Justice on Circumvention, Fraud and Abuses of EU Law. In: Andenas A, Roth WH (eds) Services and Free Movement in EU Law. Oxford University Press, Oxford, pp. 245–278.
Kochenov D, Lindeboom J (2017) Breaking Chinese Law - Making European One. The Story of Chen, or Two Winners, Two Losers, Two Truths. In: Nicola F, Davies B (eds) EU Law Stories. Contextual and Critical Histories of European Jurisprudence. Cambridge University Press, Cambridge, pp. 201–223.
Lauterfeld M (2001) "Centros" and the EC Regulation on Insolvency Proceedings: The End of the "Real Seat" Approach towards Pseudo-foreign Companies in German International Company and Insolvency Law? - The Danger of Diverging Developments of the Connecting Factors in Company and Insolvency Law. European Business Law Review 12:79–88.
Leczykiewicz D (2019) Prohibition of Abusive Practices as a "General Principle" of EU Law. Common Market Law Review 56:703–742.
Lenaerts K (2015a) The Concept of Abuse of Law in the Case Law of the European Court of Justice on Direct Taxation. Maastricht Journal of European and Comparative Law 22:329–351.
Lenaerts K (2015b) EU Citizenship and the European Court of Justice's 'Stone-by-Stone' Approach. International Comparative Jurisprudence 1:1–10.
Leopold PM (1982) Community Law-Making: Opinions of the European Parliament. Oxford Journal of Legal Studies 2:454–459.
Lettieri N (2014) L'abuso del diritto in ambito internazionale e comunitario (il dialogo delle Corti di Lussemburgo e Strasburgo). In: Lettieri N, Marini G, Merone G (eds) L'abuso del diritto nel dialogo tra corti nazionali ed internazionali. Edizioni scientifiche italiane, Naples, pp. 62–143.
Lowe V (1999) Overlapping Jurisdiction in International Tribunals. Australian Yearbook of International Law 20:191–204.
Mastroianni R, Arena A (2015) Free Movement of Lawyers and the European Court of Justice, Grand Chamber Judgment of 17 July 2014, Joined Cases C-58/13 and C-59/13. European Constitutional Law Review 11:373–388.
Munari F, Terrile P (2001) The Centros Case and the Rise of and EC Market for Corporate Law. Il Diritto dell'Unione Europea 6:1–38.
Neville Brown L (1994) Is There a General Principle of Abuse of Rights in European Community Law? In: Curtin D, Heukels T (eds) Institutional Dynamics of European Integration. Essays in Honour of Henry G. Schermers. Martinus Nijhoff, Dordrecht/Boston/London, pp. 511–525.
Neville Brown L (1994), Joined Cases C-181/91and C-248/91, European Parliament v Council and Commission, Judgment of 30 June, [1993] ECR 1–3685. Common Market Law Review 31:1347–1355.
Nic Shuibhne N (2002) Free Movement of Persons and the Wholly Internal Rule: Time to Move on? Common Market Law Review 39:731–771.
Richelle I, Schön W, Traversa E (eds) (2025) Abuse of Law in European Taxation. Springer, Berlin.
Roth WH (2000) Case C-212/97, Centros Ltd v. Erhvervs- og Selskabsstyrelsen, Judgment of 9 March 1999. Full Court. Common Market Law Review 37:143–151.
Saydé A (2016) Abuse of EU Law and Regulation of the Internal Market. Hart Publishing, Oxford/Portland.
Smith LJ (1994) Postgraduate Degrees, Vocational Training and Reverse Discrimination: the Narrow Divide. European Law Review 19:65–75.
Sørensen KE (2006) Abuse of Rights in Community Law: A Principle of Substance or Merely Rhetoric. Common Market Law Review 43:423–460.
Tridimas T (2006) The General Principles of EU Law. Oxford University Press, Oxford.

Tridimas T (2009) Abuse of Right in EU Law: Some Reflections with particular Reference to Financial Law. Queen Mary University of London, School of Law Legal Studies Research Paper No. 27/2009.
Tridimas T (2018) The Principle of Proportionality. In: Schutze R, Tridimas T (eds) Oxford Principles of European Union Law. Oxford University Press, Oxford, pp. 243–264.
Tryfonidou A (2005) C-200/02, Kunqian Catherine Zhu and Man Lavette Chen v. Secretary of State for the Home Department: Further Cracks in the "Great Wall" of the European Union? European Public Law 11:527–541.
Van den Hurk H (1999) The European Court of Justice Knows its Limits (A discussion inspired by the Gilly and ICI Cases). EC Tax Review 8:211–223.
Vanistendael F (2020) From Abuse to Base Erosion, How did it Come to This? In: Haslehner W, Pantazatou K, Kofler G, Rust A (eds) A Guide to the Anti-Tax Avoidance Directive. Edward Elgar, Cheltenham, pp. 1–31.
Van Riemsdijk M (2013) Obstacles to the Free Movement of Professionals: Mutual Recognition of Professional Qualifications in the European Union. European Journal of Migration and Law 15:47–68.
Vinther N, Werlauff E (2006) Tax Motives Are Legal Motives - The Borderline between the Use and Abuse of the Freedom of Establishment with Reference to the Cadbury Schweppes Case. European Taxation 46:383–387.
Vitale G (2009) La libertà di stabilimento degli avvocati. In: Barcellona P (ed) La società europea. Identità, simboli, politiche. Giappichelli, Turin, pp. 541–549.
Weatherhill S (2011) Fitting "Abuse of Rights" into EU Law Governing the Free Movement of Goods and Services. In: De La Feria R, Vogenauer S (eds) Prohibition of abuse of law: a new general principle of EU law? Hart, Oxford/Portland, pp. 49–62.
Weber D (2013) Abuse of Law in European Tax Law: An Overview and Some Recent Trends in the Direct and Indirect Tax Case Law of the ECJ - Part 2. European Taxation 53:313–328.
Woods L (2021) Article 54. In: Peers S, Hervey T, Kenner J, Ward A (eds) The EU Charter of Fundamental Rights. A Commentary. Hart Publishing, Oxford/Portland, pp. 1692–1708.

Chapter 4
The Scope of Application of the Principle of Abuse of Law in the EU Legal Order

Contents

Abstract This chapter distils the key insights from the case law on abuse of Union law, organising them into a coherent and logical framework to clarify the nature and scope of this general principle within the EU legal order. It defines abuse of law as a "special" general principle, explaining the reasons behind this. It also provides a typology of abuse of Union law and examines its interaction with other principles, as well as with secondary legislation. As a core part of the monograph, it presents several significant conclusions while also drawing attention to a number of questions that remain open to debate.

Keywords Abuse of Union law · Scope of application · General principle of EU law · Special general principle · Fraud · Article 50 TEU

4.1 Introduction

In the previous chapter, we conducted a thorough review of the relevant case law of the Court of Justice on abuse of Union law. As pointed out in the closing section of that chapter, the analysis allowed us to formulate a preliminary conclusion. Namely, as it happened with the case law relating to other areas of EU law, the build-up of the general principle that abuse of (Union) law is prohibited has been steady but

L. Pantaleo, *Abuse of Law in the European Union*,
https://doi.org/10.1007/978-94-6265-731-1_4

slow. Considering *Van Binsbergen* the point of departure in which the Court dealt for the first time with an abusive practice, and *Cussens* the point of arrival in which the Court unequivocally clarified its nature of a general principle of EU law, it took more than 40 years to complete the journey. A journey that is not entirely over since several aspects still need to be clarified. The purpose of this chapter is to provide an appraisal of the case law to systematise it in a coherent framework, shedding light on the scope of application of the principle as well as on the remaining grey areas.

Before getting started with the examination, a terminological clarification appears apposite. We have already mentioned in Chap. 3 that the Court of Justice has had some issues when it comes to the language employed in connection with abuse. Over the years, it has resorted to a variety of expressions, such as improper use, abusive practices, abuse of rights, circumvention, etc.[1] However, since the beginning of the third and final phase of the case law, which we have termed the consolidation stage, the ECJ seems to have settled on one expression, namely, that a general principle that abusive practices are prohibited exists in EU law. So far, I have used a number of expressions, most often the principle of abuse of Union law or the principle of prohibition of abuse of Union law. From now on, and for the remainder of this book, I will primarily use positive expressions which do not feature the negative "prohibition". Hence, I will only refer to a general principle of abuse of law, abuse of Union law,[2] or abuse of EU law. This is not just a mere professorial rumination. Words are important. The concept of abuse already implies a denial. When abuse is found in a given situation in any legal order that admits the existence of abuse of law/rights,[3] the consequence of such a finding is that the right/legal entitlement holder is normally not allowed to exercise that right or to rely on that legal entitlement. In other words, s/he is prohibited from using a right that would normally exist and being able to exercise it in a legally acceptable manner. Therefore, including the word "prohibition" creates, in my opinion, a double negative that unnecessarily weighs down the concept. To be sure, this is merely a linguistic choice, a semantic preference. It is in no way meant to distance me from the Court of Justice, which prefers to speak of the prohibition of abuse of law.

The chapter will unfold as follows. Section 4.2 will deal with the legal nature of abuse as a general principle of EU law. In this part, a number of sub-questions will be examined, such as the difference between fraud and abuse and the (partial) analogy

[1] In my view, there is no (at least intended) difference between these expressions, which the Court has used freely and interchangeably for no underlying fundamental conceptual reason. This was also the opinion submitted by AG Bobek in the *Cussens* case. See CJEU, *Cussens*, Opinion of Advocate General Bobek, 7 September 2017, case C-251/16, ECLI:EU:C:2017:648, paras 23–31, a part meaningfully titled "Terminological note". However, see the discussion in Leczykiewicz 2019, p. 734 ff., who submitted that the expressions are conceptually different and that the Court purposefully uses one or another depending on whether it intends to endorse a narrower or broader proposition of abuse, as the case may be. It should not be forgotten that this author argued against the existence of a unitary notion of abuse of EU law as a general principle.

[2] Which, by the way, was also the option preferred by AG Bobek. See CJEU, *Cussens*, Opinion of Advocate General Bobek, para 26.

[3] For a discussion of the different legal traditions, see Chap. 2.

between (some) cases of abuse and the situations dealt with in the *Keck* case law. Section 4.3 will systematise abuse into two main types, corresponding with the two most recurring situations in which abuse has manifested itself in the EU legal order. Section 4.4 will discuss how the principle in question applies to different areas of EU law in an attempt to point out similarities and differences. Section 4.5 will address the role of secondary legislation. In this part, some reflections on the general role of harmonisation in connection with abuse will be made. Section 4.6 will analyse the questions that are still open and the challenges that remain unresolved in light of the current state of development of the case law. Section 4.7 will provide a summary and proffer some conclusions.

4.2 Abuse of Law as a General Principle of EU Law

After examining the abundant case law on the matter, there is no doubt that abuse of law constitutes a general principle of EU law. Yet, it has some specificities that distinguish it from a "normal" general principle, which is why Butler and Sørensen have defined it as a "special general principle". This section will explore why and to what extent it is special.

Before doing that, a quick summary of what is a general principle of EU law is apposite. This is clearly not the place to engage in a comprehensive discussion of a topic on which much ink has already been spilt. For the purpose of this book, it is sufficient to refer to the existing scholarship. Although general principles are often categorised in different ways in the literature, we will draw on the work of a few prominent authors. A general principle is first and foremost general in the sense that it "transcends specific areas of law and underlie the legal system as a whole".[4] It is different from a concrete rule because it provides justification for its existence.[5] In EU law, the origins of general principles lie outside the EU legal order: in formulating them, "the Court of Justice draws on two main sources: (a) the national laws and constitutional traditions of the Member States; and (b) international treaties signed by the Member States".[6] The extrapolation of unwritten general principles from the laws of the Member States resembles, to a certain extent, the development of the common law by the English courts.[7] However, it should be pointed out that when the Court looks for guidance in the legal orders of the Member States, it does not search for the lowest common denominator.[8] Moreover, once a general principle enters the Union legal order, "it acquires a life of its own independent of its domestic forebears".[9] General principles of EU law typically perform two functions:

[4] See Tridimas 2006, p. 1.
[5] See Dworkin 1994, p. 24 ff.
[6] See Arnull 2011, pp. 7–8, as well as Cannizzaro 2022, pp. 238 ff.
[7] See Tridimas 2006, p. 5.
[8] See Arnull 2011, p. 9.
[9] Ibid.

first, they are interpretive instruments of written primary and secondary law, and second, they are grounds for review of Member States' measures as well as secondary legislation, both directly and indirectly, through Article 263 TFEU and Article 267 TFEU, respectively.[10] A non-exhaustive list includes legal certainty, proportionality, non-discrimination, the rule of law and respect for fundamental rights *lato sensu*.[11] They are sometimes divided into structural and substantive ones.[12] However, opinions differ on such categorisations.[13]

In light of this brief overview of the general principles of EU law, we can now assess how abuse of Union law features the attributes discussed above and to what extent it differs from the archetypical general principle. To be sure, one cannot apply a sort of checklist approach to the assessment of a general principle of EU law. That said, it does seem that the principle of abuse of Union law features most of the typical characteristics of general principles of EU law. The discussion in the previous chapter has demonstrated that it has been applied to a wide variety of areas of EU law and seems fit to apply to all areas of EU law.[14] This does not mean that it applies precisely the same way across the legal order.[15] On the contrary, the analysis evidenced that there are differences even in similar fields, as is the case with the different fundamental freedoms. However, despite these differences, it cannot be denied that it underlies the legal system as a whole, to borrow from Takis Tridimas. In principle, the abuse test developed by the Court of Justice is susceptible to be applied to the exercise of any rights derived by EU law. However, in some areas, such as the free movement of persons, it is more challenging to establish that a right has been exercised abusively.

As regards the second attribute, it seems reasonable to affirm that the principle of abuse of Union law developed by the Court of Justice provides justification for the existence of various specific EU rules that are designed to directly or indirectly combat abuse. Put differently, the many anti-abuse clauses foreseen in EU secondary law are a direct or indirect expression of the general principle that Union law cannot be used for abusive ends. We have dealt with some of these *ad hoc* provisions quite closely in Chap. 3, such as Article 35 of the Citizenship Directive. But there are many other anti-abuse clauses, all of which mirror the general principle in a more or less specific way.

Furthermore, the analysis in Chap. 2 has evidenced that many legal systems of the Member States feature a legal notion that is expressive of the same principle, although it can be said that in the EU legal order, the principle of abuse of law has

---

[10] See Tridimas 2006, pp. 29–35. In Chap. 5, we will go back to the question of the functions of general principles, with a special focus on the principle of abuse of law.

[11] See Arnull 2011, p. 7.

[12] See Walker 2015, pp. 17–18.

[13] See, for example, the different categorisation proposed by Neuvonen and Ziegler 2022, p. 9 ff, or by Strozzi and Mastroianni 2023, pp. 207 ff.

[14] Except, perhaps, the Common Foreign and Security Policy, which is an area where the relevance of the principle appears less evident.

[15] See *infra*, Sect. 4.4.

acquired a life of its own, to borrow from Anthony Arnull. This chapter will attempt to demonstrate exactly that. Therefore, it can be affirmed that, at least conceptually, the origins of abuse of Union law can be traced back to the national laws and constitutional traditions of the Member States. However, as is often the case with general principles, the Court has never explicitly grounded abuse of Union law on the doctrine of abuse taken from one or more specific Member State legal orders. According to Paul Craig, this can be explained by the fact that the normative foundations of general principles, although drawn from national legal orders, are, in reality, to be found in the Treaties.[16] For these reasons, general principles of Union law are perhaps the strongest expression of judge-made law in the Union legal order,[17] and abuse of Union law appears to be no exception to this.

The last attribute mentioned above concerns the two functions performed by general principles of EU law. To begin with, it must be emphasised that the functions performed by general principles should not be understood as conditions for their existence. That said, there is no doubt that abuse of Union law can serve as an interpretive tool of both primary and secondary law. This is probably its principal function. The issue of abuse of law as an interpretive tool will be further discussed in Sect. 4.3. For now, it is sufficient to recall the case law analysed in Chap. 3, where we have seen that in cases of abuse of rights deriving from secondary legislation, the general principle in question was used by the Court of Justice to narrow down the scope of application of the rules so as not to cover abusive practices. Hence, abuse of law was a means to restrict the scope of application of the rules by way of interpretation. The second function of general principles, that is, their ability to constitute grounds for invalidity of secondary law, will be further discussed in Sects. 4.4, 4.5 and 4.6 below. For now, suffice it to say that the Court has repeatedly used abuse of Union law as a compatibility standard of Member States measures designed to (admittedly) combat abuse. Furthermore, as will be demonstrated in Sect. 4.5, there is no reason to exclude that it can also perform the function of ground for invalidity in order to annul acts adopted by the EU institutions, as any other general principle of EU law.

The analysis above confirms that abuse of Union law features all the attributes one can usually find in a general principle of EU law, as repeatedly affirmed in the most recent case law on the matter. It remains to be seen how and to what extent it differs from other general principles. In order to understand the differences, it is necessary to go back to the very origins of general principles as an autonomous source of EU law. It is undeniable that they emerged as instruments designed to protect individuals. The Court of Justice first employed them in the early staff cases litigated in the 60s.[18] Most importantly, they represented the solution that allowed the Court to

---

[16] See Craig 2022, p. 26 ff.

[17] As recognised by this prominent author. See Craig 2022, pp. 38–39, but also Strozzi and Mastroianni 2023, p. 205, who use the expression judge-made legislation (*legislazione giurisprudenziale*, in the Italian original).

[18] See Tridimas 2006, p. 7.

recognise that the fundamental rights of individuals were binding on the Union's institutions,[19] thus alleviating the pressure that was mounting from national constitutional courts, particularly the German *Bundesverfassungsgericht*, which culminated with the formulation of the so-called *Solange* doctrine.[20] The circumstance that general principles usually serve the ultimate purpose of protecting individual rights is the main reason Anthony Arnull maintained that abuse of Union law does not possess the features of a general principle of law. In particular, he argued that "the prohibition of abuse does not protect the rights enjoyed by private parties under Union law but deprives them of advantages it would otherwise confer on them. It is typically (albeit not invariably) invoked by the administration. Unlike established general principles, the prohibition of abuse does not therefore operate as a principle of administrative law. It does not contribute to that aspect of the rule of law which requires the exercise of public power to be subject to review by the courts".[21] Butler and Sørensen also recognised that "the general principle of the prohibition of abuse of EU law is used to the opposite effect [compared to other general principles, namely] to take rights *away* from individuals".[22] However, for these authors this attribute is not an obstacle in the recognition of its nature of general principle, it is instead "what makes it special".[23]

Anthony Arnull wrote those lines before the Court of Justice handed down the landmark rulings that unequivocally clarified that abuse of law is a general principle of EU law. His position was entirely reasonable and tenable at that time. However, in light of the most recent developments, it is difficult to disagree with the idea that abuse of law is a general principle of a special nature. It is special because, on top of featuring the attributes traditionally associated with general principles, it also has an additional one: it limits the action of natural and legal persons seeking to (abusively) rely on Union law not only in (inversely) vertical situations (that is, *vis-à-vis* the administration, as pointed out by Arnull), but also in horizontal situations (that is, *vis-à-vis* other private actors). This horizontal dimension of abuse of Union law is more closely connected with the civil law tradition of abuse of rights, which is rooted in the Roman law notion of *aemulatio*. As will be argued in Chap. 5, abuse of Union law is susceptible to shedding new light on general principles of EU law, as it signals the realisation on the part of the ECJ that the European integration process can be jeopardised (also) by the conduct of individuals that are willing to exploit EU rules abusively. We will go back to this reasoning in the next chapter.

Before turning to the next section, it is worth addressing the question of whether the principle of abuse of EU law should be regarded as a structural principle of the Union's legal order. A widely accepted definition and typology of structural principles

[19] See CJEU, *Internationale Handelsgesellschaft*, Judgment of the Court, 17 December 1970, case 11/70, ECLI:EU:C:1970:114.

[20] See Claes 2015, pp. 179 ff. For a thorough analysis of the role of general principles in the protection of fundamental rights see Amalfitano 2018, *passim*.

[21] See Arnull 2011, pp. 20–21.

[22] See Butler and Sørensen 2022, p. 412 (emphasis in the original).

[23] Ibid.

is provided in the work of Marise Cremona.[24] Although her analysis focuses primarily on EU external relations law, her framework is nonetheless applicable to principles without an obvious external dimension, such as abuse of law. If structural principles are understood as those principles that are "defining and [...] inherent to the deep structure of the EU",[25] that is, its constitutional architecture, it is reasonable to argue that the principle of abuse of Union law falls within this category. The remainder of this book, more specifically Chap. 5, will further develop and substantiate this argument.

4.2.1 *The Prohibition of Fraud as a General Principle of EU Law*

We have seen in Chap. 3 a number of cases in which the Court of Justice has dealt with fraud. The idea that fraud is also prohibited by a general principle of Union law clearly emerged from that case law. In this section, we will attempt a systematisation of the Court's findings concerning fraud, with a special focus on its relation to abuse.

To begin with, the Court has referred to fraud and abuse together in almost all cases concerning fraud, while the opposite is not true: in many cases clearly concerning abuse, and not fraud, the latter was not mentioned. From this circumstance, we concluded in Chap. 3 that fraud is a specific manifestation of abuse, just like abuse of process is a specific form of abuse of law. They display different characteristics, yet they have the same DNA. Abuse is the genus, and fraud is the species. Or, put differently, abuse is the basic underlying principle from which fraud is an offspring.

What are the differences between fraud and abuse? There is one overarching difference. Abuse arises in situations where the law has been formally respected. No formal infringement of the rules has been perpetrated in cases of abuse. Conversely, fraud is premised on a false representation of reality, which can be actively or passively engendered by an action or omission, respectively. A typical fraudulent action is the forging of documents, creating an appearance of formal legality of a set of facts or circumstances that are, in reality, not in conformity with the law. A typical fraudulent omission is the concealing of legally relevant circumstances or facts that, if known, would not trigger the legal protection of the rules invoked. Examples of the two types of fraud are the *Altun* and *CRPNPAC* cases analysed in Sect. 3.4.3 of Chap. 3.

Despite this fundamental difference, the Court of Justice has almost invariably referred to fraud and abuse interchangeably. In the early cases, such as *Könecke* and *Boterlux*, this joint reference was somewhat casual: the Court would typically not elaborate on their relation. In the most recent case law, however, the Court has repeatedly proclaimed the existence of a general principle prohibiting both fraud

---

[24] See Cremona 2020, pp. 11 ff.

[25] Ibid., p. 15.

and abuse.[26] This cannot be considered a coincidence. In so doing, the ECJ has deliberately and willingly taken a position concerning the relation between these two concepts, whose "logical consequence is that fraud should not be handled by a different general principle, but rather, the general principle of the prohibition of abuse of EU law *also* covers prevention of fraud".[27] From a conceptual perspective, if fraud is a specific manifestation of abuse, as it seems to emerge from the case law, the Court's position is entirely sensible. However, as developed in *Emsland-Stärke* and adjusted over time, the abuse test appears unfit to detect fraud cases because of the fundamental difference between fraud and abuse, as clarified above. As we have seen in the previous chapter, the Court has managed to adapt the abuse test to fraud in *Altun* and *CRPNPAC*. It is helpful to recall what the ECJ said about the two-tiered abuse test in these two rulings.

As regards the objective element of fraud, the Court of Justice stated that it consisted of the fact that the conditions for obtaining the protection of EU law were not formally met. This is different from the first constitutive element of abuse, whereby the formal observance of the law is not disputed. As regards the subjective element, the Court held that it corresponded with the intention of the parties to evade or circumvent the conditions set out in EU law to obtain the advantage granted by it. This is also different from the subjective element of abuse, which consists of the intention to obtain an advantage from EU rules by artificially creating the conditions for obtaining it (or, alternatively, by carrying out a transaction whose essential aim is to obtain an advantage deriving from EU law). When it comes to fraud, the Court established that the parties involved were to have a very specific mental element, that is, the intent to evade or circumvent the rules. Regrettably, the same distinctions have not been made in the more recent *Matmut* ruling, which was also a case of potential fraud rather than abuse.

Despite this last, partially contradictory precedent, it seems reasonable to conclude that while abuse and fraud are covered by the same general principle of EU law, they are subject to a similar yet different detection test. In both cases, the assessment aims to verify the existence of an objective and a subjective element. However, these two constitutive elements are fundamentally different, reflecting the fundamental difference between fraud and abuse that was pointed out above. For these reasons, the abuse test, as coined in *Emsland-Stärke,* is unfit for fraud and vice versa.

4.3 Abuse of Union Law: A Typology

We have seen in the previous chapter that abuse of Union law has manifested itself in many different areas and contexts and has taken three main forms: abuse of law proper, abuse of process and fraud. Leaving aside abuse of process and fraud, which

[26] The Court has phrased the general principle in these terms in *Altun*, *CRPNPAC*, and *N Luxembourg 1*.

[27] See Butler and Sørensen 2022, p. 411 (italics in the original text).

are specific manifestations of the same general legal phenomenon, it is reasonable to affirm that the manifestation of abuse of Union law (proper) ultimately comes down to two main contexts: (a) where a natural or legal person attempts to circumvent national law by relying on EU law, and (b) where a natural or legal person attempts to abusively (that is, in a manner that contrasts with its purpose) rely on EU law to obtain an undue advantage.[28] In brief, it seems reasonable to affirm that there are only two main types of abuse. Interestingly, two Advocate Generals have expressly endorsed this construction in almost identical terms. One is AG Maduro in his much-celebrated Opinion in *Halifax*;[29] the other is AG Szpunar in *Matmut*.[30] Although the Court of Justice has never endorsed this distinction, it has employed two different anti-abuse strategies depending on the type of abuse at stake. For the sake of brevity, in this section, we will refer to the attempt to circumvent national law by relying on EU law as type 1 abuse and the attempt to abusively derive undue advantage from EU law as type 2 abuse.

When it comes to type 1 abuse, that is, in a *Van Binsbergen* situation, the Court of Justice has found that the need to combat abuse constitutes a justification for the imposition of a restriction on free movement on the part of the Member States. Take this example. Citizen A is a professional providing consultancy in her home Member State. She decides to transfer the place of her activity to the neighbouring Member State, which becomes her host Member State. All her consultancy, however, continues to be offered in the territory of her home Member State. By doing so, she formally becomes a professional providing cross-border consultancy services. By establishing herself in the host Member State, Citizen A merely intends to evade the stricter rules of her home Member State concerning, say, the use of professional titles. Unfortunately, her home Member State has a residence requirement to prevent its citizens from circumventing national rules by (artificially) establishing themselves in another EU Member State. In accordance with the case law of the Court of Justice, that is a situation typically falling under type 1 abuse, where the national rule in question (the residence requirement) constitutes a restriction to free movement justified by the need to combat abuse (provided it is proportionate, of course). In brief, in similar situations, the need to combat abuse justifies the imposition of restrictions that would otherwise be incompatible with the fundamental freedoms. This is the first anti-abuse strategy accepted by the Court, and it is used exclusively in type 1 abuse cases where an operation of circumvention of national law is at stake.

---

[28] This is, by and large, the same typology outlined by Munari 2015, p. 520.

[29] CJEU, *Halifax plc*, Opinion of Advocate General Maduro, para 63, according to whom there are "two main contexts in which the notion of abuse has been analysed by the Court. First, when [Union] law provisions are abusively invoked in order to evade national law. Second, when [Union] law provisions are abusively relied upon in order to gain advantages in a manner that conflicts with the purposes and aims of those same provisions".

[30] CJEU, *Matmut*, Opinion of Advocate General Szpunar, para 61, who stated that there are "two main contexts in which the concept of abuse may be analysed, that is to say, when EU law is invoked in order to evade national law and when provisions of EU law are relied upon to gain advantages in a manner which runs counter to the objectives and the aims of those same provisions".

When it comes to type 2 abuse, the Court of Justice has found that the existence of abuse triggers a restriction of the scope of application of the rules invoked so that the abusive practice in question does not fall within the coverage of those rules. Take this example. Corporation A has its primary establishment in the Member State in which it is incorporated and a number of subsidiaries (secondary establishments) in various host Member States. Corporation A disguises most of its profits in the form of interest and royalty payments made to its controlled subsidiaries in the other Member States under Directive 2003/49, so that its (taxable) revenue in the home Member State is significantly reduced. The transactions in question have no other justification than obtaining a tax advantage. Suppose the tax authorities of the Member State of incorporation issue additional tax assessments to Corporation A in order to recover the taxes that were unduly evaded. In accordance with the case law of the Court of Justice, that situation typically falls under type 2 abuse. In such a case, the ECJ would endorse the decisions of the national tax authorities to issue additional tax statements by holding that the EU rules in question cannot be extended to cover abusive practices such as those at stake. EU rules would apply to transactions with an economic justification but not to transactions whose sole or principal aim is to obtain a tax advantage. In this way, the Court would sanction abuse on the level of interpretation. Therefore, the second anti-abuse strategy accepted by the Court is purely interpretive and only used in type 2 abuse cases where natural or legal persons attempt to derive an undue advantage from EU law.

In fairness, in type 2 abuse cases, there might also be an element of circumvention of national law. In the example made here, and more generally in most tax evasion cases, the circumvention is actually *in re ipsa*.[31] One may, therefore, wonder what makes type 1 and type 2 abuse different. The difference, in my opinion, is quite clear. In type 1 abuse cases, a natural or legal person typically seeks to obtain an advantage deriving from the national law of another Member State and not from EU law directly. In type 1 abuse cases, EU law serves as a means to trigger the application of more favourable national rules. In the example made here, Citizen A intends to benefit from a more permissive legal framework concerning the use of professional titles. The EU rules on free movement offer her the means to obtain that advantage. Conversely, the advantage sought in type 2 abuse cases derives directly from EU law.[32] The invocation of EU rules may entail the circumvention of national rules. In the example, Corporation A attempts to evade taxes in its home Member States. However, the more favourable treatment in question is a direct consequence of EU law.[33]

One may wonder why the Court of Justice has resorted to two different anti-abuse strategies. In particular, the interpretive strategy used for type 2 abuse seems fit for

---

[31] The only circumstance where there appears to be no circumvention of national law is an *Emsland-Stärke* situation. In such case, the EU right claimed, namely, the right to receive a subsidy, is entirely based on EU law and does not involve any national rules.

[32] For this reason, this type of abuse has also been referred to as a U-turn or triangular situation. See Butler and Sørensen 2022, p. 404.

[33] A similar systematisation is offered by Vogenauer 2011, pp. 525–530.

type 1 abuse as well, at least at first scrutiny. For the sake of clarity, we will apply the interpretive strategy to the type 1 abuse mentioned above. If abuse entails restricting the scope of EU law so as not to cover abusive practices, formally speaking, the conduct of Citizen A could be said to fall outside the scope of the fundamental freedoms involved, namely establishment and services. She is not genuinely established in the host Member State. Likewise, she is not a genuine cross-border service provider in the home Member State. Consequently, it could be said that EU law does not cover her conduct, so she derives no rights from it. This reasoning is formally logical and correct. However, if one looks under the surface, one problem clearly arises. Without a restriction imposed by her home Member State (namely, the residence requirement), her conduct would most likely remain undetected. Neither the EU legal order nor the Member State legal order would be able to catch such an abusive situation. It would simply go unnoticed. This aspect of type 1 abuse is inextricably connected with the legal nature of the fundamental freedoms and of the EU legal order. Just like any other freedom, the EU fundamental freedoms typically impose negative obligations on the Member States, that is, an obligation to abstain from creating obstacles or barriers (restrictions, in EU law parlance) to the exercise of those freedoms. Hence, in order to combat an abusive practice, it is necessary to breach that negative obligation to abstain by positively imposing a restriction. It is, therefore, logical that the strategy used to combat abuse is the imposition of an otherwise unlawful restriction.

The situation is different for rights directly derived from EU law, especially secondary legislation. These rights typically impose positive obligations on the Member States, like the obligation to grant something to a natural or legal person. In our example above, Corporation A claims a tax exemption on the payments made to its subsidiary. In an *Emsland-Stärke* situation, a natural or legal person claims the granting of a subsidy. And so forth. In order to combat abuse, it is necessary to breach the positive obligation to grant an export subsidy or a tax advantage by making a negative decision, such as an *ex-ante* denial or an *ex-post* restitution claim. The technique used to assess the lawfulness of such denial or restitution is genuinely a matter of interpretation of the rules in question: the scope of the right to a subsidy or to a tax exemption does not cover mock transactions such as fictitious exports or artificial intragroup payments. The determination of a transaction as a fictitious or artificial one is entirely a matter of factual and legal interpretation of the circumstances of the case.

It is, therefore, reasonable to affirm that each type of abuse has its own anti-abuse strategy. That said, it should be pointed out that despite the use of different anti-abuse strategies, the result is always the same: the natural or legal person who perpetrates abuse, no matter what type, is denied the possibility to rely on EU law,[34] either as a means to obtain an advantage or as an advantage in and of itself. That is because the ultimate underlying rationale for both anti-abuse strategies is a teleologically

---

[34] See in this sense Adinolfi 2012, p. 330.

oriented interpretation of EU law.[35] Put differently, what is ultimately decisive in abuse cases is the (defeat of the) purpose of the EU rules invoked, whether primary or secondary.

The decisiveness of teleological interpretation is self-evident in type 2 abuse cases, which are by far the most common ones.[36] It is no accident that the Court of Justice has coined the abuse test precisely in a type 2 abuse case. In such cases, the attainment of the objective pursued by the rules constitutes the first constitutive element of abuse, namely the objective one. This is typically the first thing the Court looks at, and only if the purpose of the rules has not been attained would the ECJ move to the second tier of the test, which is aimed at assessing the subjective element. In other words, defeating the purpose of the rules is a necessary precondition to a finding of abuse. It is necessary but not sufficient, as we know from the case law. The existence of the subjective element must also be found.

In the less common type 1 abuse cases, to which the Court has never explicitly applied the two-tiered abuse test, the purpose of the rules in question also plays a central, if only less noticeable, role in the finding of abuse. If we look at cases such as *Van Binsbergen*, *Leclerc*, *Veronica*, *Centros* and *Akrich*, the purpose of the rules was always decisive, albeit indirectly. We have already mentioned this aspect in the previous chapter, especially when commenting on the *Akrich* ruling.[37] It should be recalled that in *Van Binsbergen*, the service in question was provided entirely or principally towards the territory of another Member State. This suggested that the conditions for the application of the freedom to provide services were created artificially in order to circumvent national rules. What made that scheme artificial is precisely the purpose of those rules, as demonstrated by the teleological interpretation endorsed by the Court. Since the purpose of the freedom to provide services is to allow providers across the EU to pursue their activity in another Member State *on an occasional and temporary basis*, the conduct of someone who carried out no activity in the Member State of establishment, as was the case in *Van Binsbergen*, clearly defeated that purpose. The same holds true in relation to the free movement of persons. When it comes to the free movement of workers, the purpose of the freedom in question is to allow EU workers to take up employment in another Member State under the same conditions as the nationals of that Member State, provided such employment is effective and genuine. When Mrs Akrich took up employment in Ireland, the Court was satisfied with the finding that her employment was effective and genuine in accordance with the purpose of the free movement of persons. Since the objective was attained, the motives that prompted her to take up a job in Ireland were immaterial. That is so because no abuse of EU law can exist, whereby the

---

[35] See Iliopoulou-Penot 2013, p. 188, who affirmed that "appreciation de l'abus et interprétation téléologique son intrinsèquement liée".

[36] Among the decisions commented on in Chap. 3, only around 10 of them constitute type 1 abuse cases.

[37] See Chap. 3, Sect. 3.3.2.

purpose of the rules has been attained. If the purpose of the rules has been attained, the two-tiered abuse test fails on the first tier.[38]

For this reason, there is a clear analogy between the case law on abuse of Union law and the *Keck* case law concerning selling arrangements.[39] Although the concept of abuse is not explicitly discussed in *Keck* and remains somewhat in the background, it has clearly shaped the Court's reasoning. Without dwelling on the details of that case,[40] *Keck* was the ECJ's reaction to "the increasing tendency of traders to invoke Article [34] of the Treaty as a means of challenging any rules whose effect is to limit their commercial freedom even where such rules are not aimed at products from other Member States".[41] In this statement, the Court seemed to imply that the free movement of goods was being invoked speciously in a manner incompatible with its very purpose, which was not to eliminate whatever rules limiting commercial freedom, but only those rules affecting intra-Union trade in goods.[42] *Keck* was, in other words, the Court's reaction against abusive reliance on the free movement of goods, to which it responded by narrowing down the scope of application of Article 34 TFEU. By virtue of this (teleological) interpretation, selling arrangements were declared to fall outside the scope of EU law in much the same way as abusive practices do.[43]

The inherently interpretive dimension of abuse of Union law fits squarely in line with its being a general principle of EU law. As we have seen above, all general principles of EU law serve first and foremost as means of interpreting EU primary and secondary law. In Sects. 4.5 and 4.6 below, we will discuss how abuse of Union law performs the second typical function of general principles, namely that of constituting a ground for invalidity.

4.3.1 The Role of Proportionality

As we have seen from the analysis of the case law, in abuse cases, the Court of Justice has resorted to proportionality, in essence, in order to assess the lawfulness of the anti-abuse measures adopted by the Member States. This is coherent with the general application of proportionality as a ground for the review of national measures.[44]

---

[38] See also Koutrakos 2011, p. 210, who correctly pointed out that "the definition of the objective of the relevant EU rules is the starting point for any analysis of the abuse issue".

[39] The same view is held by Adinolfi 2012, p. 332.

[40] On which the literature is quite abundant. See, among many, Edward 2019, pp. 164 ff.; Purnhagen 2019, pp. 176 ff.; Sharpston 2019, pp. 150 ff.

[41] CJEU, *Keck and Mithouard*, Judgment of the Court, 24 November 1993, joined cases C-267/91 and C-268/91, ECLI:EU:C:1993:905, para 14.

[42] See, in this sense, Iliopoulou-Penot 2013, pp. 188–189.

[43] Under the systematisation offered here, *Keck* would be a case of type 2 abuse, where the advantage sought is derived directly from EU law. Hence, the relevant anti-abuse strategy is the restriction of the scope of the rules in question, which is in keeping with the Court's case law on abuse.

[44] See Tridimas 2006, pp. 193 ff.

Proportionality has been applied in this way in many abuse cases, mainly to find that the national measures imposed were not compatible with EU law. The textbook illustration is *Marks & Spencer*, where the Court found that the national measures were, in principle, justified but went beyond what was necessary to prevent abusive practices because they were too broad and risked capturing non-abusive practices as well.[45] The ECJ has found that the use of presumptions on the part of the Member States in order to prevent abuse is not disproportionate, provided that the presumptions are rebuttable.[46] However, the Member States cannot go as far as automatically excluding *a priori* entire categories of transactions.[47]

As already mentioned in Chap. 3, the proportionality and the abuse test somewhat overlapped in *Cadbury-Schweppes*. In that case, the Court of Justice recognised that the CFC rules constituted restrictions to the freedom of establishment justified by the need to prevent abuse. However, when assessing their conformity with the proportionality principle, the Court stated that the rules in question could be considered compatible with it only if they targeted purely artificial arrangements, that is, transactions with no economic justification other than obtaining a tax advantage.[48] It should be noted that the determination of the artificial nature of a transaction is also decisive for the second constitutive element of abuse (the subjective one). For the subjective element to exist, it is necessary to demonstrate that a person has artificially created the conditions to obtain a given advantage. This effectively led to a situation whereby the existence of an abusive practice, which is based on the premise that a transaction is purely artificial, automatically ensured conformity of the rules in question with the proportionality principle. This is somewhat anomalous because proportionality is supposed to operate after it is established that an abuse exists as a means to assess whether the restriction imposed is not excessively burdensome.[49]

The partial confusion generated by this ruling goes hand in hand with the Court's difficulty in defining the second constitutive element of abuse, which has been more problematic than the first one. This paves the way for the discussion of the next subsection, in which the two constitutive elements will be examined more closely.

[45] See *Marks & Spencer*, para 57.

[46] See *Leur-Bloem*, paras 41 ff.

[47] See *ICI*, paras 26–28.

[48] See CJEU, *Cadbury-Schweppes*, paras 65–75.

[49] But see the considerations made by Neville Brown, who highlighted the existence of a clear analogy between proportionality and the doctrine of abuse of rights. More specifically, this author observed that "[a]buse of rights carries with it an idea of excess; the right ceases to be protected in law where it is exercised in a manner which is disproportionate" (see Neville Brown 1994, p. 521). However, he conceded that "the general principle of proportionality needs to be complemented by a distinct and separate general principle of abuse of rights. Hitherto an offshoot, as it were, of proportionality, abuse of rights should now be recognized as a principle that stands on its own" (see Neville Brown 1994, p. 522).

4.3.2 *The Two Constitutive Elements of Abuse of Union Law: An Appraisal*

Since the creation of the abuse test in *Emsland-Stärke*, we know that abuse of Union law consists of two constitutive elements. While the Court of Justice has been quite consistent in relation to the first one, the second one has been more difficult to delineate fully.

The objective element of abuse implies that despite the formal observance of the conditions laid down by EU rules, the purpose of those rules has not been achieved. This first element has two components. First, it must be determined that the rules have been formally complied with. As we have seen above, verifying this component is crucial to distinguish abuse from fraud. In fraud cases, EU rules are not formally observed. Their application is triggered by making false statements or hiding relevant information that would make the rules, by definition, inapplicable. In abuse cases, there is no misrepresentation or concealment involved. Second, it must be determined that the purpose of the rules invoked has not been achieved. We have already discussed above how central the purpose of the rules is for any finding that abuse exists. Those considerations will not be repeated here. Suffice it to note that the second component of the objective element of abuse is what makes it particularly difficult to find that abuse exists in some specific areas of EU law, namely the establishment of companies and the free movement of persons. We will go back to this issue in Sect. 4.4.

As regards the second constitutive element of abuse, the Court of Justice has essentially oscillated between two alternative formulations. The original version was coined in the foundational *Emsland-Stärke* and referred to *the intention to obtain an advantage* from the EU rules by artificially creating the conditions laid down for obtaining it. A variation to this was introduced in *Halifax*, where the Court held that the subjective element is satisfied, whereby the *essential aim of the transaction* is to obtain a given advantage. Therefore, the *intention of the party* was replaced by the *aim of the transaction.* We have already observed in Chap. 3 that this adjustment was most likely prompted by the criticism raised by the first formulation, which appeared too uncertain to verify to many observers. We also stated that this recalibration had the effect of objectifying the subjective element. These considerations are certainly true and reasonable. However, as also noted in Chap. 3, the ECJ continued to use both expressions interchangeably and without any apparent logical explanations. It is true that, for some time, it seemed to prefer the reference to the intention of the party, as opposed to the aim of the transaction, in cases where natural persons were involved, such as *O* and *Commission v. Spain*, while favouring the more objective formulation in cases involving legal persons, whose intention might be more difficult to establish. However, the Court returned to the original formulation in *N Luxembourg 1*, which was a case of tax evasion carried out by corporations. Hence, in the absence of clearer guidance from the Kirchberg Plateau, both expressions must be recognised as suitable.

Leaving aside the lexical aspects, it is important to clarify under what circumstances the subjective element can be considered satisfied. The first indication came from a ruling predating the creation of the abuse test. In *Leur-Bloem*, which concerned tax evasion, the Court of Justice held that a transaction not carried out for valid commercial reasons could be considered abusive, where valid commercial reason was understood as any transaction aiming to attain more than a purely fiscal advantage.[50] To put it in positive terms, in *Leur-Bloem,* the ECJ found that a transaction carried out to attain a purely fiscal advantage was commercially invalid. In *ICI*, another ruling predating *Emsland-Stärke*, the Court coined the expression *wholly artificial arrangements* without clarifying what it meant. Over the years, it provided some guidance on what constitutes an artificial transaction for the purpose of abuse of Union law, sometimes a *contrario*, that is, by stating what does not constitute an artificial transaction. In *Marks & Spencer*, the Court stated (at least indirectly) that intragroup transactions whose sole purpose is to transfer losses to the Member State with the highest tax rate are artificial ones. In contrast, transactions that are part and parcel of genuine economic activity are not, even if they are designed to minimise tax liability.[51] The most comprehensive elucidation of the concept of artificial transaction was arguably provided in *N Luxembourg 1*. By way of example, the Court held that "[i]ndications of an artificial arrangement may […] be constituted by the various contracts existing between the companies involved in the financial transactions at issue, giving rise to intragroup flows of funds which […] may have the aim of transferring profits from a profit-making commercial company to shareholding entities in order to avoid the tax burden or reduce it as much as possible",[52] or "by the simultaneity or closeness in time of, on the one hand, the entry into force of major new tax legislation […] which some of the groups of companies strive to circumvent and, on the other hand, the setting up of complex financial transactions and the grant of intragroup loans".[53]

In brief, it is safe to conclude that, based on the Court's case law, the second constitutive element of abuse is to be ascertained on a case-by-case basis, and its content may vary depending on the context. However, the *leitmotiv* of the subjective element is the concept of artificiality, or lack of genuineness, applied to the transaction or the intention of the parties involved. Attempting to define this element of abuse *in abstracto* might be a pointless effort.

4.4 The Application of Abuse of Law to Different Areas of EU Law

As we have seen in Chap. 3, the most recent case law has unequivocally clarified that abuse of Union law can potentially apply to all areas of EU law, which is normal for a general principle. However, an examination of the areas in which it has effectively

[50] See *Leur-Bloem*, para 48(c).

[51] See *RBS Deutschland*, para 54.

[52] See N Luxembourg 1, para 132.

[53] Ibid., para 133.

been applied suggests that the principle in question, while having a unitary core, is not a monolith.

A list of the areas to which abuse of Union law has been applied was provided by the Court of Justice in *N Luxembourg 1*. It includes free movement of goods, freedom to provide services, public service contracts, freedom of establishment, company law, social security, transport, social policy, restrictive measures and VAT. More areas should be added to this list, such as the common agricultural policy, free movement of persons, and the insurance of motor vehicles. The main difference in the application of the principle to different areas of EU law can be identified in the fact that in some of them, it has been very difficult to successfully demonstrate the existence of abuse. It is argued that this is not an accident but a logical consequence of (a) the structural features of the principle of abuse of Union law and (b) the Court's extensive interpretation of the purpose of the rules in question.

As previously mentioned, the starting point for any analysis concerning abuse, to borrow from Panos Koutrakos, is precisely the purpose of the supposedly abused rules. Finding that abuse of Union law exists means that the purpose of EU rules has not been attained, which, in turn, presupposes the determination of what the purpose of those rules is, which is why teleological interpretation plays such a central role in applying this general principle. In some areas of EU law, the purpose of the rules as interpreted by the Court is such that their defeat through abusive conduct is very unlikely. The prime examples are the rules on the free movement of workers and on the establishment of companies.

Let's start with the free movement of workers, where the ECJ has traditionally settled on strongly pro-free movement positions. The Court of Justice has famously held in the *Levin* ruling that the purpose of those rules is to eliminate any discrimination based on nationality between workers of the Member States regarding employment, remuneration and other conditions of work, provided the employment is genuine and effective.[54] More specifically, the Court held that the purpose of the rules in question is "promoting throughout the [Union] a harmonious development of economic activities and a raising of the standard of living".[55] The Court clarified that precarious work, such as seasonal and part-time jobs, was also included because "although it may provide an income lower than what is considered to be the minimum required for subsistence, constitutes for a large number of persons an effective means of improving their living conditions".[56] Against this background, the possibility of abusing these rules appears to be quite limited. Even though real life is often unpredictable, it seems plausible to affirm that the main, and perhaps only, possibility to defeat the purpose of these rules is to disguise as employment an activity that, in reality, is not employment as (extensively) interpreted by the ECJ. If the purpose is to allow Union workers to take up employment in another Member State under the same conditions as the nationals of that Member State, irrespective of its duration,

---

[54] See *Levin*, paras 7–17.

[55] Ibid., para 15.

[56] Ibid.

stability and pay, then the possibility of improperly using these rules is limited to borderline situations such as so-called social tourism,[57] or outright frauds.[58]

The same holds true in relation to the rules on the freedom of establishment of companies. The Court has interpreted the purpose of such rules in an extensive, strongly liberal fashion. In *Centros*, the ECJ famously held that the purpose of the rules in question is "to enable companies formed in accordance with the law of a Member State and having their registered office, central administration or principal place of business within the [Union] to pursue activities in other Member States through an agency, branch or subsidiary".[59] From this statement, the Court drew the consequence that the "right to form a company in accordance with the law of a Member State and to set up branches in other Member States is inherent in the exercise, in a single market, of the freedom of establishment guaranteed by the Treaty".[60] We have already mentioned in Chap. 3 that this assertion, which was confirmed in later cases concerning the free movement of companies, implies the acceptance of regulatory arbitrage in the field of company law, which had almost immediate repercussions on the single market.[61] Against this broad, pro-market interpretation of the purpose of the Treaty rules on the establishment of companies, the room left for their abusive exploitation is quite limited. This is not to say that companies are given a blank cheque under this freedom. As demonstrated by *Cadbury-Schweppes*, the rules in question cannot be used to purposefully reduce tax liability by virtue of artificial intragroup transactions. However, *Cadbury-Schweppes* was a case of abuse perpetrated through subsidiaries (i.e. secondary establishment), not a case concerning the inherent exercise of the freedom of establishment as affirmed in *Centros*.

It is precisely this last aspect that constitutes the umbilical cord connecting the free movement of workers and the free movement of companies as far as abuse of Union law is concerned. This analogy was correctly identified by Katja Ziegler, who pointed out that "it is nigh impossible to draw the dividing line between use of a right (or EU law) for a purpose for which it was not foreseen and misuse of EU law where the unforeseen purpose directly results from the exercise of a freedom".[62] Put differently, the intrinsic characteristics of these two freedoms, whose purpose has been broadly interpreted by the Court of Justice, render abuse of Union law almost impossible to occur. This is so because any unforeseen use of the rules, such as the incorporation of a company in a Member State with the sole aim of benefiting from

---

[57] See Bartoloni 2015, p. 475 ff.

[58] Such as the cases of EU workers who exploit the rules on the free movement of workers to unduly receive social benefits in two different Member States, or for wrong periods. See Directorate-General for Employment, Social Affairs and Inclusion 2022, pp. 30 ff. At any rate, these are cases of fraud of the secondary rules implementing the free movement of workers and not fraud of the fundamental freedom as such.

[59] See *Centros*, para 26.

[60] Ibid., para 27.

[61] See Ringe 2011, p. 118, who pointed out that "national lawmakers responded to the challenge posed by English company law that was triggered by the Court's case law", for example by making the national rules concerning the incorporation of companies more competitive.

[62] See Ziegler 2011, p. 308.

more favourable legislation (*Centros*), or the taking up of temporary employment in another Member State with the sole aim of getting one's partner the residence right upon returning to the home State (*Akrich*), is conceptually inseparable from the normal use of the freedom in question.[63]

4.5 What Is the Role of Secondary Legislation?

EU secondary legislation may or may not feature an anti-abuse clause. Some anti-abuse clauses are well known and have been expressly examined in Chap. 3 through the case law analysis. That is the case of the most prominent one, which is Article 35 of the Citizenship Directive. But we have also already encountered Article 11 of Council Directive 90/434/EEC (now no longer in force), as well as Article 13(B) of the Sixth Council Directive 77/388/EEC (now no longer in force).

In general terms, two alternative situations can be identified where secondary legislation features an *ad hoc* anti-abuse provision. If the scope of the provision corresponds with, or is broader than, the imperative content of the general principle of abuse of Union law, it is reasonable to believe that the general principle no longer applies.[64] Conversely, if the scope of the provision is narrower than the general principle, it would mean that the specific anti-abuse clause can potentially allow conduct that is instead caught by the imperative content of the general principle. In this case, it is reasonable to believe that, if a consistent interpretation of the anti-abuse clause is not possible, the general principle of Union law would serve as a ground

[63] Commenting on the implications of this line of case law, Ionescu maintained that it deprives national decisions concerning the expulsion of foreigners of "*toute valeur juridique*". See Ionescu 2012, p. 180. While not entirely untenable, this view is, in my opinion, partly misplaced. It is true that, based on the *Akrich* case law, an individual who has been subject to an expulsion decision in Member State A can obtain the right to reside in that same Member State lawfully by virtue of EU law. However, it should be pointed out that to achieve that, such individual has to (a) marry a national of Member State A, (b) temporarily move to Member State B in order for his spouse to take up employment there, and (c) return to Member State A, after a period of effective and genuine employment, as a family member of a national of Member State A. If the individual in question does all that, it is undeniable that the prior expulsion decision that was issued against him ceases to be effective. However, that is the consequence of the fact that the individual in question has, in the meantime, acquired new rights, deriving from EU law, that he did not have when he received the expulsion decision. Had the individual in question been a family member of an EU national lawfully residing in her spouse's country, an expulsion decision would have been simply impossible to issue against him. Furthermore, it should not be forgotten that EU law features an *ad hoc* clause sanctioning marriages of convenience as abusive, which is enough to protect the Member States from artificial arrangements. If the arrangement (that is, the marriage) is not artificial but genuine, it would be absurd to deny the rights to a family member who has previously received an expulsion decision solely on this basis. As a result, I believe that the concerns relating to the effectiveness of the Member States' powers in the field of migration control are largely misplaced.

[64] This is also the opinion of Sørensen 2006, p. 438.

for the invalidity of secondary law, which is the second function typically performed by general principles of EU law.[65]

In practice, *ad hoc* anti-abuse provisions are usually included in directives, meaning that the Member States must transpose them into national law. If the Member States adopt an anti-abuse clause whose scope corresponds with, or is broader than, the general principle of EU law, there would be no issue. However, sometimes, such provisions allow the Member States to adopt anti-abuse measures without compelling them to do so. The Member States may, therefore, not avail themselves of this possibility, which is exactly the situation that arose in *Kofoed*. However, the Member States may also not transpose the directive or adopt an anti-abuse provision that is narrower than the general principle. What happens in these cases? Does abuse of Union law perform the typical gap-filling function of general principles of Union law?[66]

The most logical answer to this question is yes. There are a number of systemic reasons to admit that abuse of Union law, as a general principle, can be used to fill gaps in the Member States' legal order. It can entail the deduction of a rule of law in a situation where a *lacuna* exists in the national law, whether that *lacuna* is caused by a lack of transposition or an incorrect implementation of EU rules. First, general principles of EU law are part and parcel of primary law, so it is only logical that they prevail over sources of law that are lower in the hierarchy, as is the case with national law. So, if the national anti-abuse provision is narrower than the general principle, the broader scope of the latter would prevail. Second, we have seen that abuse of Union law can constitute a ground for review of the measures of the Member States. In this context, the general principle of abuse of EU law can lead to a finding of incompatibility with EU law of the national rule in question, which will eventually lead to its removal from the Member State's legal order. This has been affirmed by the Court of Justice repeatedly. If the application of abuse of Union law can have such a disruptive effect on national law, it is all the more logical to admit that it can have the (less disruptive) effect of complementing the interpretation of national rules whenever there is a (intended or unintended) gap in the Member State legislation.

However, this problem is inextricably connected with the issue of whether general principles of EU law have direct effects. Speaking of this, AG Sharpston held that "[i]t is trite [Union] law that general principles of law are capable of being invoked *vertically* against the State. Thus for example the Court has held that various national measures were precluded by [Union] law on the basis that they were incompatible with the general principle of equal treatment or with specific manifestations of that principle, such as the prohibition of discrimination on grounds of nationality in various contexts, respect for fundamental rights, the principle of the protection of legitimate expectations and the principle of proportionality".[67] That is certainly true.

---

[65] See, along the same lines, Butler and Sørensen 2022, p. 418.

[66] For an overview of how general principles are used to fill a gap in written law, see Tridimas 2006, pp. 17 ff.

[67] CJEU, *Birgit Bartsch*, Opinion of Advocate General Sharpston, 22 May 2008, case C-427/06, ECLI:EU:C:2008:297, para 79 (emphasis added).

Yet, it has been pointed out that the case law has been rather ambivalent when it comes to the horizontal direct effects of general principles.[68] The Court has unequivocally admitted that some general principles are capable of being invoked in a dispute between private parties.[69] For example, it can now be considered established case law that the prohibition of discrimination on grounds of age, as a specific expression of the principle of equal treatment, is invokable in the context of fully horizontal disputes, as firstly affirmed in *Mangold* and later confirmed in *Kücükdevici* and *Dansk Industri.*[70] However, the Court of Justice has been traditionally more hesitant or cautious in recognising inverse direct effects, which is precisely what happens when abuse of Union law is applied to take away rights from individuals, as already mentioned above.

In this respect, it has been submitted that only general principles of fundamental rights should be applied horizontally for the benefit of the right holder. Otherwise, general principles "cannot be relied upon by a State of an EU institution against a private party".[71] The author in question suggested that other mechanisms, such as consistent interpretation, would suffice. In principle, this view is not entirely erroneous. After all, it goes back to the very origins of general principles, which, as mentioned above, have always been regarded as a judge-made safeguard of individual rights. However, the Court of Justice has now unequivocally acknowledged that abuse of Union law can have inverse vertical direct effects. As we said above, this is what makes this general principle a special one. We have discussed this issue in Chap. 3 when commenting on the *Kofoed*, *Italmoda* and *Cussens* rulings. In that context, we pointed out that if *Kofoed* had raised some doubts on the horizontal applicability of abuse of Union law, the Court of Justice has removed those doubts in the following two judgments by unequivocally holding that the application of the general principle of abuse of Union law is not "subject to a requirement of transposition".[72]

It is, therefore, reasonable to conclude that the general principle in question is fully capable of performing the typical gap-filling function with respect to both EU secondary legislation and national transposition measures. What is more, and differently from other general principles, it can be directly applied to the detriment of individuals in the absence of secondary law and national rules.

There is one final question concerning the relation between abuse of Union law and secondary rules, namely the potential role of harmonisation as an alternative way to combat abuse. We have seen in Chap. 3 that in at least two cases, the Court

[68] See the thoughtful considerations made by Arnull 2011, pp. 13–18. For a discussion on the horizontal direct effects of provisions of the EUCFR, see Lazzerini 2014, pp. 907 ff.

[69] See, along the same lines, Lazzerini 2022, p. 185, who stated that "one has to acknowledge that the general principles of EU law (some of them, at least) may be directly relevant to inter-individual relationships falling within the scope of Union law".

[70] For a comment on the development of this line of case law, see Gualco and Lourenço 2016, p. 648 ff.

[71] See Leczykiewicz 2019, p. 741.

[72] See *Cussens*, para 28.

of Justice has expressly cited the availability of harmonisation as a preventive anti-abuse strategy.[73] This circumstance suggests that the ECJ is at least open to this idea.[74] It is undeniable that more harmonisation would lower the risk of type 1 abuse cases, that is, cases in which an individual attempts to exploit Union law as a means to fly into the legal order of another Member State because of its more favourable provisions. In our example above, Citizen A would have no reason to transfer her activity to the host Member State if the rules on using professional titles were the same in all Member States. At the same time, the case law analysis has demonstrated that harmonisation may not be decisive, especially in type 2 abuse cases. Abuse of Union law has arisen in harmonised fields, sometimes even despite the existence of an express anti-abuse provision. The difficulties that often surround the interpretation of such provisions, coupled with the risk that the Member States may implement them incorrectly or not implement them at all, suggest that, in most cases, harmonisation does not constitute a real alternative to combat abuse. Rather, it can be useful to complement the general principle of EU law prohibiting abuse. Not to mention that "harmonization undertaken only to prevent abuse seems to be harmonization based on the wrong premises" to which "a broader application of the principle of abuse of rights may be preferable".[75]

4.6 Open Questions and Outstanding Challenges

In the previous pages, we have dealt with the legal issues surrounding abuse of Union law that the Court of Justice has directly or indirectly clarified in its case law. There are, however, a number of issues that still have to be clarified.

Let us start with abuse of process. We have seen in Sect. 3.2.3 of Chap. 3 that the Court of Justice has recognised the existence of abuse of process in two early decisions, namely the *Simmenthal* and *Albertini and Montagnani* rulings. We have clarified that, based on this (limited) case law, abuse of process in EU law can be considered a specific expression of the general principle of abuse of Union law, which manifests itself at the procedural level. As we have seen in Chap. 3, the ECJ had little problem recognising abuse of process and even calling it by its name from the outset. We observed that the kind of abuse that emerged in *Simmenthal* and in *Albertini and Montagnani* is reminiscent of the concept of abuse of rights in the strict sense, which has its direct roots in Roman law. Its main feature is an abusive exercise of an individual right characterised by an element of harmfulness (*aemulatio*) on the part of the individual exercising the right in question. In such cases, the existence of an individual right is not questionable. It is the way in which it is exercised that becomes problematic. In *Albertini and Montagnani*, for example, there was no doubt that they had the right to bring an action before the Court of Justice. However, by

---

[73] The Court has done that in *Knoors* and *Marks & Spencer*.

[74] See, in this sense, Butler and Sørensen 2022, p. 417.

[75] See Sørensen 2006, p. 459.

filing abnormally lengthy complaints filled with insulting allegations, they exercised that right in an abusive manner. This is an abuse of rights *stricto sensu*, which was easy for the Court to recognise also in light of the case law of the ECtHR under Article 35(3)(a) referred to in Chap. 3, Sect. 3.2.3.

There are, in reality, other cases in which the Court has admitted the possibility that procedural rights are used in an abnormal or abusive manner. More specifically, according to established case law, the Court can decline to rule under Article 267 TFEU what it regards as fabricated references specifically designed to artificially bring before it EU law questions that are irrelevant for the resolution of the dispute in the main proceedings.[76] Although not expressly qualified as abusive by the Court, the referral to it of hypothetical or specious questions carries with it an idea of improper or excessive use of the procedural instruments available in the EU legal order.[77] While considerations concerning the sustainability of the caseload certainly play a role in the Court's decisions concerning the admissibility of preliminary ruling requests,[78] the idea of abuse of process is not foreign to this line of case law. As is well-known, the Court can reject as inadmissible the preliminary references in a number of situations that, at least on the theoretical and logical level, seem to imply an abuse or misuse of the instrument of the preliminary reference. One can think of questions deemed manifestly irrelevant for the resolution of the national dispute, or questions having manifestly no connection with the national dispute, or hypothetical questions.[79] Even though the Court of Justice does not label these instances as abusive, the scholarship has always considered them as abusive exercises of this peculiar procedural instrument available in the EU legal order,[80] namely the preliminary reference. As we have seen in Chap. 2, abuse of process in other legal orders, such as international investment law, usually also leads to a declaration of inadmissibility of the claim. This further confirms and strengthens the analogy in this context.

Another aspect that deserves some attention is the existence of a duty to prevent abuse of Union law, next to the right to combat abuse (whose existence has been abundantly demonstrated). As a matter of principle, as has been correctly pointed out, "[i]t does not make sense to have a general principle that may only be applied by a Member State on a discretionary basis".[81] Yet, it has been suggested that this duty only applies to the prevention of abuse of secondary law.[82] While certainly interesting, this view does not seem to find support in the case law, and it contrasts with systemic considerations concerning the functions of abuse of Union law as a general principle of the legal order. Hence, the duty to refuse the benefits of EU law

---

[76] CJEU, *Manuel José Lourenço Dias*, Judgment of the Court, 16 July 1992, case C-343/90, ECLI:EU:C:1992:327, paras 16 ff.

[77] See, along the same lines, Neville Brown 1994, p. 521.

[78] See Pereira Coutinho 2017, p. 398.

[79] For an overview of the case law on the matter, see Strozzi and Mastroianni 2023, pp. 397 ff.

[80] See Mancini and Curti Gialdino 1988, p. 246 ff.

[81] See Butler and Sørensen 2022, p. 418.

[82] See Weber 2013, p. 263.

in case of abuse along the lines affirmed in *N Luxembourg 1*,[83] mandatorily applies to the Member States in a general manner.

Moving on to the next question, one may wonder whether abuse of Union law applies to the EU institutions and the Member States. The EU institutions and the Member States have rights conferred on them by EU law. If abuse is a general principle of EU law, which it is, it should logically apply to any rights granted by the EU legal order, no matter who the rights holder is. It has been observed that the concept of misuse of powers, which is a ground for invalidity of EU acts under Article 263(2) TFEU, has an affinity with abuse of law.[84] The idea is that the misuse of discretionary powers is the equivalent of the abuse of individual rights at the institutional level. A power can be used for a purpose other than that for which it was created, in much the same way a right can be exercised for a purpose other than that for which it was granted. In other words, the rationale underlying misuse of powers and abuse of rights is conceptually analogous. This construction is fascinating and pregnant with logical coherence. However, it must be pointed out that the link between misuse of powers and abuse of rights finds no express support in the case law.[85]

Another indication that the EU institutions and the Member States can also commit abuse of their prerogatives can be found in the anti-abuse clause of the Charter of Fundamental Rights, which is also addressed to the institutions and the Member States, as is Article 17 ECHR.[86] However, as seen in Chap. 2, Sect. 2.4.3, abuse of rights within the framework of human rights law has an autonomous meaning, which shares only the *nomen iuris* with the general principle of abuse of EU law analysed in this book.

The most telling indication that the Member States, and consequently the EU institutions, can exercise their EU rights abusively possibly comes from the practice concerning Article 50 TEU. In the context of Brexit, AG Sánchez-Bordona, when discussing the exercise of the right to withdraw of the UK under this provision, appeared open, at least in principle, to the idea that the "general principle [of abuse of Union law] could be applied in the context of Article 50 TEU, if a Member State engaged in an abusive practice of using successive notifications and revocations in order to improve the terms of its withdrawal from the European Union".[87] However, in the remainder of her Opinion, AG Sánchez-Bordona narrowed down the likelihood that abuse could occur in practice in such a way as to make it almost irrelevant in that context.[88] In any case, there appears to be broad consensus in the academic

[83] See *N Luxembourg 1*, para 97.

[84] See Neville Brown 1994, p. 520.

[85] This is also recognised by Sørensen 2006, p. 441, who, despite this, still considered "most likely that EU institutions and Member States could be challenged under the principle if they were to abuse Community rights" (see Sørensen 2006, p. 442).

[86] See Woods 2021, p. 1697.

[87] See CJEU, *Andy Wightman and Others*, Opinion of Advocate General Sánchez-Bordona, 4 December 2018, case C-621/18, ECLI:EU:C:2018:978, para 153.

[88] Ibid., para 155–156.

literature that the prerogatives conferred by Article 50 TEU, though rooted in the sovereign right of Member States to withdraw, must be exercised in accordance with the principle of good faith[89]—which, as amply demonstrated in this book, is inextricably connected with abuse of law. If even such a special right as the right to withdraw is susceptible of being exercised abusively, there seems to be no logical reason to rule out that other EU rights cannot be used improperly. At the moment, however, this argument is not supported by the Court's case law. Therefore, for now, it can only be assumed that, by virtue of its nature as a general principle, abuse of Union law is theoretically applicable to the conduct of the EU institutions and the Member States alike. That is a reasonable and logical assumption to make in the absence of explicit recognition from the Court of Justice.

4.7 Conclusions

At the end of this attempt to systematise the ample case law of the Court of Justice on abuse of Union law, it is possible to provide a succinct summary of the main conclusions reached regarding the features of this special general principle of EU law.

Number one, there is no doubt that abuse of Union law constitutes a general principle of EU law. It features all the typical characteristics of general principles, namely: (a) it satisfies the requirement of generality, (b) its origins lie in the national laws and constitutional traditions of the Member States, and (c) like other general principles, once entered the EU legal order it has acquired a life of its own.

Number two, it performs the two functions typically performed by general principles: (a) it serves as an interpretive instrument of written primary and secondary law, and (b) it is a ground for review of Member States' measures as well as of secondary legislation, both directly and indirectly, through Article 263 TFEU and Article 267 TFEU, respectively.

Number three, abuse of Union law has some specificities that distinguish it from a "normal" general principle. It is a special general principle that, on top of performing the functions traditionally performed by general principles, also performs an additional one: it limits the action of natural and legal persons seeking to (abusively) rely on Union law not only in (inversely) vertical situations (that is, *vis-à-vis* the administration), but also in horizontal situations (that is, *vis-à-vis* other private actors).

Number four, fraud is also prohibited by the same general principle of Union law. More specifically, fraud is a specific manifestation of abuse, just like abuse of process is a specific form of abuse of law. They display different characteristics, yet they have the same DNA. Abuse is the genus, and fraud is the species. Or, put differently, abuse is the basic underlying principle from which fraud is an offspring. Fraud is different from abuse for one overarching reason. Abuse arises in situations

[89] See Benrath 2018, pp. 234 ff.; Casolari 2022, p. 173 fn. 221.

where the law has been formally respected. Conversely, fraud is premised on a false representation of reality. Despite this fundamental difference, the Court of Justice has managed to adapt the abuse test to fraud in *Altun* and *CRPNPAC*. As regards the objective element of fraud, the Court stated that it consisted of the fact that the conditions for obtaining the protection of EU law were not formally met. This is different from the first constitutive element of abuse, whereby the formal observance of the law is not disputed. As regards the subjective element, the Court held that it corresponded with the intention of the parties to evade or circumvent the conditions set out in EU law to obtain the advantage granted by it. This is also different from the subjective element of abuse, which consists of the intention to obtain an advantage from EU rules by artificially creating the conditions for obtaining it (or, in some areas of EU law, by carrying out a transaction whose essential aim is to obtain an advantage deriving from EU law). When it comes to fraud, the Court established that the parties involved were to have a very specific mental element, that is, the intent to evade or circumvent the rules.

Number five, although abuse of Union law has manifested itself in many different areas and contexts and has taken three main forms (abuse of law proper, abuse of process and fraud), it is reasonable to affirm that the manifestation of abuse of Union law (proper) ultimately comes down to two main contexts: (a) where a natural or legal person attempts to circumvent national law by relying on EU law, and (b) where a natural or legal person attempts to abusively (that is, in a manner that contrasts with its purpose) rely on EU law to obtain an undue advantage. We referred to these situations as type 1 abuse and type 2 abuse, respectively.

Number six, we concluded that for each type of abuse, there is a different anti-abuse strategy. When it comes to type 1 abuse, the Court of Justice has found that the need to combat abuse justifies the imposition of restrictions by the Member States that would otherwise be incompatible with the fundamental freedoms. When it comes to type 2 abuse, the Court of Justice has found that the existence of abuse triggers a restriction of the scope of application of the rules invoked so that the abusive practice in question does not fall within the coverage of those rules. What makes type 1 abuse cases different from type 2 abuse cases is that in the former, a natural or legal person typically seeks to obtain an advantage deriving from the national law of another Member State and not from EU law directly. In type 1 abuse cases, EU law serves as a means to trigger the application of more favourable national rules. Conversely, the advantage sought in type 2 abuse cases derives directly from EU law.

Number seven, we pointed out that despite the different anti-abuse strategies, the finding that abuse exists leads inevitably to the same result: the natural or legal person who perpetrates abuse, no matter what type, is denied the possibility to rely on EU law.

Number eight, we argued that what is ultimately decisive in abuse cases is the (defeat of the) purpose of the EU rules invoked, whether primary or secondary. For this reason, teleological interpretation plays a central role in the development of the principle in question.

Number nine, we observed that proportionality has the function of assessing the lawfulness of the anti-abuse measures adopted by the Member States, which is coherent with the general application of proportionality as a ground for the review of national measures.

Number ten, starting from the foundational *Emsland-Stärke* ruling, we highlighted that the Court of Justice has been quite consistent in relation to the first constitutive element of abuse, while the second one has been more difficult to define. The objective element of abuse implies that despite the formal observance of the conditions laid down by EU rules, the purpose of those rules has not been achieved. As regards the second constitutive element of abuse, the Court of Justice has essentially oscillated between two alternative formulations. The original version was coined in the foundational *Emsland-Stärke* and referred to *the intention to obtain an advantage* from the EU rules by artificially creating the conditions laid down for obtaining it. A variation to this was introduced in *Halifax*, where the Court held that the subjective element is satisfied, whereby the *essential aim of the transaction* is to obtain a given advantage. The ECJ has continued to use both expressions interchangeably and without any apparent logical explanations. Hence, in the absence of clearer guidance from the Kirchberg Plateau, we concluded that both expressions must be recognised as suitable. Despite the lexical aspects, the second constitutive element of abuse is to be ascertained on a case-by-case basis, and its content may vary depending on the context. However, the *leitmotiv* of the subjective element is the concept of artificiality, or lack of genuineness, applied to the transaction or the intention of the parties involved.

Number eleven, we clarified that abuse of Union law applies to all areas of EU law, which is normal for a general principle. However, we concluded that because of the intrinsic characteristics of the free movement of workers and of the freedom of establishment of companies, whose purpose has been broadly interpreted by the Court of Justice, abuse of Union law is very difficult to occur in those areas. Similarly, there might be other areas of EU law where finding abuse may prove challenging or where the relevance of the principle is less obvious (i.e. the CFSP).

Number twelve, we examined in-depth the role of EU secondary legislation. In general terms, we identified two alternative situations where secondary legislation features an *ad hoc* anti-abuse provision. If the scope of the provision corresponds with, or is broader than, the imperative content of the general principle of abuse of Union law, we argued that the general principle no longer applies. Conversely, if the scope of the provision is narrower than the general principle, the latter would serve as a ground for the invalidity of secondary law, if consistent interpretation is not possible. The same holds true for any anti-abuse measures adopted by the Member States. If the Member States adopt an anti-abuse clause whose scope corresponds with the general principle of EU law, there is no issue. If the Member States have no anti-abuse provision or a provision that is narrower than the general principle, the broader scope of the latter would prevail. We observed that this problem is inextricably connected with the issue of whether general principles of EU law have direct effects. We pointed out that the Court of Justice has unequivocally acknowledged that abuse of Union law can have direct effects, including in horizontal and inverse vertical situations. This last aspect is what makes this general principle a special one.

Number thirteen, we explored the potential role of harmonisation as an alternative way to combat abuse. We concluded that harmonisation does not constitute a real alternative but rather a useful complement to the general principle of EU law prohibiting abuse, which can work in some cases and might not work, or even backfire, in other cases.

Finally, we have addressed a number of questions that are still open to discussion. First, we pointed out that abuse of process can be considered a specific expression of the general principle of abuse of Union law, which manifests itself at the procedural level. We observed that the Court's case law on the inadmissibility of preliminary questions is also connected with the idea of abuse of process, even though the Court has not expressly framed inadmissible preliminary references as abusive. Second, we concluded that, next to the right to combat abuse, there is also a duty to refuse the benefits of EU law in case of abuse, which mandatorily applies to the Member States in a general manner. Third, we concluded that at the moment, there is no express confirmation in the case law that abuse of Union law can be perpetrated by the EU institutions and the Member States. However, we opined that, by virtue of its nature as a general principle, and on the basis of the (few) indications found in the practice, abuse of Union law is theoretically applicable to the conduct of the EU institutions and the Member States alike.

In light of all this, it seems apposite to conclude this chapter by citing one of the most erudite statements on abuse of Union law. In his already mentioned Opinion in *Cussens*, AG Bobek declared his scepticism towards the existence of a unitary doctrine of abuse in EU law. He held that "[a]t a high level of abstraction, there might indeed be one unifying proto-idea of the principle of abuse, its blurry shadow flickering somewhere on the wall of Plato's allegorical cave. However, once one seeks to gain a sharper picture, and looks in particular into the individual conditions of abuse in the specific areas of law, then considerable diversity becomes apparent".[90] The analysis in this chapter and in the previous one has certainly demonstrated that abuse of Union law is not monolithic, to borrow from AG Bobek again.[91] There are differences in the way in which it operates in different areas of EU law, and it has manifested itself in different ways depending on the context. Sometimes, it has remained in the background, as is the case for the *Keck* line of case law. Other times, it has been disguised by other concepts that share the same rationale but go under different names, as is the case for inadmissible preliminary references. AG Bobek's words capture quite elegantly the difficulties that are intrinsic in the definition of a general principle of such a special nature. However, to continue with Plato's allegorical cave, it is submitted that abuse of Union law is not just a blurry shadow. It has a very distinct shape, but it is indeed true that when you zoom in to focus on the details, its multiform nature becomes apparent.

[90] See CJEU, *Cussens*, Opinion of Advocate General Bobek, para 30.

[91] He used that expression in para 29 of the same Opinion.

References

Adinolfi A (2012) La nozione di "abuso di diritto" nell'ordinamento dell'Unione Europea. Rivista di diritto internazionale 95:329–353.

Amalfitano C (2018) General Principles of EU Law and the Protection of Fundamental Rights. Edward Elgar, Cheltenham.

Arnull A (2011) What is a General Principle of EU Law? In: De la Feria R, Vogenauer S (eds) Prohibition of Abuse of Law. A New General Principle of EU Law? Hart Publishing, Oxford/Portland, pp. 7–23.

Bartoloni E (2015) La libera circolazione dei cittadini europei economicamente inattivi tra principio di non discriminazione e tutela dei sistemi nazionali di welfare. Diritti umani e diritto internazionale 10:474–480.

Benrath D (2018) Bona Fide and Revocation of Withdrawal. How Article 50 TEU Handles with the Potential Abuses of a Unilateral Revocation of Withdrawal. European Law Review 2:234–248 ss.

Butler G, Sørensen KE (2022) The Prohibition of Abuse of EU Law: a Special General Principle. In: Ziegler K, Neuvonen PJ, Moreno-Lax V (eds) Research Handbook on General Principles in EU Law. Edward Elgar, Cheltenham, pp. 402–422.

Cannizzaro E (2022) Il diritto dell'integrazione europea. Giappichelli, Turin.

Casolari F (2022) Il principio di leale cooperazione tra Stati membri e Unione europea. Studio sulla partecipazione all'Unione al tempo delle crisi. Editoriale scientifica, Naples.

Claes M (2015) The Primacy of EU Law in European and National Law. In: Arnull A, Chalmers D (eds) The Oxford Handbook of European Union Law. Oxford University Press, Oxford, pp. 178–211.

Craig P (2022) General Principles of Law: Treaty, Historical, and Normative Foundations. In: Ziegler K, Neuvonen PJ, Moreno-Lax V (eds) Research Handbook on General Principles in EU Law. Edward Elgar, Cheltenham, pp. 25–39.

Cremona M (2020) Structural Principles and their Role in EU External Relations Law. In: Cremona M (ed) Structural Principles in EU External Relations Law. Hart, Oxford/London/New York/New Delhi/Sydney.

Directorate-General for Employment, Social Affairs and Inclusion (2022) Fraud and Error in the Field of EU Social Security Coordination. Publication Office of the European Union, Brussels.

Dworkin R (1994) Taking Rights Seriously. Duckworth, London.

Edward D (2019) What Was *Keck* Really About. In: Amtenbrink F, Davies G, Kochenov D, Lindeboom J (eds) The Internal Market and the Future of European Integration Essays in Honour of Laurence W. Gormley. Cambridge University Press, Cambridge, pp. 164–175.

Gualco E, Lourenço L (2016) "Clash of Titans". General Principles of EU Law: Balancing and Horizontal Direct Effect. European Papers 1:643–652.

Iliopoulou-Penot A (2013) Liberté de circulation et abus de droit. In: Dubout E, Maitrot de la Motte A (eds) L'unité des libertés de circulation. *In varietate concordia*? Bruylant, Brussels, pp. 185–204.

Ionescu RN (2012) L'abus de droit en droit de l'Union européenne. Bruylant, Brussels.

Koutrakos P (2011) The Emsland-Stärke Abuse of Law Test in the Law of Agriculture and Free Movement of Goods. In: De la Feria R, Vogenauer S (eds) Prohibition of Abuse of Law. A New General Principle of EU Law? Hart Publishing, Oxford/Portland, pp. 203–217.

Lazzerini N (2014) (Some of) the Fundamental Rights Granted by the Charter May be a Source of Obligations for Private Parties: AMS. Common Market Law Review 51:907–933.

Lazzerini N (2022) The Horizontal Application of the General Principles of EU Law: Nothing Less than Direct Effect. In: Ziegler K, Neuvonen PJ, Moreno-Lax V (eds) Research Handbook on General Principles in EU Law. Edward Elgar, Cheltenham, pp. 173–190.

Leczykiewicz D (2019) Prohibition of Abusive Practices as a "General Principle" of EU Law. Common Market Law Review 56:703–742.

Mancini GF, Curti Gialdino C (1988) Brevi note in tema di abuso del processo comunitario. Rivista di diritto europeo 1:245–253.
Munari F (2015) Il divieto di abuso del diritto nell'ordinamento dell'Unione europea. Diritto e Pratica Tributaria 4:519–534.
Neuvonen PJ, Ziegler K (2022), General Principles in the EU Legal Order: Past, Present and Future Directions. In: Ziegler K, Neuvonen PJ, Moreno-Lax V (eds) Research Handbook on General Principles in EU Law. Edward Elgar, Cheltenham, pp. 7–24.
Neville Brown L (1994) Is There a General Principle of Abuse of Rights in European Community Law? In: Curtin D, Heukels T (eds) Institutional Dynamics of European Integration. Essays in Honour of Henry G. Schermers. Martinus Nijhoff, Dordrecht/Boston/London, pp. 511–525.
Pereira Coutinho F (2017) Protecting the Jewel in the Crown: The *Ognyanov* Case and the Preliminary Reference Procedure. European Papers 2:393–401.
Purnhagen K (2019) *Keck* Is Dead, Long Live *Keck*? How the Court of Justice Tries to Avoid a Sunday Trading Saga 2.0. In: Amtenbrink F, Davies G, Kochenov D, Lindeboom J (eds) The Internal Market and the Future of European Integration Essays in Honour of Laurence W. Gormley. Cambridge University Press, Cambridge, pp. 164–175.
Ringe WG (2011) Sparking Regulatory Competition in European Company Law: The Impact of *Centros* Line of Case Law and its Concept of 'Abuse of Law'. In: De la Feria R, Vogenauer S (eds) Prohibition of Abuse of Law. A New General Principle of EU Law? Hart Publishing, Oxford/Portland, pp. 521–571.
Sharpston E (2019) About that Sunday Trading Mess... In: Amtenbrink F, Davies G, Kochenov D, Lindeboom J (eds) The Internal Market and the Future of European Integration Essays in Honour of Laurence W. Gormley. Cambridge University Press, Cambridge, pp. 164–175.
Sørensen KE (2006) Abuse of Rights in Community Law: A Principle of Substance or Merely Rhetoric. Common Market Law Review 43:423–460.
Strozzi G, Mastroianni R (2023) Diritto dell'Unione Europea. Parte istituzionale. Giappichelli, Turin.
Tridimas T (2006) The General Principles of EU Law. Oxford University Press, Oxford.
Vogenauer S (2011) The Prohibition of Abuse of Law: An Emerging General Principle of EU Law. In: De la Feria R, Vogenauer S (eds) Prohibition of Abuse of Law. A New General Principle of EU Law? Hart Publishing, Oxford/Portland, pp. 521–571.
Walker N (2015) The Philosophy of European Union Law. In: Arnull A, Chalmers D (eds) The Oxford Handbook of European Union Law. Oxford University Press, Oxford, pp. 3–27.
Weber D (2013), Abuse of Law in European Tax Law: An Overview and Some Recent Trends in the Direct and Indirect Tax Case Law of the ECJ – Part 1. European Taxation 53:251–264.
Woods L (2021) Article 54. In: Peers S, Hervey T, Kenner J, Ward A (eds) The EU Charter of Fundamental Rights. A Commentary. Hart Publishing, Oxford/Portland, pp. 1692–1708.
Ziegler K (2011) 'Abuse of Law' in the Context of the Free Movement of Workers. In: De la Feria R, Vogenauer S (eds) Prohibition of Abuse of Law. A New General Principle of EU Law? Hart Publishing, Oxford/Portland, pp. 295–314.

Chapter 5
The Purpose and Function of Abuse of Law in the Union Legal Order

Contents

Abstract Building on the conclusions reached in the preceding chapters, particularly in Chap. 4, this chapter advances the analysis by shifting the focus to its theoretical underpinnings. It explores the purpose and function of abuse of law within the Union legal order and examines its broader implications for the general concept of abuse of law. The chapter seeks to address several fundamental questions, including: what is the normative role of abuse of law in the Union's legal architecture? What contribution does it make to the broader understanding of abuse of law as a legal concept? It argues that abuse of Union law ultimately serves to safeguard the internal coherence of the EU legal order and promote overall justice and fairness, in line with analogous doctrines found in other legal systems.

Keywords Normative function of abuse of law · Ultimate purpose of abuse of law · Justice and fairness · Internal coherence · Law evolution

5.1 Introduction

In the previous chapter, we examined the ECJ's case law, aiming to systematise it within a coherent and logical framework. This analysis allowed us to delineate abuse of Union law as a general principle of the EU legal order. In that context, we proposed a typology, clarified its scope of application, and examined the anti-abuse strategies developed by the Court. Building on that foundation, this chapter takes the analysis one step further, shifting to its theoretical dimension. We will explore the purpose and function of abuse of law in the Union legal order, as well as its implications for the broader concept of abuse of law. In other words, having demonstrated that abuse

L. Pantaleo, *Abuse of Law in the European Union*,
https://doi.org/10.1007/978-94-6265-731-1_5

of EU law exists, clarified when it occurs, and examined how it should be countered, we now turn to a fundamental question: what is the normative function of abuse of law in the Union's legal order? From this, a second, related question arises: what contribution does a theory of abuse of Union law make to the overall understanding of abuse of law as a general legal concept? These overarching questions can be further articulated into the following four inquiries: what are the underlying legal reasons that led the ECJ to develop the principle of abuse of Union law? What is the ultimate purpose of this legal principle? Does it align with the traditional function of abuse of law in other legal orders? How does the theory of abuse of Union law enhance the broader conceptual understanding of abuse in legal discourse?

To address these questions, this chapter is structured as follows. Section 5.2 examines the purpose and function of abuse of law in the EU legal order. Section 5.3 builds on the comparative analysis conducted in Chap. 2 by providing an overview of the purpose and function of abuse of law in other legal systems and evaluating the contribution of a theory of abuse of Union law to the broader understanding of abuse of law. Section 5.4 concludes with final remarks.

5.2 The Purpose and Function of Abuse of Law in the Union Legal Order

As the analysis in previous chapters has demonstrated, the Court of Justice identified two situations where abuse of Union law can typically occur. We termed those situations type 1 and type 2 abuse. The former occurs when a natural or legal person attempts to circumvent national law by abusively relying on EU law. The latter occurs when a natural or legal person attempts to abusively rely on EU law to obtain an undue advantage directly from it. We have seen that, in principle, it cannot be excluded that the principle in question also applies to the conduct of the EU institutions and the Member States. However, this hypothesis is, at the moment, not supported by the case law. We also opined that, in both abuse types, in order to assess whether the reliance on EU law is abusive, one must look at the purpose of the rules and evaluate whether it has been successfully achieved.

Behind the concept of abuse of Union law seems to lie the idea that there exist situations in which the purpose of EU law can be defeated or distorted by the conduct of individuals, whether natural or legal persons. In this sense, abuse of Union law constitutes a clear limit to the interests of individuals when they conflict with the general interest of the legal order. This is perhaps a novelty for the EU legal order, but it is a commonly accepted concept in other legal systems. As we shall see in Sect. 5.3, in both the domestic and international contexts, abuse of law constitutes an instrument that leads to the eventual sacrifice of individual prerogatives to safeguard the general interests of the system. In domestic legal orders, abuse constitutes a general limitation to party autonomy, which is the foundational stone of a legal system based on liberal principles. In the international legal order, abuse constitutes a general limitation to

State sovereign rights, which, *mutatis mutandis*, can be considered the equivalent of party autonomy in public international law. The main consequence of the existence of abuse is, therefore, that the exercise of otherwise lawful individual prerogatives is exceptionally restricted by the system to preserve its intrinsic coherence.

In the EU legal order, the Court of Justice is the guardian of the system and a significant factor in preserving the integration process. Moreover, the Court has admittedly pursued an integration agenda throughout its history.[1] Traditionally, natural and legal persons have been the natural allies of the Court in this effort. The typical situation is that of Mr Flaminio Costa, whose intricate legal case against Italian authorities gave the Court a chance to come up with the principle of primacy and lay the foundations of the principle of autonomy.[2] Or Ms Gabrielle Defrenne, whose watershed court case gave the Court a chance to affirm the horizontal applicability of the principle of equal pay and lay the foundations of the general non-discrimination principle.[3] The history of EU law is full of similar examples. However, this perspective is twisted when it comes to abuse of Union law. The emergence of this principle is linked with the Court's recognition that the integration process can be jeopardised by individual behaviours that counter this process, undermining its integrity. It was realised that Emsland-Stärke had attempted to obtain export subsidies without effectively exporting goods to third States. Or that individuals arranged mock relocations of their businesses solely to escape from national law and not to benefit from the wonders of the common market in a genuine manner. These practices revealed that sometimes natural and legal persons, longstanding allies of the Court, could disrupt the legal system. Abuse of Union law was the tool the ECJ needed to tackle this issue.

Put this way, it is easier to see why the general principle of abuse of Union law has been termed "special" in the previous chapter. Traditionally, general principles are legal safeguards for individuals. Their very origins, as analysed in Chap. 4, trace them back to this function. They represented a judge-made device to protect individuals from the deficiencies of the legal order, such as the Member States' non-compliant legislation or the *lacunae* of EU law (think about the initial lack of explicit protection of fundamental rights). Abuse of Union law has the opposite effect, at least at first scrutiny. Even when applied to horizontal situations such as *Kratzer*, it entails a restriction of individual prerogatives in order to safeguard the general interests of the system. Upon closer examination, however, the picture appears more nuanced. The principle of abuse of Union law is not unique in serving to preserve the integrity of the EU legal order. Principles such as primacy and sincere cooperation fulfil a comparable role.[4] Given the very nature of the EU legal system, the very operation

---

[1] Rosas 2007, p. 1037.

[2] The reference here is to the much celebrated CJEU, *Flaminio Costa v. E.N.E.L.*, Judgment of the Court, 15 July 1964, case 6/64, ECLI:EU:C:1964:66.

[3] The reference here is to the other much celebrated *Defrenne* saga, and more specifically to CJEU, *Gabrielle Defrenne v. Sabena*, Judgment of the Court, 8 April 1976, case 43/75, ECLI:EU:C1976:65.

[4] On the principle of sincere cooperation, see the thoughtful considerations made by Casolari 2022, pp. 252 ff.

of these principles can, in and of itself, function as a safeguard for individuals. It is therefore more accurate to distinguish between general principles that offer direct legal protection to individuals and those that pursue this objective indirectly, through their systemic role.[5] From this perspective, abuse of Union law is perhaps less exceptional than it might initially seem.

Furthermore, the operation of the principle of abuse of EU law can be considered a sign of the maturity of the Union's legal order, which becomes more complex as it evolves and ripens over time. In his seminal early study of the concept of abuse of (then) Community law, Gestri argued that the principle in question is somewhat inherent to exercising the judicial function. He wrote that "it is reasonable to consider that the control of the exercise of individual prerogatives based on the notion of abuse of law is the expression of a principle inherent to the judicial function, as such an integral part of the Community legal order, as well as of national legal orders".[6] It is an indispensable feature of any fully-fledged legal system. It is only logical that, in the gradual development of the Union's legal order, abuse of law has come into existence, even if it defies, at least to a certain extent, the original rationale underlying the general principles of EU law.

The inherent nature of abuse of law clearly emerges in connection with its application to the exercise of the fundamental freedoms. It is a truism to say that normative choices are integral to a common market. From a free market perspective, law can be a cost which businesses may take into consideration as part of their strategic planning. As observed in Chap. 3, the ECJ took a bold position on this matter. It knowingly chose to allow regulatory arbitrage in the common market. For example, the Court has accepted that companies can be established in a legal order based exclusively on considerations concerning what national legislation is more favourable to the business. Or that a given professional qualification is obtained in a Member State where the requirements are perceived as less demanding by the individuals willing to qualify for that profession. The Court's stance on these issues is based on the acceptance that these practices are inherent to a (common) free market. The Court of Justice could allow market dynamics to play out freely precisely because the judicial oversight it exercises features the emergency brake (namely, abuse of Union law) that is necessary to guarantee the integrity of the market and, with it, of the system as a whole. Abuse of Union law ensures that normative choices are protected only inasmuch as they align with the purpose of the rules in question. The exact dividing line between normal market dynamics and abusive situations is precisely the purpose of the rules being relied on. If that purpose is not genuinely achieved, it is inherent in the judicial scrutiny carried out by the Court that formal compliance with the law is insufficient to recognise a given conduct as lawful.

---

[5] I am especially grateful to Federico Casolari for bringing this point to my attention, as I had not fully appreciated it on my own.

[6] See Gestri 2003, p. 199. The translation is mine. The original Italian text reads as follows: "*è ragionevole ritenere che la tecnica di controllo dell'esercizio delle prerogative individuali fondata sulla nozione di abuso del diritto costituisca espressione di un principio immanente alla funzione giurisdizionale, che come tale fa parte dell'ordinamento comunitario, oltre che degli ordinamenti nazionali*".

The developments that occurred in the two fields mentioned above confirm the soundness of the Court's approach. As regards professional qualifications, as we have already seen in Chap. 3, the ECJ's position has led some Member States to change their rules to make it less easy and, most importantly, more in line with the situation of other Member States, to obtain the qualifications needed for some professions. In the field of company law, the Court's liberal attitude has been associated with increased mobility of companies and with positive regulatory competition between Member States, which mobilised in order to render their company law more attractive (so-called responsive lawmaking).[7] As also seen in Chap. 3, in recent times, the Court of Justice has clearly affirmed that market actors *have the right* to make normative choices and take advantage of the competition engaged in by the Member States. In this way, the Luxembourg Court clarified that abuse of Union law cannot be used as a general anti-free market tool. It is an exceptional remedy that can be triggered where the purpose of EU rules has been defeated or distorted (or both), leading to outcomes that contradict their original intent.

From this perspective, I agree with Butler and Sørensen that abuse of Union law "is conceived of as a narrow, exceptional recourse",[8] not only for the reasons just mentioned but also to avoid it being used differently or even abused by national authorities of the Member States. As we have seen in Chap. 3, the free movement of persons is the field where abuse has more frequently been invoked in a pretextual manner. This explains the ECJ's particularly strong posture regarding possible abuses of this freedom.[9] In Chap. 3, we concluded that relying on the principle of abuse of Union law to restrict this freedom is very difficult. It can be said that the free movement of persons is the area of EU law where the exceptional nature of abuse of law is most visible.

In light of the foregoing, it seems reasonable to put forward the following arguments regarding the function and purpose of abuse of law in the Union legal order. Firstly, abuse of law aims to ensure that the genuine purpose of the Union rules is achieved and safeguarded against the risk of pretextual individual exploitation. The defeat or distortion of such a purpose turns the use of a right into an abuse. Secondly, and as a consequence, the principle in question inherently safeguards the general interests of the legal order, particularly when they collide with individual interests. When the invocation of EU law results in a situation where the social disadvantage (general interest) outweighs the individual advantage (personal interest), the system favours the former. That said, while the principle of abuse indeed safeguards general interests, it should be borne in mind that the Court often engages in a balancing exercise. In other words, this is not to say that the system favours the general interest in every conflict. Instead, the ECJ assesses whether the individual is misusing EU law in the sense of defeating or distorting its purpose, and there has to be clear evidence of abuse. Finally, the more fundamental consequence of the previous point is that abuse of Union law ultimately safeguards the coherence of the integration process

[7] See Ringe 2011, pp. 108–120; for the opposite view, see Vella 2011, pp. 131 ff.

[8] See Butler and Sørensen 2022, p. 412.

[9] See the considerations made by Poli 2017, pp. 30 ff.

and the integrity of the legal order. Here, coherence should be understood broadly to include not only the prevention of negative externalities for all the actors involved but also the advancement of mutual trust in the EU system. If Member States or other private parties (for example, in horizontal cases) suspect that EU law can be twisted to create artificial advantages, further integration may be resisted. By asserting that the application of EU law cannot protect the individual at the expense of the general interest, the principle of abuse of Union law ensures that EU law, like any other legal system, is intrinsically fair and just. To be sure, the Court itself usually frames abuse of Union law in terms of protecting the purpose of EU law or ensuring no undue advantage. Direct references to concepts such as intrinsic fairness and overall justice are to be found nowhere in the ECJ's own language. In this sense, fairness and justice should be understood as the underlying rationale, not the Court's explicit pursuit.

This final point aligns perfectly with the nature of abuse of Union law as a general principle of the EU legal order. In its recent work on general principles of international law,[10] the ILC has recognised that such principles "contribute to the coherence of the international legal system".[11] According to the Special Rapporteur Vázquez-Bermúdez, this function "is a natural consequence of the fact that this source of international law is essentially aimed at filling gaps in the international legal system".[12] While explicit references to this attribute in practice are limited, legal scholarship frequently emphasises the systemic function of general principles of law across different areas of international law.[13] The underlying idea is that general principles serve as a unifying force, ensuring: (a) the systemic nature of the legal order, (b) intra-systemic convergence, and (c) in the case of international law, the inter-systemic coherence between international and domestic legal systems.[14] As Vázquez-Bermúdez observed, "while all general principles of law [...] could be regarded as ensuring in some way the coherence of the international legal system, certain general principles appear to be aimed at performing this function in a more direct manner".[15] Among them, he included good faith,[16] which, as demonstrated throughout this book, is inextricably linked to the concept of abuse of law. It follows, therefore, that *mutatis mutandis*, these same considerations regarding the systemic role of general principles in international law can also be applied to the EU legal order, particularly in relation to abuse of law.

This conclusion leads to the discussion in Sect. 5.3, where the ultimate goal of abuse of law as a legal concept will be examined in the broader context of domestic legal orders and international law.

[10] For a general comment, see Jalloh 2023; for a discussion on what appears to be the most contentious issue debated at the ILC, see Bjørge 2023.

[11] See ILC, General principles of law. Text of the draft conclusions provisionally adopted by the Drafting Committee on first reading, A/CN.4/L.982, 12 May 2023, Draft conclusion n. 10.

[12] See Vázquez-Bermúdez 2023, p. 50.

[13] See Kolb 2019, p. 136; Gazzini 2009, p. 106.

[14] See Andenas and Chiussi 2019, p. 10.

[15] See Vázquez-Bermúdez 2023, p. 52.

[16] Ibid.

5.3 The Purpose and Function of Abuse of Law in General: A Theory of Abuse of Law

As the analysis in Chap. 2 has evidenced, virtually all legal systems analysed in this monograph have their own version of abuse of law. However, despite the existing differences already seen in Chap. 2, to which we will not go back in this section, it is reasonable to say that, at some level of abstraction, abuse of law has a similar systemic purpose in all national legal systems featuring abuse of law, as well as in international law.

We will start with domestic legal orders. Taking the Italian system as the leading example, given my familiarity with it for apparent reasons, authors have expressed a variety of opinions about the function of abuse of law. Leaving aside the outright deniers of its existence,[17] according to one author, abuse of law expresses the idea that the law must be just,[18] and, as a consequence, its social function inherently limits the exercise of individual rights. A more nuanced view equally recognises that abuse of law represents the tool with which the legal system realigns the exercise of individual rights with their legitimate aim, but does not connect this function to the realisation of a superior ideal of justice. Instead, abuse of rights is seen as a rationalising force.[19] According to a more positivist approach, concepts such as justice and fairness are inherent to the idea of law. Something, like an action, is unjust as long as it is carried out *non iure*, that is, without a norm authorising that action.[20] While not denying the existence of abuse of law and its relevance for the legal order, this author connects it with the concept of good faith.[21] Another scholar has expressed a similar position, arguing that an abusive act is outside the remit of the law and, as such, deprived of legal protection.[22] The *leitmotiv* emerging from the literature, which consists mainly of private lawyers, is that abuse of law constitutes a limit of general application to the exercise of individual rights and freedoms. It is a mechanism that introduces an element of flexibility in the otherwise potentially inflexible application of individual rights as absolute prerogatives.

As far as international law is concerned—leaving aside the outright deniers of its existence[23]—abuse of law serves the same purpose as in the domestic context, *mutatis mutandis*. It functions as a limitation on the exercise of rights on the part of States. Such rights can be exercised directly or indirectly (as seen in the field of investment law in Chap. 2). From this perspective, abuse of law can be regarded as

[17] Which can, nowadays, be considered out of date, given that, as seen in Chap. 2, the existence of abuse of rights is generally accepted by established case law. For a classic rejection of the theory of abuse of law, see Rotondi 1923, p. 105 ff.

[18] See Astone 2017, p. 12.

[19] See Restivo 2007, pp. 112–113 and 127.

[20] See Rescigno 1998, p. 113.

[21] Ibid., p. 277.

[22] See Galgano 2011, p. 317.

[23] For a particularly erudite example, see the classic Schwarzenberger 1956, pp. 149–150.

a general limitation on State sovereignty inherent to the rights conferred by international law. According to Politis, who has meaningfully assessed abuse of law in a study on *les limitations de la souveraineté*, abuse arises in international law when the general interest of the international community is sacrificed to satisfy the individual interest of a single sovereign State. Abuse of law thus operates as a mechanism for restoring balance, ensuring the protection of the general interest over that of a single State.[24] Similarly, Lauterpacht observed that the prohibition of abuse of law is triggered only when the "interests injuriously affected by the exercise of the hitherto perfectly legal right are socially and morally more important" than the individual interests underpinning that right.[25] By the same token, Lemey, in the most comprehensive recent study on abuse of law in international law, argued that "*[l]a function essentielle de l'abus de droit consiste à assurer une regulation dans l'ordre juridique international en restreignant l'exercice des prerogatives juridiques afin qu'elles ne soient pas employées de façon arbitraire*".[26] She further asserted that abuse of law contributes to preserving the international rule of law,[27] and that, ultimately, "*permet de preserver la function sociale du droit*" in the international context.[28] Therefore, it is fair to conclude that, for international lawyers too, much like for domestic law scholars, the prevailing view is that even an individual entitlement as strong as a State's sovereign right cannot take precedence over the general interests of the community as a whole. Consequently, the idea that abuse of law is intrinsically linked to concepts such as fairness and justice emerges in international legal discourse as well.

In light of the foregoing, it seems reasonable to affirm that, in both the domestic and international context, abuse of law is conceived of as a legal mechanism that allows interpreters to look beyond formal compliance with legal rules and address situations where adherence to the letter of the law results in manifestly unjust outcomes. In other words, it reflects the idea that, even when a right holder exercises its rights, the application and interpretation of the law should always lead to fair and just outcomes *lato sensu*, ensuring the inherent systemic coherence of the legal order.

This very notion was advanced by Louis Josserand, who is widely regarded as the founder of the modern understanding of abuse of law. In his foundational study, he argued that the principle *summum ius summa iniuria* ("the highest law is the highest injustice") should prevail over "*la maxime haïssable* ***Dura lex sed lex***".[29] He presented abuse of law as a "*notion profondément moral*", aimed at ensuring "*le triomphe de l'esprit de la loi sur son texte*",[30] but also as a "*notion sociale*" designed

---

[24] See Politis 1925, p. 89.

[25] See Lauterpacht 2011, p. 304.

[26] See Lemey 2021, p. 398.

[27] Ibid., p. 387 ff. Politis also argued that abuse of law is an instrument at the service of *la légalité*. See Politis 1925, p. 78.

[28] Ibid., p. 400.

[29] See Josserand 1905, p. 86 (emphasis in the original text). The maxim in question can be translated as "the law is harsh, but it is the law".

[30] Ibid., p. 6.

to guarantee "*la réalisation des droits pour le plus grand bien de la collectivité, loyalement, opportunément,* ***civiliter***".[31] For Josserand, the very legitimacy of the law was at stake. His words remain profoundly relevant and deserve to be cited in full: "*il s'agit de savoir si le droit est susceptible, par une interpretation outrancière et draconienne, d'abriter indéfiniment l'injustice ou s'il ne doit pas se vivifier, s'humaniser profondément au souffle de l'équité*".[32] Accepting the notion of abuse of law allows the legal system to fulfil its fundamental promise of delivering fairness and justice. In other words, its promise to be a coherent legal system.

At this stage of the analysis, it seems appropriate to clarify the meaning of concepts such as fairness and justice for the purpose of understanding the principle of abuse of law. Their interpretation inevitably depends on one's fundamental legal convictions. Accordingly, I will present an account that reflects my positivist approach and situate it within the broader framework of EU law. I align with those scholars cited above who argue that justice and fairness are inherent to the very concept of law.[33] Consequently, an abusive action is one that exceeds the boundaries set by the posited norm—an action carried out *non iure* (without legal right). As Gestri aptly put it, "acting abusively is tantamount to acting with no right".[34] From this perspective, the moral dimension of abuse of law lies in ensuring that the legal boundaries are not stretched to encompass actions that fall outside the purpose(s) pursued by the posited norm, as determined, at least in the EU legal order, through the Court's teleological interpretation. The demarcation line is thus determined by the law's purpose, and that lawful purpose is intrinsically moral.

The interpretation presented here aligns squarely with the Court of Justice's case law. The ECJ's analysis of abuse does not engage in moral considerations; instead, it is firmly rooted in assessing whether the purpose of EU law has been achieved. The legitimacy of that purpose is never questioned—it is assumed as a given, and rightly so, in my view. Moreover, it is important to recall that the Court of Justice's strategy is to place abusive conduct outside the remit of EU law. In what we have termed type 2 abuse cases, the ECJ does so explicitly, stating that the secondary legislation invoked by the abuser does not extend to abusive practices. However, beneath the surface, the same approach is evident in type 1 abuse cases, where the Court's anti-abuse strategy consists of validating a Member State's otherwise unlawful restriction, thereby excluding the abuser from EU law's protective scope. Restrictions on EU law effectively narrow down its scope, reducing the range of situations that fall within its protection. Thus, underlying the Court's reasoning in both categories of abuse appears to be the conviction that acting abusively is tantamount to acting outside the law. This reinforces the idea that an abusive action is carried out *non iure*. If you are a trader applying for an export subsidy, not to export something but to achieve some

[31] Ibid. (emphasis in the original text).

[32] Ibid.

[33] For an erudite positivist account of the "built-in dash of moral merit in every law" see Gardner 2012, p. 48 ff.

[34] See Gestri 2003, p. 202. In the original Italian text: "*abusare di un diritto equivale ad agire 'senza diritto'*".

other purpose not recognised by the posited norm, you are effectively outside the protective shield offered by that norm.

That said, I also contend that abuse of law may exert an inevitable reforming impulse on the legal order. In 1957, Bobbio, who described the principle of abuse of law as "controversial", argued that principles of this kind enable interpreters to "auscultate" society—in the metaphorical sense of attentively listening—to capture emerging moral and political ideas and advance them over those in decline.[35] In other words, Bobbio conceived of abuse of law as a natural drive of (legal) progress, a view that clearly builds on Josserand's approach.

This perspective, in my opinion, also resonates with Lowe's construction of abuse of law as an interstitial principle in international law. As is well-known, Lowe referred to the "emergence of normative concepts operating in the interstices between [...] primary norms [which] do not themselves have a normative force of the traditional kind but instead operate by modifying the normative effect of other, primary norms of international law".[36] These interstitial principles, far from being mere interpretive tools, serve a primary function: resolving conflicts between primary norms by directing "the manner in which competing or conflicting norms that do have their own normativity should interact in practice".[37] A defining feature of such principles is their capacity to be "redefined with infinite flexibility in order to accommodate social change".[38] Furthermore, Lowe observed that "[t]hrough the influence of these principles, the whole character of international law and its relation to the most pressing problems of fairness and justice can be materially altered".[39] Thus, in Lowe's view, the function of abuse of law previously discussed—namely, that of serving fairness and justice—converges with the driver-for-change function identified by Bobbio. In summary, both Bobbio and Lowe see abuse of law as not merely a defensive tool designed to combat abusive practices but also as a proactive force for evolving the law. Interestingly, this was also the primary function of abuse of law in international law according to Lauterpacht. In his seminal 1933 work, *The Function of Law in the International Community*, recently reprinted, he notably titled the section on abuse of law as *The doctrine of abuse as an instrument of change*. Lauterpacht argued that "[i]n many cases the use of a right degenerates into a socially reprehensible abuse of right, not because of the sinister intention of the person exercising the right, but owing to the fact that, as the result of social changes unaccompanied by corresponding developments in the law, an assertion of a right grounded in the existing law becomes mischievous and intolerable".[40] Thus, abuse of law was conceived as a mechanism to address this imbalance and adapt the law to evolving social realities.

I do not fully align with the moral dimension of Bobbio's approach (or Lauterpacht's), nor do I entirely endorse Lowe's characterisation of abuse of law as an

[35] See Bobbio 1957, p. 895.

[36] See Lowe 2000, p. 213.

[37] Ibid., p. 216.

[38] Ibid., p. 217.

[39] Ibid., p. 218.

[40] See Lauterpacht 2011, pp. 294–295.

interstitial principle. However, I share their fundamental belief that abuse of law may function as a driver of legal and social change beyond ensuring fair and just outcomes, including in the Union legal order. As we have seen, the purpose of a norm is central to abuse of law. The lawmaker defines this purpose, while the interpreter bears the responsibility of ensuring that natural and legal persons do not defeat or distort it through abusive actions. By taking into account emerging societal trends, the interpreter can construe the lawful purpose of a norm accordingly, thereby accommodating social change. What is considered acceptable today may be abusive in the future, and vice versa. Abuse of law is the instrument that questions whether the literal application of norms has become outdated or misaligned with societal values.

5.4 Conclusions: Abuse of Union Law as an Integral Part of a Complete Legal System

The analysis carried out in this chapter has allowed us to dig deep into the systemic functions and theoretical foundations of abuse of Union law. We started off in Sect. 5.1 with a number of questions and sub-questions, which we are now in a position to answer.

Regarding the normative function of abuse of law in the Union's legal order, it is safe to conclude that the principle in question operates as a safeguard against abusive reliance on EU law, ensuring that rights derived from EU rules, though valid on their face, are not invoked in ways that defeat the underlying purpose of the rules in question. Its central normative function is thus twofold. On the one hand, it preserves the integrity and coherence of the legal system; on the other hand, and as a consequence thereof, it upholds fundamental values like fairness and justice by denying protection where the established purpose of the law is defeated or distorted. In this sense, the principle ensures that the spirit of the law prevails over its text, taken at face value, preserving the coherence of the integration process and reinforcing the general trust in it.

When it comes to the contribution that abuse of Union law makes to understanding abuse of law as a general legal concept, the following observations can be made. Traditionally, municipal legal systems, as well as international law, have recognised abuse of law precisely to curtail overly formalistic uses of legal prerogatives, thus avoiding despicable and unjust outcomes. The development of abuse of law in the Union legal order is consistent with this framework. The Court of Justice resorted to abuse in order to respond to situations where strict adherence to the text risked subverting the purpose of EU rules, resulting in unjust outcomes. Faced with artificial arrangements in taxation, corporate structures, free movement, or other fields, the ECJ recognised the need to deny the exercise of rights if those rights were pursued solely to gain an undue advantage and undermine the genuine purpose pursued by the rules. Thus, at its core, the principle of abuse of Union law mirrors the traditional rationale found in domestic systems, as well as in international law, which likewise seeks to limit formal legal entitlements based on considerations of good faith, justice and fairness, with a view to preserving the inherent systemic coherence of the legal order. In the EU context, as we have seen, an abuse doctrine can also become a driver of integration—an ally of the Court, as we put it above. At any rate, the Union's version of abuse of law seems to be firmly grounded in universal notions of justice and fairness. Moreover, it may contribute to the further development and progress of the law over time.

The overarching purpose of abuse of Union law is, therefore, to protect the coherent and effective functioning of EU law. It ensures that EU rules are interpreted and applied in line with their genuine aim, thus maintaining fairness, avoiding negative externalities, and promoting trust in the system among Member States, as well as EU citizens and companies. As we have seen, the Court balances individual rights against the general interest, emphasising that private advantage cannot prevail over the foundational goals of the system taken as a whole. The Court of Justice's stance, guided by teleological interpretation, vividly demonstrates how a supranational, *sui generis* legal order can refine and even reinvigorate the concept of abuse of law.

The reach of this principle further underscores the maturation of the EU legal order into a fully-fledged system. In his Opinion in *Kefalas*, AG Tesauro famously observed that "any legal order which aspires to achieve a minimum level of completion must contain self-protection measures, so to speak, to ensure that the rights it confers are not exercised in a manner which is abusive, excessive or distorted".[41] At the time, AG Tesauro believed that the conditions for enshrining a general principle in the Union legal order, one that would allow the denial of recognition to abusive exercises of rights conferred by EU rules, had not yet been met.[42] Much has changed since then. Today, the consecration of this general principle is indisputable, illustrating the significant evolution of the EU legal order compared to AG Tesauro's time. Far from having achieved *just a minimum level* of completion, the Union has now developed the capacity to preserve both legal coherence and its overarching commitment to justice through the principle of abuse of law. This principle not only reinforces the integrity of EU law but also enhances its ability to evolve in response to shifting social and economic realities, affirming the Union's ascension to a fully-fledged legal system.

In his 1993 landmark study, *Fairness in the International Legal and Institutional System*, Thomas Franck linked the need to assess the fairness of international law to the idea that it had "matured into a complete legal system".[43] He observed that "humanity wants to be reassured that the emerging legal system is capable of ensuring both stability and progressive change. Any legal system which is not perceived as fair

[41] CJEU, *Kefalas*, Opinion of Advocate General Tesauro, 4 February 1998, case C-367/96, ECLI:EU:C:1998:41, para 24.

[42] Ibid., para 21.

[43] See Franck 1993, p. 24.

will eventually cease to evolve and may shrivel",[44] regardless of how mature or well-developed it may be. While fairness is inherently "a product of social context and history",[45] making it "relative and subjective",[46] it remains a fundamental attribute of any fully-fledged legal system. In both the EU legal order and other legal systems, abuse of law functions as a mechanism that upholds this core principle, ensuring not only legitimacy and fairness but also the ability to foster progressive change in line with prevailing societal trends.

References

Andenas M, Chiussi L (2019) Cohesion, Convergence and Coherence of International Law. In: Andenas M, Fitzmaurice M, Tanzi T, Wouters J (eds) General Principles and the Coherence of International Law. Brill-Nijhoff, Leiden, pp. 9–34.

Astone A (2017) Il divieto di abuso del diritto. Giuffrè, Milan.

Bjørge E (2023) General Principles of Law Formed within the International Legal System. International and Comparative Law Quarterly 72:845–867.

Bobbio R (1957) Principi Generali di Diritto. In: Novissimo Digesto Italiano. Giappichelli, Turin, 888–896.

Butler G, Sørensen KE (2022) The Prohibition of Abuse of EU Law: a Special General Principle. In: Ziegler K, Neuvonen PJ, Moreno-Lax V (eds) Research Handbook on General Principles in EU Law. Edward Elgar, Cheltenham, pp. 402–422.

Casolari F (2022) Il principio di leale cooperazione tra Stati membri e Unione europea. Studio sulla partecipazione all'Unione al tempo delle crisi. Editoriale scientifica, Naples.

Franck T (1993) Fairness in the International Legal and Institutional System. Recueil des cours 240: 23–498.

Galgano F (2011) Qui suo iure abutitur neminem laedit? Contratto e impresa 27:311–319.

Gardner J (2012) Law as a Leap of Faith: Essays on Law in General. Oxford University Press, Oxford.

Gazzini T (2009) General Principles of Law in the Field of Foreign Investment. Journal of World Investment and Trade 10:103–119.

Gestri M (2003) Abuso del diritto e frode alla legge nell'ordinamento comunitario. Giuffrè, Milan.

Jalloh CC (2023) The International Law Commission's Seventy-Fourth (2023) Session: General Principles of Law and Other Topics. The American Journal of International Law 118:120–144.

Josserand L (1905) L'abus des droits. Rousseau, Paris.

Kolb R (2019) Theory of International Law. Hart, Oxford.

Lauterpacht H (2011) The Function of Law in the International Community. Oxford University Press, Oxford.

Lemey M (2021) L'abus de droit en droit international public. LGDJ, Paris.

Lowe V (2000) The Politics of Law-Making: Are the Method and Character of Norm Creation Changing? In: Byers M (ed) The Role of Law in International Politics: Essays in International Relations and International Law. Oxford University Press, Oxford, pp. 207–226.

Poli S (2017) L'abuso delle libertà di circolazione delle persone nel quadro complessivo della giurisprudenza della Corte di giustizia. In: Calamia AM (ed) L'Abuso del diritto. Casi scelti tra principi, regole e giurisprudenza. Giappichelli, Turin, pp. 21–51.

[44] Ibid., p. 26.

[45] Ibid., p. 31.

[46] Ibid., p. 32.

Politis N (1925) Le problème des limitations de la souveraineté et la théorie de l'abus des droits dans les rapports internationaux. Recueil des Cours de l'Académie de droit international de La Haye 6:1–122.
Rescigno P (1998) L'abuso del diritto. Il Mulino, Bologna.
Restivo C (2007) Contributo ad una teoria dell'abuso del diritto. Giuffrè, Milan.
Ringe WG (2011) Sparking Regulatory Competition in European Company Law: The Impact of the *Centros* Line of Case Law and its Concept of 'Abuse of Law'. In: De la Feria R, Vogenauer S (eds) Prohibition of Abuse of Law. A New General Principle of EU Law? Hart Publishing, Oxford/Portland, pp. 107–125.
Rosas A (2007) Separation of Powers in the European Union. The International Lawyer 41:1033–1046.
Rotondi M (1923) L'abuso del diritto. Rivista di diritto civile 15:105–124.
Schwarzenberger G (1956) Uses and Abuses of the "Abuse of Rights" in International Law. Transactions of the Grotius Society 42:147–179.
Vázquez-Bermúdez M (2023) Third Report on General Principles of Law. International Law Commission, Seventy-Third Session, A/CN.4/753.
Vella J (2011) Sparking Regulatory Competition in European Company Law: A Response. In: De la Feria R, Vogenauer S (eds) Prohibition of Abuse of Law. A New General Principle of EU Law? Hart Publishing, Oxford/Portland, pp. 127–136.

Chapter 6
Concluding Reflections: Abuse of Law and the Maturation of the EU Legal Order

Contents

Abstract This concluding chapter summarises the book's main findings and closes with a reflection on whether the emergence of the principle of abuse of law signals the maturation of the EU legal order or, conversely, represents a sign of immaturity. It argues in favour of the former.

Keywords Key findings · Fully-fledged legal order · Principle of abuse of law · EU legal order

6.1 The Principle of Abuse of Law in the EU Legal Order: From the Uncertain First Steps of the Early Case Law to the Formulation of a Fully-Fledged Doctrine of Abuse

This monograph has analysed the doctrine of abuse of law in the EU legal order, as it developed from the foundational *Van Binsbergen* case to the most recent judgments that have allowed the ECJ to formulate a comprehensive doctrine of abuse of Union law. It has done so with a twofold approach. On the one hand, it has taken a practical perspective by carefully examining the extensive case law of the Court of Justice, which has slowly extrapolated a general principle prohibiting the abusive exercise of rights granted by EU law. On the other hand, it has taken a more scholarly approach by analysing the theoretical foundations of such principle and placing it against the broader background of abuse of law as a general legal concept beyond the EU legal order.

L. Pantaleo, *Abuse of Law in the European Union*,
https://doi.org/10.1007/978-94-6265-731-1_6

Chapter 1 began by distinguishing between abuse of law and other legal concepts that may share some affinities with it and serve similar purposes but are nonetheless intrinsically distinct from it. This holds true for legitimate expectations, estoppel, proportionality, and legal certainty. A special place is occupied by the principle of good faith, which, as demonstrated by the analysis in the following chapters, is profoundly connected with abuse of law.

Chapter 2 examined the concept of abuse of law as it has emerged in legal orders other than the EU. In this chapter, a number of interim conclusions were reached that paved the way for the examination of EU law, the central focus of this book. We saw in that chapter that the concept of abuse of law originated in Roman law as a response to the rigid, absolute conception of individual rights. It evolved gradually as a limitation to the exercise of rights in some areas. However, Roman law stopped short of developing a fully-fledged doctrine of abuse of law. Moreover, Chap. 2 highlighted how the French case law and legal scholarship in the 19th and early 20th centuries took the issue further, laying the foundations for the modern understanding of abuse of law. From the watershed 1855 judgment of the Court of Appeal of Colmar to the erudite scholarly reflections of Louis Josserand, the abuse of law doctrine was expanded to cover seemingly all areas of law, acquiring the general scope it holds today.

The analysis further demonstrated that nearly all continental European jurisdictions in the civil law tradition recognise a principle of abuse of law, although in different ways and with some nuances from one system to another. The chapter showed that even common law jurisdictions, which are traditionally perceived as resistant to the concept of abuse of law, nonetheless feature legal doctrines that align with the underlying rationale of abuse of law. Furthermore, the analysis elaborated on how different jurisdictions, such as Japan, Islamic legal systems and the Nordic countries, despite their specific attributes, have gradually shaped a functional doctrine of abuse of law that aligns with the versions of it that can be found elsewhere. Finally, that chapter dealt with international law, which remains the field where the doctrine of abuse of law has faced the most significant difficulties in gaining explicit recognition. However, developments in some specific areas of international law, such as investment law and WTO law, as well as State practice outside these domains and the prevailing opinion in the scholarship, all pointed to the conclusion that abuse of law in international law features the same essential attributes as its domestic counterparts. In essence, the analysis in Chap. 2 confirmed that the idea that legal entitlements cannot be exercised abusively is as old as the very concept of legal systems and, as such, inherent to them.

Chapter 3 provided an in-depth examination of the extensive case law of the Court of Justice on the matter. Cases were presented in chronological order in an attempt to demonstrate the trajectory followed by the ECJ in developing a fully-fledged doctrine of abuse of Union law. The analysis demonstrated that despite some initial uncertainties and a reasonable amount of bewilderment, the Court adopted its typical stone-by-stone approach observed in the construction of other important EU law concepts. The case law was divided into three main stages, named the foundational period (starting from the "first stone", that is, the *Van Binsbergen* ruling), the structural development period (where an abuse test was introduced in *Emsland-Stärke* and fine-tuned over time), and the consolidation stage (starting from *Cussens*, where the systematisation of the general principle of abuse of EU law began).

Chapter 4 synthesised the key insights from the case law, structuring them into a coherent and logical framework to clarify the nature and scope of abuse of Union law. As this chapter is central to the monograph, it presented several important conclusions, which will now be reiterated here for clarity and better understanding.

First, there is no doubt that abuse of EU law constitutes a general principle of EU law, featuring all the typical characteristics of general principles. Second, it performs the two main functions typically performed by general principles, such as being an interpretive instrument of written primary and secondary law and a ground for review of Member States' measures, as well as of secondary legislation. Third, abuse of Union law has some specificities that distinguish it from a "normal" general principle. In particular, it is a special general principle that also performs an additional function: it limits the action of natural and legal persons seeking to abusively rely on Union law in horizontal situations (that is, *vis-à-vis* other private actors). Fourth, fraud is also prohibited by the same general principle of Union law, being a specific manifestation of it. Abuse is the basic underlying principle from which fraud is an offshoot. Fraud, however, has one crucial difference: while abuse arises when the law has been formally respected, fraud is premised on a false representation of reality. Despite this fundamental difference, the Court of Justice has managed to adapt the abuse test to fraud, considering such a difference. Fifth, although abuse of Union law has manifested itself in many different areas and contexts and has taken different forms, it eventually comes down to two types of abuse: (a) where a natural or legal person attempts to circumvent national law by relying on EU law (type 1 abuse), and (b) where a natural or legal person attempts to abusively (that is, in a manner that contrasts with its purpose) rely on EU law to obtain an undue advantage directly from it (type 2 abuse). Sixth, each type of abuse is countered by a different anti-abuse strategy. For type 1 abuses, the Court of Justice allows the Member States to impose restrictions that would otherwise be incompatible with the fundamental freedoms. For type 2 abuses, the ECJ narrows down the scope of application of the rules invoked so that abusive practices do not fall within the coverage of EU law. Seventh, in both type 1 and type 2, a finding of abuse leads to the same consequence: the natural or legal person who perpetrates abuse is denied the benefit of EU law. Eighth, for abuse of Union law to materialise, it is necessary that the purpose of the EU rules invoked is defeated or distorted. Hence, the importance of teleological interpretation. Ninth, in type 1 abuse cases, proportionality is used to assess the lawfulness of the anti-abuse measures adopted by the Member States, in line with the general application of the proportionality principle. Tenth, the Court of Justice has been quite consistent in highlighting that abuse of Union law has two constitutive elements, a subjective and an objective one. While the second one has not led to much controversy, the first one has been more difficult to define. The objective element of abuse implies that despite the formal observance of the conditions laid down by EU rules, the purpose of those rules has not been achieved. As regards the subjective element of abuse, the Court of Justice has essentially oscillated between two alternative formulations.

The subjective element was found where there was an *intention to obtain an undue advantage* from the EU rules or where the *essential aim of the transaction* was to obtain such an *undue advantage*. Both expressions are used by the Court and must be recognised as suitable. The *leitmotiv* between them is the concept of artificiality, or lack of genuineness, applied to the transaction or the intention of the parties involved, as the case may be. Eleventh, while abuse of Union law in principle applies to all areas of EU law, it is very difficult to occur in some areas of it (such as the free movement of workers and the freedom of establishment of companies) because of the prevailing teleological interpretations of the ECJ. Twelfth, abuse of Union law has a clear gap-filling role not only when there is a legal vacuum but also where *ad hoc* anti-abuse rules exist (either in secondary legislation or in Member States' domestic law), yet their scope is narrower than the general principle. Thirteenth and final conclusion, harmonisation does not constitute a real alternative to combat abuse, but it is instead a helpful complement to the general principle of EU law prohibiting it.

In Chap. 4, we have also underscored the existence of a number of questions that are still open to discussion. First, there seems to be a logical connection between the ECJ's case law on the inadmissibility of preliminary questions and the idea of abuse of process. This connection, however, has not fully emerged in practice. Second, next to the right to combat abuse, there is also a duty to refuse the benefits of EU law in case of abuse. While there has been some discussion, especially in the scholarship, on the scope of this duty, the case law seems to suggest that it applies to the Member States in a general manner. Third, while there is no confirmation in the case law that abuse of Union law can be perpetrated by the EU institutions and the Member States, this seems to be a likely development that may occur in the future in light of the nature of abuse of law as a general principle and its connection with good faith.

In Chap. 5, the analysis turned to the purpose and function of abuse of law in the Union's legal order. In very short terms, we claimed that it has two overarching functions. The first and most apparent one is to ensure that EU rights are exercised in a manner that is consistent with the purpose for which they have been granted. Therefore, an abusive exercise of a right is the use of such a right in a manner that defeats or distorts its purpose. If EU law grants the right to an export subsidy, one can only benefit from it if exporting goods is effectively taking place. However, we emphasised that abuse of Union law has a second and more fundamental purpose. It is aimed at guaranteeing the systemic coherence of the system, ultimately serving the universal notions of justice and fairness, contributing to the further development and progress of the law over time. It ensures that the European integration process remains in line with its genuine intent so that deceitful exploitations of the law are prevented, and trust in the systemic coherence is maintained.

6.2 Abuse of EU Law: A Childhood Disease or an Inevitable Consequence of Maturity?

Earlier in this book, we have already mentioned the idea that the development of some legal concepts is traditionally associated with the maturation of the legal order. We have referred to AG Tesauro's Opinion in *Kefalas*, as well as to Franck's considerations on fairness in international law.[1] Building on Tesauro, we argued that abuse of law belongs to this category of legal concepts that render a legal order complete, fully-fledged, and, in short, truly a legal system. In this section, which concludes the book, we will critically reflect on this consideration. Is abuse of law really a byproduct of the maturation of the EU legal order, or the opposite? Is it, as the title of this section suggests, using an age-related analogy, an inevitable consequence of maturity or a childhood disease?

In his seminal article focused on abuse of process in international investment law, Emmanuel Gaillard concluded with a sour note. He argued that "[w]here certain types of conduct generate a sense of unease, they are first addressed through the application of general principles such as 'abuse of rights' or 'good faith'. Over time, new legal rules will emerge that are specifically designed to tackle particular types of […] conduct".[2] Based on these words only, it is impossible to say whether this prominent author indeed intended to conclude that abuse of law is a childhood disease of underdeveloped (better: developing) legal orders. But let us assume, for the sake of argument, that this was the implication. It would essentially mean that abuse of law is a residual remedy, perhaps a temporary one, that operates so long as the legal system does not develop more specific rules to address certain types of (reprehensible) conduct.

This idea is not entirely new to the reader of this book. When commenting on the Soviet Civil Code in Chap. 2, we observed that abuse of law in the socialist system became affected by desuetude. Since Soviet laws were presumed to be morally impeccable, malevolence within the boundaries of the law became theoretically impossible when socialist law took hold in the system, leading to abuse of law progressively losing significance. A similar position was expressed by Nazi legal theory. The doctrine of abuse of law was endorsed by several influential Nazi scholars, who thought it would promote a less individualistic society, admittedly more in line with national-socialist principles.[3] However, the general understanding was that its relevance would gradually diminish as the national-socialist idea of law took hold in the German legal order.[4] *Mutatis mutandis*, the idea that abuse of law

[1] See Chap. 5.

[2] See Gaillard 2017, p. 37.

[3] See Gordley 2011, p. 42.

[4] Ibid.

is superfluous in a fully developed legal system, is not foreign to those common lawyers who are sceptical about its existence and relevance in common law jurisdictions.[5] To be absolutely clear, I am in no way equating distinguished legal scholars such as Gaillard, Gutteridge, and Schwarzenberger to Nazi or Soviet legal theorists. What I am suggesting is that a recurring argument in legal scholarship, expressed by a diverse range of scholars across different contexts, maintains that abuse of law, along with other legal principles, is ill-suited to regulate legally relevant situations in a fully developed legal order. If it has a role to play, it is usually a temporary or fallback one, which will fade away so long as the system comes to maturation.

I am, however, convinced of the opposite. It is undoubtedly true that abuse of law has ancient roots. It is also true that it has been decisively boosted by the French case law and scholarship of the 19th and early 20th centuries, as well as the codifications that followed between the 19th and the 20th centuries. However, its veritable success is more recent and has to do, in my opinion, with the advent of liberal democracies. More specifically, it has only fully established itself across legal orders with the emergence of constitutional democracies based on the rule of law. In the past, individual rights were, at best, conceded by absolute rulers such as the God-appointed monarchs of the 19th century or the brutal tyrants of the early 20th century. In those days, the private and the public spheres were inherently mutually hostile. Individuals mistrusted the State, and individual rights were therefore seen as the last line of defence against governmental authority. Against this background, it is easy to see the reasons that led Gutteridge to conclude in 1933 that the principle of abuse of law could potentially "get out of hand and result in serious inroads on individual rights, thus becoming an instrument of dangerous potency in the hands of the demagogue and the revolutionary".[6]

Gutteridge's very reasonable concerns cease to exist in a constitutional democracy based on the rule of law. In this system, the citizens and the public authorities no longer need to stare each other down in mutual hostility because the latter find their legitimacy in the former's democratic participation in the exercise of power.[7] In this system, there is no need to conceive of individual rights as absolute prerogatives whose main purpose is to protect the individual from the despotic interference of the government. Hence, the idea that an individual right is not absolute but needs to be exercised in a manner compatible with its purpose, established by laws enacted in accordance with the rule of law, becomes acceptable. For this fundamental reason, I submit that abuse of law is not an infant disease of the legal order. It is the contrary.

---

[5] See Chap. 2.

[6] See Gutteridge 1933, pp. 43–44.

[7] See Calamandrei 2018, p. 57. This is my English-language paraphrase of the original Italian text, which read as follows: "*[l]a libertà e l'autorità possono guardarsi in cagnesco e diffidare l'una dell'altra, fino a quando l'autorità vanti la sua legittimazione in un titolo diverso da quello della volontà del popolo*".

It is, therefore, only logical that the EU legal order, as a mature system based on the rule of law,[8] has developed its own version of the principle of abuse of law.

References

Calamandrei P (2018) L'avvenire dei diritti di libertà. Galaad Edizioni, Gorgonzola.
Gaillard E (2017) Abuse of Process in International Arbitration. ICSID Review 32:17–37.
Gordley J (2011) The Abuse of Rights in the Civil Law Tradition. In: De la Feria R, Vogenauer S (eds) Prohibition of Abuse of Law. A New General Principle of EU Law? Hart Publishing, Oxford/Portland, pp. 33–46.
Gutteridge HC (1933) Abuse of Rights. Cambridge Law Journal 5:22–45.

[8] See CJEU, *Parti écologiste Les Verts v European Parliament*, Judgment of the Court, 23 April 1986, case 294/83, ECLI:EU:C:1986:166, para 23.

Index

L. Pantaleo, *Abuse of Law in the European Union*,
https://doi.org/10.1007/978-94-6265-731-1

MIX
Papier aus verantwortungsvollen Quellen
Paper from responsible sources
FSC® C105338

If you have any concerns about our products,
you can contact us on
ProductSafety@springernature.com

In case Publisher is established outside the EU,
the EU authorized representative is:
Springer Nature Customer Service Center GmbH
Europaplatz 3, 69115 Heidelberg, Germany

Printed by Libri Plureos GmbH
in Hamburg, Germany